ISBN 978-1-331-45075-7
PIBN 10191873

Similar Books Are Available from
www.forgottenbooks.com

THE GALLOWS,

THE PRISON, AND THE POOR-HOUSE.

A PLEA FOR HUMANITY;

SHOWING THE DEMANDS OF CHRISTIANITY IN BEHALF OF THE CRIMINAL AND PERISHING CLASSES.

BY G. W. QUINBY.

"IT is not the will of your Father which is in Heaven that one of these little ones should perish." CHRIST.

CINCINNATI:

G. W. QUINBY, PUBLISHER,

74 WEST FOURTH STREET.

1856.

TO THE HUMANE, BENEVOLENT AND HOPEFUL

OF EVERY SECT, PARTY AND CREED,

RELIGIOUS AND POLITICAL,

Of Every Country and Clime,

WHO FEELS HIMSELF CONNECTED BY THE TIES OF A COMMON ORIGIN
AND A COMMON HUMANITY,

TO EVERY OTHER HUMAN BEING,

AND WHO NOT ONLY SEES THE WRONGS OF SOCIETY, BUT HAS FAITH
THAT THEY CAN BE REMOVED, AND IS WILLING TO
AID IN THEIR REMOVAL,

This Volume is Respectfully and Affectionately Dedicated,

BY THE AUTHOR

PREFACE.

The Author of the following pages, if he knows himself, would place nothing upon paper to injure society. What he writes is the result of years of investigation and observation, and is given to the world with a desire alone to benefit his fellow-men, especially the little ones and weak of the human family. "Have we not all one Father, hath not one God created us?" is a question asked by the ancient servant of God, and answered in the affirmative by the Teachings, the Sympathies, and the Cross of Christ as well as the divine within us. I am, therefore, a constituent member of the "Great Brotherhood," and if a true follower of my Master, must not injure the weakest, the most sinful, or the most ignorant of the race, but labor for the welfare and happiness of all. Humanity is never dangerous. In all my investigation, my observation and experience, I have never learned that the study, the cultivation or the practice of this divine principle would injure any one. No one, therefore, need fear harm from a perusal of these chapters, or a practical observance of the principles which they illustrate.

Society, throughout the civilized world, has advanced in its humanities; but is there not room for still greater advancement? Is not our Christianity still dogmatic rather than practical? These important questions are considered at length in this work. Crucifixion, burning, roasting, starving, sawing asunder, were once deemed indispensable to the safety and purity of society and the Church, while at a later day the whipping-post, pillory and the stocks were regarded as equally indispensable. But we have learned to live without these relics of barbarism. Can we not learn to live without other things, equally unnecessary, even if they are less cruel than the customs and institutions of our fathers? The Inquisition is not so dreadful as endless hell-fire, but shall we, therefore, sustain the Inquisition? Shall we maintain the gibbet, if unnecessary, because the gibbet is less cruel than the faggot? Shall we practice *any* cruelty in the punishment of our fellow-men, or refuse to aid the poor and unfortunate, with the plea that our practices are more benevolent than those of our ancestors, if a full and free play of our humanity would be more Christian and better for them, for us, and for society? The author of this work is fully convinced, by reading, and more especially, by personal investigation in jails and prisons, among prisoners, and his intercourse with the poor, the ignorant and unfortunate, that the Christian world is yet governed too generally by revenge, and too little by the spirit of Christ and a true humanity. The result of our investigations are before the reader. Our philosophy is based upon *facts*. It is not utilitarian but *Christian*. "Let God be true but every man a liar."

In what we have said we have studied for clearness rather than ornament in style. We have written for the heads and hearts of men seeking for truth. To all such is this book respectfully dedicated, and given to the world with the prayer to God that, as imperfect as it is, it may be instrumental in helping on the great cause of humanity.

Cincinnati, October, 1856.

CONTENTS.

PART I

CHAPTER I. Growth of Humanity.

CHAPTER II. Progress in the Last two Centuries.

CHAPTER III. Appeal to Christians.

CHAPTER IV. Abolishment of the Gallows.

CHAPTER V. Vengeance of the Gallows.

CHAPTER VI. Individual Responsibility

PART II.

THE PRISON.

CHAPTER V. The Jail and the Penitentiary.

PART III

THE POOR HOUSE.

CHAPTER I. Perishing Ones.

CHAPTER II. Jesus and the Poor.

CHAPTER III. Character of our Christianity.

CHAPTER IV. An Appeal.

THE GALLOWS, THE PRISON, AND THE POOR-HOUSE.

CHAPTER I.

THE GROWTH OF HUMANITY.

Growth, a law of Nature—Man in his rude State—Progress of Art, Science, Education—Power, destitute of Benevolence, a Curse—The certainty of Progression in Humanity—The Hope of doomed Millions—Savageness of Society on the introduction of Christianity—Herod the cruel—Titus, "the Darling of Mankind"—Nero—Savage condition of the most refined Women—The Beauty of the Gospel amidst this Deformity.

Growth, improvement, progression, seem a law of nature, and the destiny of our race. Even the earth, itself, is not destitute of active forces. Each moment the old is passing into newness of life. The mass of matter which, in the beginning, is said to have been " without form and void," has become the beautiful world which surrounds us. In this perpetual recreation, noble forests, luxuriant meadows, beautiful shrubbery and fragrant flowers of a thousand tints have sprung into being, rendering charming the earth-home which our good Father has given us for a brief time.

Man, too, is progressive in the elements of his being—in his INTELLECT and his HEART. At first he was rude. His ideas were simple and his wants few. The bear was better fed, and the panther better armed, than he

Thus was he thrown upon his own resources. Necessity gave him energy. He sewed fig leaves and covered his nakedness. He had, too, his brain and his two hands with which to *labor;* but no work-shop—no mill, and no

(11)

steam-engine.   At length he constructed his stone axe,
and, by degrees, his saw and sledge-hammer.   Then he
forsook his cave-home and dwelt in his rude hut.   But
he tarried not here; for while the bear is only and always
a bear, no more and no less, from age to age—boasting
only of his fur coat, his claws and his teeth—there is
something divine in man which prompts him to activity
and improvement, and to look beyond the mere supply of
his necessities, and aim at comfort, elegance and beauty.
Hence the rude hut gradually passed into a habitation
of refinement. ˙ Simple studs and rafters became columns, arches and domes; and so, at length, followed out in
all their detail of order and beauty, the plinth, die, cor-
nice, base, capital, architrave and mouldings, to give
symmetry, finish and perfection to the structure; and
thus architecture became, by degrees, a fine art.   And
what have we now?   Lift up your eyes and behold the
thousands of magnificent cities that dot the earth;—the
grandeur of their temples and public edifices;—our mills,
with their millions of spindles and thundering looms;—
our work-shops, with their multiplied implements for
construction;—our improvements in the arts of hus-
bandry and in the modes of commerce.   Behold oceans
spanned, and nations linked by steam-ships—and countries welded by iron bars, over which people of a thous-
and realms pass in flying palaces drawn by fiery steeds.

The same law of development prevails in Philosophy
and Science.

The crucible and the telescope, the galvanic battery
and the revelations of philosophy, as directed by human
research and ingenuity, have astonished the world.   The
earth, once thought to be the center and bulk of the universe, now dwindles beneath our feet to a mere point;
while the twinkling stars, regarded by the ancients as

so many lamps suspended in the midway heavens for the convenience of our earth, now burst upon us with all the grandeur of stupendous worlds, peopled with millions of sentient beings, and spinning through the heavens with the velocity of lightning, and the order and precision of mathematical certainty.

I suppose there are but few or none in any community disposed to contradict, or even to doubt, the development of which I speak, as connected with the Material or the Intellectual. All men of thought, who know anything of the past, are certain that the world is progressing in learning, philosophy, science, art, political economy and a true civilization. But all men of thought are not certain that the race is progressing in HUMANITY. On the contrary, many affirm that the world, like a patient hopelessly sick, is getting no better, but worse continually; more corrupt, wicked and oppressive, and less kind, benevolent and humane. Such persons are always doubting the mollifying influences of the Christian religion, and the prophetic declarations of the Bible with reference to the growth of humanity among the nations. And not only so, but they are constantly regretting that they were born into the world at so late a period. " Ah !" they groan, " the times are not what they once were ! The days of our good old fathers were happy days. There was less oppression and more humanity than now, and a great deal more true enjoyment." So chime the croakers.

It is strange that while society is moving forward with eager speed, that so many should be filled with doubt, and, dissatisfied with the present, should look back and with regrets so tender, sigh for the " good old days" of the *dark ages.*

I desire, then, in the beginning, to show to this class, and to all, the sure growth of the human soul in the divine principle of benevolence. I wish to demonstrate to every reader the *certainty* of such a growth; and further, that the developments of humanity are never deleterious to society, but, on the contrary, serve to soften and subdue the sinful. I am specially desirous to impress this important truth on the hearts of all professed Christians, and to convince them that Christianity has something to do with the progression of which I speak.

Now, to me, the thought is a glorious one, and full of encouragement, that while the public mind of all civilized society is ripening with wisdom, it is softening with benevolence. What are nations and communities, destitute of benevolence or humanity ? What the power of millions of men—each as learned as the seven wise men —boasting of philosophy, science, riches, without humanity to control and direct their energies ? Such power would prove but a dreadful engine of cruelty and oppression. What every good man desires above all else, is to behold a development that, while it mollifies and civilizes society generally, it shall benefit man, especially the poor and unfortunate classes of our race,—the criminal,— the little ones and the weak, by kindness, instruction and assistance. There is hope in such a progression—hope for the suffering, toiling poor, inhabiting the wretched cellars and garrets of our pent up cities—hope for the intemperate and ignorant—hope for the "widow and the fatherless," cursed with poverty, rags and tears ; in short, hope for the doomed millions of enslaved Europe and America, who live beneath the very spires, and sit in the very shadow of our thousand churches, consecrated to Him who was the "sinner's friend," and who exclaimed, when on earth—" The spirit of the Lord is upon me, *because he hath anointed me to preach the Gospel to the poor ; he hath sent me to heal the broken-hearted, to*

*preach deliverance to the captives, and recovering of sight to
the blind; to set at liberty them that are bruised, and to
preach the acceptable year of the Lord."*

Is there such a progression now going forward in the
heart of all civilized society?

Let us see. We shall appeal to facts, and shall demonstrate by contrasting the past with the present. And
look you, first, at a few historical relations showing the
want of humanity—the extreme cruelty, that existed in
the most civilized and enlightened nations, on the introduction of Christianity into the world, eighteen centuries ago.

We have all read, in the Gospel, the simple but touching account of the massacre which took place by the order of Herod the Great, on the birth of Christ, in Bethlehem of Judea; but did we ever reflect on the inhumanity—the perfect savageness of the society and the
age, which could have tolerated an act so terribly cruel?
This man was born in Judea, of one of the first fam
ilies of that realm, and was regarded as one of the greatest men of his time. His abilities as a politician and
commander were of the first order, and such was the magnificence he displayed in decorating his palace and other
public buildings, that Augustus said, "His soul was too
great for his kingdom." And yet, in the 33d year of
his reign as king of Judea, when Christ was born, being
unable to find the infant Savior that he might destroy
him, "he sent forth and slew all the children that were
in Bethlehem and all the coasts thereof, from two years
old and under," in order to make sure of his victim.

Can we conceive of a more cruel and heartless act?
And yet we are not told that the people, being filled with
horror, arose *en masse* and tore the unfeeling wretch from
his throne and consigned him to the flames. To be sure,

weeping and lamentations were heard throughout the land, by wretched mothers who refused to be comforted. But what then ? This was of no consequence ! Cruelty and blood were common with kings, and familiar with the people ; and the terrible act was passed without note or comment. Herod was still reverenced and lauded as the king of Judea. He put to death his innocent wife, and butchered his sons, and still was reverenced and lauded as the king of Judea. And, according to Josephus, he planned a scene of posthumous cruelty which shows how barbarous must have been the age that would suggest a thought so terrible. It was this : He summoned the chief persons among the Jews to the city of Jericho, and caused them to be shut up in the royal circus. He was now near seventy years of age and very sick, and he gave strict orders to his sister Salome, to have all the men massacred at his death, that every great family in Judea might weep at his funeral. His savage order, however, was never executed.

Now here is a question : Is there a Prince on earth in our age who would be guilty of acts so dreadfully cruel ? Or if so, is there a people on earth, civilized or savage, that would not execrate the monster who could be thus heartless? If not, then has not the world progressed in humanity since that religion, which is peace on earth, good will to men, was proclaimed?

I am aware that Herod bears the character of having been a very cruel and blood-thirsty wretch, far worse than most men of his time. Permit me, therefore, to mention one other historical fact to show the inhumanity of society at that period. About thirty years subsequently to the death of Christ, the Roman army invaded Judea and destroyed the great city of the Jews, under Titus, the Roman general, who in consequence of his many

virtues, was called " *the darling of mankind.*" This man
Titus, who was the darling of mankind eighteen hundred
years ago, took ninety-seven thousand of the Jews
captive; six thousand of whom, chosen young men, he
sent to Nero, the Roman Emperor; the same Nero it was
who subsequently, for the gra ification of an insane caprice, set fire to Rome that he might have a real represeu-
tation of the burning of Troy, and who afterward trans-
ferred the guilt of the act to the Christians, and caused
them to be butchered by thousands throughout his do-
mains. But let this pass. I am not recounting the doings of *bad* men ; I was just speaking of an act perpetrated by Titus, " the darling of mankind." I repeat : Titus
sent six thousand of his ninety-seven thousand captives
to Rome, as slaves for Nero. Thirty thousand were sold
as bond-men into Egypt; eleven thousand in one place, he
caused to perish by starvation. At Cesarea he murdered
two thousand five hundred in honor of his brother's birthday, and a greater number at Berytus in honor of his
father's; while he distributed nearly thirty thousand
through the provinces of Rome, to be destroyed in their
theatres by the sword or torn in pieces by wild beasts.
And all this was perpetrated, not by a man recognized as
a *savage* by the age in which he lived, but one who was the
very quintessence of perfection, the *"the darling of mankind!"*
and I know not but the darling of *womankind* also, if any
distinction is allowed, for I am very sorry to say the women were as savage as the men. The reader is doubtless
familiar with the account, in the Gospel, of the dancing
of a beautiful damsel in the presence of a certain king,
on the occasion of his birthday, and how charmed he was
with her person and performance;—so charmed that he
declared with an oath, that he would give her whatever
she asked, even to the half of his kingdom. And do you

2

not recollect what she demanded as a present? "Give me here," said she, "the head of John the Baptist in a charger;"—that is, in a bowl or platter. What a present for a young damsel, charming in her person, all decorated for the dance, to ask of a king enamored with her beauty. The bloody head of the murdered fore-runner of the Lord Jesus! But, astounding as it may seem, her wishes were gratified. "The king sent and beheaded John in his prison; and the head was brought in a charger and given to the damsel, and she brought it to her mother." Perhaps the reader is ready to exclaim— "Why this damsel must have been educated a savage, and was summoned to dance in the presence of the king, *because of her remarkable agility or beauty.* Instead of this, she was herself of the royal family. Herod Phillip was her father, Aristobulus her grandfather, and Herodias her mother, the woman to whom she carried the bleeding, ghastly head of John, when she had received it from the hand of the executioner. She was, therefore, educated a member of the royal palace, and had all the advantages which the most refined and polished society in that age could afford.

But here we have a specimen of what constituted refinement eighteen hundred years ago, in one of the most civilized nations on earth. We see the nature of the influences brought to bear on the minds of youthful females. Herodias, the mother of the young woman who so delighted the king, was offended with John the Baptist, because he had the boldness to condemn her incestuous intercourse with the king. She, therefore, instructed her daughter to ask the head of John as a present, if opportunity should present itself. And when she received it, it is said that she gazed with exulting pleasure on the speechless mouth that had dared to utter such words of condemnation against her, and offered in-dignities to the tongue from which she could no longer dread reproof. St. Jerome positively asserts that "when she got the head, she drew out the tongue and thrust it through with her bodkin."

Such was the moral condition of the world eighteen hundred years ago. The apostle described it when he said: "Their feet are swift to shed blood."

How shocking are these exhibitions of barbarity to the humanity and refinement of the present age! Indeed, has there been no growth of the element of humanity in the human soul for the last eighteen centuries? Why the man who is unable to discover this change, would light a candle at noonday to find the sun.

And I will add in this place, that if there was nothing divine in the mission of Christ, the circumstance is most remarkable, and to my mind wholly unaccountable, that he should inculcate a religion so pure, and a philosophy so divine, in the midst of a darkness so gross! His very life—his spirit—his teachings, and the manner in which he bore his sufferings and his death, were all in direct op-position to the prevailing sentiments and customs of the age in which he lived. His breathings of love and for-giveness—of tenderness and compassion—of benevo-lence and humanity, when contrasted with the predomi-nant principles of that age, were like a resplendent star in the midst of surrounding darkness—or a blooming paradise in a howling wilderness.

CHAPTER II.

THE MARCH OF HUMANITY DURING THE LAST TWO CENTURIES.

Inhumanity of France and England two Hundred Years ago--Cruelty of Persecution gradually softened--Inhumanity of Louis XIV--Inhumanity of the Pilgrim Fathers--Persecution of the Quakers--The softening of Penal Codes--One Hundred and Sixty offenses Punishable with Death in England—Codes of England, Sweden, Germany, France and Poland—The Cruelty of their Punishments—Hanging for stealing forty Shillings--Touching case of the Execution of a Young Woman in England—Laws of the New England Colonies--Case of a Young Girl--Progress of Humanity in the more kindly Treatment of Criminals, and in the Improvement of the Poor, Ignorant, Sick and Suffering--Extract from Macaulay.

But let us come forward to a more recent age, and mark the growth of humanity in the hearts of those who stand more closely connected with us on the pages of history. We will limit our investigations to the last two centuries.

In 1650 we find France and England, two of the most enlightened and civilized nations on the globe, governed by principles, both in war and peace, that would utterly shock the humanity of the present age.

Men regarded as great and good, both in Church and State, gave their sanction to laws, practices and customs so unjust and inhuman, as to strike the worst man now living in civilized society dumb with astonishment and horror! This will be seen as we proceed.

Notice the unmistakable change which has been produced within the last two hundred years, with reference to the cruelty of proscription and persecution in consequence of religious faith. Christians have now very gen-

(20)

erally learned the folly of attempting to convert men to a love of Christian truth, and inspire them with benevolence, by prisons, chains, fire and torture. But two hundred years ago, these were the principal means employed in the dissemination and defense of the Christian religion. Two hundred years ago, the inquisition, that tribunal of horror and cruelty, which drank the blood of nearly four hundred thousand innocent victims, was in full force in France, Spain, Portugal and other countries. An accredited English writer says, in describing the inhumanity of priests and potentates in their persecution of heretics: "If the least shadow of proof appeared against any pretended criminal, he was condemned to death at once, and was clothed with a garment painted with flames, and with his own figure surrounded with dogs, serpents, and devils, all open-mouthed, as if ready to devour him. If the offenders died in any other faith than that of Rome, they were burned alive, the priests telling them that they left them to the devil who was standing at their elbow waiting to receive their souls and bear them to the flames of hell.

Flaming furzes, fastened to poles, were thrust against their faces till their faces were burned to a coal, and this was accompanied with the loudest acclamations of joy among the thousands of spectators. At last, fire was set to the furze at the bottom of the stake, over which the criminals were chained so high that the top of the flame seldom reached higher than the seat they sat on, so that they seemed to be roasted, rather than burned. There could not be a more lamentable spectacle; the sufferers continually crying out, so long as they were able—"Pity, for the love of God!" Yet it was beheld by all sexes and ages, with transports of joy and satisfaction. And even monarchs, surrounded by their courtiers, sometimes graced the scene with their presence, imagining that they were performing an act highly acceptable to the Deity.*

Two hundred years ago, Louis the XIV. filled the throne of France. He was basely ignorant, but is described as possessing many virtues for a sovereign of his time. Among his virtues is enumerated that of his strong religious prejudices, and boldness in support of the established Church. He manifested a marked desire to convert supposed heretics to Catholicism, and introduced a method to accomplish his purpose which seems to have been original with him. We have no account of its ever having been practiced by Christ or his apostles, or any of the early fathers. He *beat* religion into them with the battle-ax. It is a literal fact that he sent forth his troopers, soldiers and dragoons, with orders to go from house to house, and from town to town, and with the sword and battle-axe, *force* men and women into the Catholic Church. " These blood-thirsty wretches entered the Protestant houses in France, where they broke and trampled under foot furniture, destroyed provisions, turned dining-rooms into stables for their horses, and treated the owners with the highest indignation and cruelty. They bound to posts, mothers that gave suck, and let their little infants lie languishing in their sight, for several days and nights, crying, mourning and gasping for life. Some they bound before large fires, and when they were half roasted, let them go. Some they hung by the hair and some by the feet in chimneys, and smoked them with hay till they were suffocated. Women and maids were hung up by their feet or by their armpits, and exposed stark naked to public view. Some they cut and slashed with knives, and after stripping them naked, stuck their bodies full of pins and needles, from

*Dr. Dick's Philosophy of Religion.

head to foot : or with red hot pinchers took hold of them by the nose and other parts of the body, and dragged them around their rooms till they promised to be *good Catholics*, or actually expired beneath their sufferings. If any endeavored to save themselves from these barbarities by flight, they were pursued into fields and woods where they were shot like wild beasts.

On such scenes of desoltation and horror the Popish clergy feasted their eyes, and made them simply a matter of laughter and sport."*

All this was done less than two hundred years ago, in refined and accomplished France, and simply for a difference of opinion in religious faith. In the civil wars on account of religion, which happened in France in the seventeenth century, above a million of men lost their lives; four hundred villages, nine cities, two thousand churches, and ten thousand dwellings, were burnt or destroyed. The inhumanity of the soldiers when set on by the priests, filled with the ranklings of an unrelenting religion, was utterly beyond description. Thousands of men, women, and children died by starvation, by being torn asunder, by butchery and by the flames. It is said of Louis XIII., who carried on the war, that what gave him greater pleasure than all things else, was the thought of driving heretics out of his kingdom, and thereby purging the Church of God of its corruptions.

In other countries the flames of persecution raged with nearly the same fury. In the Netherlands alone, not long previous to the time of which I speak, one hundred thousand persons were hanged, beheaded, buried alive or burned on account of their religious belief!

Even England, who has always acted with more calmness and humanity than any other nation, was not guilt-

*Dr. Dick's Philosophy of Religion.

less. During two or three years of the short reign of Mary, in the sixteenth century, two hundred and seventy-seven persons were committed to the flames, besides those who perished by fines, confiscations, and imprisonment. And "scarcely a century and a half has elapsed, since the Presbyterians of Scotland were hunted across moors and morasses, like partridges in the wilderness, slaughtered by bands of ruffian dragoons, and forced to seek their spiritual food in dens and mountains at the peril of their lives."*

It was the inhumanity of persecution that drove the pilgrim fathers from their homes in the old world, to seek an asylum among the savage men and beasts of the new. They were banished from their homes, and in their turn, they banished others.

Two hundred years ago, Roger Williams, the founder of the sect of Calvinist Baptists in this country, preached in Plymouth, Boston and Salem. But his doctrine and ideas of Church government were not pleasing to the Puritan fathers, and he was banished to Rhode Island—he and his wife and children, in the dead of winter, where he was dependent on the very savages for the means of subsistence!

Two hundred years ago, the magistrates of Massachusetts Colony cropped the ears, scourged the backs, and bored the tongues of the Quakers with a hot iron. More than this, they incarcerated them in jails and dungeons —whipped them through the streets at the tail of a cart, and banished them from the country on pain of death. And when they returned, they actually seized them, and put them to death by hanging.

Such is a sort of bird's eye view of the inhumanity and intolerance which has been rife in the Christian world within the last two hundred years.

---

*Dr. Dick's Philosophy of Religion.

Has not an unmistakable change taken place in society in this time? Where is the Inquisition? Some say it is still in use. If so, the progress of society cheats it of its victims. The spirit of persecution may still be burning in the hearts of some of the leading Papists, but it is confined there by the growing intelligence, humanity, and love of liberty of the masses.

Where is the king or the potentate, in this age, that dares to take the first step in the maintenance of any system of faith by the inquisition, the stake, the rack, or the scaffold? How would the public mind be struck with horror, in England, Scotland, or the United States, if men and women were beheaded or burned for their religious faith! Suppose that to-day, in Boston, or Cincinnati, a Quaker should be arraigned, tried, and executed, *"without benefit of clergy;"*—executed, simply because he repudiated wars, believed in the efficacy of kindness, —the brotherhood of man, and thought fit to wear a drab coat and broad-brimmed hat;—hanged for such an offense! What would the people think? What would they say? What would they *do?* Why, the whole nation—yea, the whole Christian world—would be shocked in every nerve! There is, probably, no deed that could be perpetrated by any party or sect, that would produce a more fearful excitement, in any civilized society, than to *hang* or *burn* a man for *his religious belief!* So great and palpable is the change which has been wrought in the popular mind, within the last two hundred years, in favor of tolerance and humanity!

2. An unmistakable change in favor of humanity is seen in the softening of the Penal Codes of nations.

We are told, by Judge Story, that less than one hundred years ago England punished *one hundred and sixty* offenses with death. Dr. Dick says: "In our country it is

3

a melancholy truth, that among the variety of actions which men are daily liable to commit, no less than *one hundred and sixty* have been declared, by act of Parliament, to be felonies *without benefit of clergy*, or in other words, *to be worthy of instant death.*" A writer in the London Morning *Herald*, puts the number at *rising two hundred.* France, Germany, Poland and Italy were still more unjust and cruel in their punishments. Now, England makes but *five* offenses punishable with death; and France, Germany and Poland have modified their codes in like manner.

Sixty years ago, England, Sweden, Germany and Poland, not only put to death for certain offenses, but prolonged the torments of the offender by cruel tortures. In Sweden, for instance, murder was punished first by chopping off the hand, then beheading and quartering. In Great Britain, "those guilty of high treason were condemned to be hung on a gallows for some minutes; then cut down while yet alive, the heart to be taken out, and exposed to view, and the entrails burned."

The following account is given, by a traveler who was in Berlin in 1819, of the execution of a man for murder, which shows that the execution of criminals in Prussia is frequently distinguished by a species of cruelty worthy of the worst days of the inquisition. Amidst the parade of executioners, officers of police, and other judicial authorities, the beating of drums, and the waving of flags and colors, the criminal mounted the scaffold. No ministers of religion appeared to gild the horrors of eternity, and to soothe the agonies of the criminal; and no repentant prayer closed his quivering lips.

" Never," says the narrator, "shall I forget the one bitter look of imploring agony that he threw around him, as, immediately on stepping on the scaffold, his coat was rudely torn from his shoulders. He was then thrown down, the cords fixed round his neck, which were drawn until strangulation almost commenced. Another execu- tioner then approached, bearing in his hands a heavy wheel, bound with iron, with which he violently struck the legs, arms, and chest, and lastly the head, of the crim- inal. I was, unfortunately, near enough to witness his mangled and bleeding body still convulsed. It was then carried down for interment, and, in less than a quarter of an hour from the beginning of his torture, the corpse was completely covered with earth. Several large stones, which were thrown upon him, hastened his last gasp: *he was mangled into eternity!*"

Now, all such barbarities are expunged from the penal code of nearly every civilized nation on earth. Only forty years since, the crime of cutting a small tree, or of shoot- ing a deer within the enclosure of an English lord, was punishable with death. If a man stole more than forty shillings from a dwelling in that country, the law clam- ored for his blood. He must be strangled. And, as in- credible as the fact may appear to some in our time, this inhuman law was not abolished till the year 1827—less than thirty years ago; and then it was not fully abolished: for the legislative body simply raised the capital indict- ment to five pounds, instead of four—or to *sixty* shillings, instead of *forty*. Since, England has wiped all such acts from her statute books; and now in no case punishes with death for theft.

Shop-lifting was also a crime punishable with death in England but a few years since. And from an extract taken from a speech by the Hon. Sir William Meredeth in 1777, on a bill creating a new capital felony, a glimpse may be obtained of public sentiment on this subject at that time—eighty years ago. This gentleman, in opposing the inhumanity of the laws, produced many touching instances where the grossest injustice had been perpetrated in the punishment of offenders. Amongst others, he mentioned the case of a young woman, of good family and beautiful person, who had just been executed for attempting to steal a small piece of cloth from a dry-goods establishment.

"Her husband," said Mr. Meredeth, "had been pressed on board of a man-of-war ship, by the officers of government. The poor woman's goods had been sold to pay some debt of her husband, and she, together with her two little children, were turned into the streets, penniless beggars.

" 'T is a circumstance," said he, "not to be forgotten, that she was very young, but little more than eighteen, and remarkably handsome. She went to a linen draper's —took some coarse linen from the counter, and slipped it under her cloak. The shop-man saw her, and she laid it down. FOR THIS SHE WAS EXECUTED. Her defense was, that she had lived in credit and wanted nothing, till a press-gang came, who were under the orders of the government, and bore away her husband. But since then, she was deprived of a home, or even a bed; had nothing to prevent the starvation of her children, or to keep them from perishing with cold; and she might have done something wrong, for she scarcely knew what she did. The parish officers testified to the truth of this declaration, but there had been a good deal of shop-lifting in that vicinity, notwithstanding the penalty was death, and it became necessary to make an example of some one. So this unfortunate woman was carried to the gibbet, hung up by the neck, and choked like a cat, for the special comfort and accommodation of the shop-keepers in Ludgate street, London.

"When brought into court to receive her sentence," said Mr. Meredeth, "she behaved like one frantic. And it was enough to break one's heart to see her set out for the gallows, with her poor babe nursing at the breast." It seems hardly credible that so heartless, inhuman and unjust an act could have been perpetrated by the authorities of England—enlightened, Christian England —within the last century!

And yet the same code of criminal law was once in vogue in the New-England colonies. Hanging for stealing forty shillings—for shop-lifting—for worshipping any god but the true God—for blaspheming the name of God—for stealing a man—or for smiting father or mother—was the law of Massachusetts and Connecticut, one hundred and fifty years ago.

The following is copied from the penal code of the Connecticut Colony, and was in vogue in 1690:

"If any man shall have or worship any other god but the true God, he shall be put to death.

"If any man or woman be a witch, that is, hath or consulteth with a familiar spirit, he or she shall be put to death.

"If any man shall blaspheme the name of God, shall curse the Father, Son, or Holy Ghost, he shall be put to death.

"If any man stealeth a man, or mankind, he shall be put to death.

"If any child or children above sixteen years, and of sufficient understanding, shall curse or smite father or mother, he shall be put to death.

"If any man have a stubborn and rebellious son of sufficient years and understanding, viz: sixteen years of age, who will not obey the voice of his father or the voice of his mother, and when they have chastened him will not hearken unto them; then may his father and his mother lay hold on him and bring him to the Magistrates assembled at court, and testify unto them, and such a son shall be put to death."

These laws were but too effectually enforced. No less than nineteen persons, as innocent of any crime as the "spirit-rappers" and "table-tippers" of our day, were hung, and one pressed to death, in Salem, Mass., in 1692, for witchcraft. And the estimated number put to death in England for the same offense, was thirty thousand; while in Germany not less than one hundred thousand suffered death by the scaffold, the flames, by being drawn assunder, and by other methods, for the same crime.

In the colonies, even parents were instrumental in the condemnation and execution of their own children:

An English lady of much repute who visited New England not long previous to the war of '76, says in her diary of 22d March, 1769, that a maid of nineteen years of age was put upon her trial for life, in Connecticut, by the complaint of her parents, both of whom were present and swore against her—saying that "she was stubborn and had violated their commands."

The diary states that "at first the mother testified strongly against her child; but when she had spoken a few words, the daughter cried out in great agony of grief, 'Oh! I shall be destroyed in my youth by the words of my own mother!' On which the woman did so soften her testimony, that the court being in doubt upon the matter, had a consultation with the ministers present, as to whether the accused girl had made herself justly liable to the punishment prescribed for stubborn and rebellious children in Deuteronomy, 21: 20."

When it was decided that this law applied only to a rebellious *son*, and that a daughter could not be put to death under its sanction; to which the court did assent, and the girl, after being admonished, was set at liberty. Thereupon she ran sobbing into the arms of her mother, who did rejoice over her as one raised from the dead; and moreover did mightily blame herself for putting her child in so great peril, by complaining of disobedience."

Has not a change, then, been wrought in behalf of humanity? Has not much of inhumanity been expunged from our statute books? Is not human life regarded by all legislators as a thing far more sacred? The humanity of every Christian heart rises up against even *legalized* killing. The offender may have wickedly violated the law; his deeds of blood may have been many and appalling; but we ask, is it wise or Christian to strangle him? —to imitate his own deeds of vengeance?

In Russia, Bombay, Belgium and Tuscany, the punishment of death has been *totally abolished.* It is also abolished in the States of Michigan and Wisconsin in our own country; while in Maine, Vermont and Massachusetts, it is *virtually* abolished.* In eight of our other States, but two offenses are punishable with death; while in Ohio, Pennsylvania and Tennessee, their codes contain but one crime for which death is the penalty.† And what is remarkable, crime is never increased by such exhibitions of humanity on the part of communities and nations. Clemency always softens, while cruelty hardens, as I will demonstrate in the progress of these

---

* In each of these States the law requires that the offender, on conviction, shall be imprisoned in the State Penitentiary for at least one year; after which the Governor of the State shall issue his warrant for his execution. But as no *time* is specified *when* the warrant shall be issued, the executive, with a single exception, has failed to act in the premises, and the consequence is, the offender is permitted to live.

† The penal code of Virginia has but *one* capital offense, when committed by a white man, and that is duelling; but *seventy-one,* when committed by a slave. When regarded as applied to the slave, her code is the most bloody now existing in the world.

pages. In the reign of Henry the VIII. of England, the laws were never more severe; and it is a fact well worthy the consideration of every man interested in jurisprudence or moral philosophy, that crime in Great Britain was never so rife nor so terrible as during the reign of Henry. No less than seventy-two thousand executions took place for *robbery alone*, amounting, on an average, to *more than six a day*, Sundays included.

3. The progress of humanity is also seen in the more kindly treatment of criminals and all other offenders, when contrasted with the past. The change in this direction within the last half-century, has been truly wonderful.

One hundred years ago, men and women guilty of minor offenses, were punished with pillory—galleys—whipping—stocks—mutilation, by cutting off the ears and the nose, cutting out the tongue, putting out the eyes, shaving off the hair, and branding—and with imprisonment.*

Fifty years ago, prisons were merely stone pens, and dark, dismal dungeons, filled with filth and vermin. Into these pens and dungeons were criminals thrust, chained to their stone floors, and fed like our hogs, with worse fare. Now, men have learned, in all civilized communities, that such treatment was barbarous—that *even the convict* is entitled to the humanity of his brother, and is worth something. So his loathsome prison has, in a measure, been converted into a workshop and school of

---

* In 1833 it was estimated that no less than SEVENTY-FIVE THOUSAND were confined in jail in the United States for debt. A poor man of my native town lay in prison all winter for a debt of six dollars only, while his wife and large family of little children were suffering at home for the provisions which his labor would have brought. An instance is reported in one State, where a man was imprisoned for *two cents* only. Even Massachusetts did not wipe this cruel and foolish law from her statute books till 1853.

reform—a hospital for the body, the mind, the soul. In nearly all our State prisons and penitentiaries, in the Free States, there is the chaplain, the library, and in some States the school of instruction; and efforts are made not only to instruct the criminal in some useful trade, that he may have the means of livelihood when he returns to the world, but to instruct his heart and mind in whatever will serve to guide and benefit him in after life, and render him a virtuous member of society.

To me, there is something beautiful, Christian, divine, in these displays of humanity. From the cleanly, well-regulated school of reform, which we find in many States of our Union, called the House of Refuge, instituted for the unfortunate youth of both sexes, through the house of correction and the improved jail, to the cleanly and well-regulated penitentiary, when contrasted with the filth and brutality connected with the prisons of but half a century ago, there is a growth in true benevolence and Christian kindness manifested, that is full of hope and exceedingly cheering to the benevolent Christian.

4. Again; the development of which I am speaking is seen in the growing interest of nearly all classes, in the improvement of the condition of the poor, the unfortunate, the sick, ignorant and suffering, of our earth. We behold the blessed Jesus, at the pool of Bethesda, administering to the wants of the sick, lame, halt and blind; so in our day, many of his followers have come to learn that works of humanity and mercy are demanded of them by the common interests of a common race. "Have we not all one Father; hath not one God created us?" and if so, are we not ALL BRETHREN? Feeling the force of this beautiful principle, a broad philanthropy has sprung up, which manifests itself in noble charities and perpetual appeals in behalf of humanity. Behold our

Hospitals—our Asylums for the Blind, Deaf and Dumb; and for the Insane;—our Homes for the Widow, the Orphan, the friendless and outcasts—our societies to assist the poor—our Peace associations—our Temperance societies—our Prison associations, Howard associations, and Ragged Schools! Behold what is being done for the most wretched and filthy in Field Lane, London, and at the Five Points, New-York! and what *was* done, but a few years ago, in sending ships and frigates, loaded with clothing, and barrels of flour and meal and hams, to the starving people of Greece and Ireland.

Our fathers erected the gallows, the whipping-post, the stocks and the pillory, by the church-side; but where did they ever organize the benevolent societies, and erect the benevolent institutions which I have enumerated? These belong alone to the present age, and mark the age as one of philanthropy and Christian benevolence, beyond every thing the world has ever witnessed. And the more the human soul is brought to contemplate the condition of the criminal and perishing classes, and what society can accomplish with no injury to itself, for suffering humanity—the more it beholds what there is yet to be done—the more tender is it in its sympathies, and disposed to combine the elements of its forces to contribute to their relief. And thus is the present an age full of joyful hopes—an age softened and mellowed by charity—an age of advancement, not only in science, art, political economy and material development, but of a universal humanity; in a word, it is an age, when contrasted with the past, which is full of glory

Macaulay, the eloquent English historian, in speaking of the growth of humanity in England, says: "There is scarcely a page of the history, or the lighter literature of the seventeeth century, which does not contain some

proof that our ancestors were less humane than their posterity. The discipline of work-shops, of schools, of private families, though not more efficient than at present,
was infinitely harsher. Masters, well born and bred, were
in the habit of beating their servants. Pedagogues knew
of no way of imparting knowledge but by beating their
pupils. Husbands of decent station were not ashamed
to beat their wives. The implacability of hostile factions
was such as we can scarcely conceive.

"Whigs were disposed to murmur because Stafford was
suffered to die without having his bowels burned before
his face. Tories reviled and insulted Russell, as his coach
passed from the Tower to the scaffold where he was put
to death. As little mercy was shown by the populace to
the sufferers of humble rank. If an offender was put
into the pillory, it was well if he escaped with his life from
brick-bats and paving-stones. If he was tied on to the
cart's tail, the crowd pressed around him, imploring the
hangman to give it to the fellow well and make him howl.

"A man pressed to death for stealing a trifle, or a woman burned for coining, excited less sympathy than is
now felt for a galled horse, or an over-driven ox.* The
prisons were hells on earth—seminaries of every crime
and of every disease. The lean and yellow culprits, when
they were brought into court from their cells, brought an
atmosphere of stench and pestilence with them, which
sometimes signally avenged them on the bench, bar and
jury. But on all this misery society looked with indifference. Nowhere could be found that sensitive and
restless compassion which has, in our time, extended a
powerful protection to the factory-child—to the Hindoo

---

*Two men were sentenced to one month's imprisonment at hard labor
in London, during the year 1853, for the crime of causing unnecessary
pain to a cat while killing it.

widow—to the negro-slave;—a compassion which winces
at every lash laid on the back of drunken soldiers;—
which will not suffer the thief in the hulks to be ill-fed
or over-worked, and which has repeatedly endeavored to
save the life of the murderer.   It is true, that compassion
ought, like other feelings, to be under the government
of reason, and has for the want of such government, produced some ridiculous and some deplorable effects.   But
the more we study the annals of the past, the more shall
we rejoice that we live in a merciful age—in an age in
which cruelty is abhorred, and in which pain, even when
deserved, is inflicted reluctantly, and from a sense of duty.
Every class, doubtless, has gained largely by this great
moral change ; but the class which has gained most is
THE POOREST, THE MOST DEPENDENT AND THE MOST
DEFENCELESS.''

And it may be added, these are the very classes that
most need the gain.   They are the very classes for whom
the blessed Jesus specially labored; and never since he
returned to his Father, and our Father, has there been a
time when they so occupied the thoughts of the humane,
and when all the elements and forces of the world's life
so contributed to their improvement and happiness as the
present.

CHAPTER III.

APPEAL TO CHRISTIANS.

Humanity is not yet "full grown"—Dreadful evils still exist—The Conservative has no desire to go back, and will not advance—Opinions of Generations to come of our Barbarities—The Duty of the Christian to the Living—Christians must labor in the Cause of Humanity or the Work must stop.—The Growth of Humanity confined to Christian Countries—Dreadful Barbarities of the Chinese—Where Christianity prevails in its purest and most living form, there is the largest Benevolence.

Thus have we demonstrated the sure progress of humanity. But let not the reader infer from what we have said, that humanity is yet "full grown." There are still dreadful evils, moral and social, in our world, and a vast amount of human suffering—suffering arising from poverty, crime, ignorance and cruelty, which can and *must* be ameliorated. We appeal to the reader for his co-operation—his sympathy, advice and assistance. You look back upon the past as exhibited in these pages, and you say, " Really the world has progressed in its humanities. I have no desire to go back and live under the customs and laws which held rule two centuries ago. Our fathers must have suffered extreme anxiety and great peril constantly. I rejoice that reforms so important to the interest and happiness of man, have been effected " All this is very well. But do you think it ‹ probable that all needed good has been effected? Is there nothing more that Christianity and humanity demand at our hands? Have we arrived at the *ne plus ultra* of reform? If not, should we not go forward? You do not desire to go back, but will **you** *advance?* Everybody is opposed to going back. Thousands of sticklers for the death pen

(37)

alty for *murder*, condemn the rigid laws of our fathers, and thank God that they did not live in the seventeenth century. It is difficult to get the conservative to move willingly. He *holds back*, but like a horse in a ferry-boat, no matter how stubbornly he pulls back, the boat moves, and he goes with it in spite of himself, and when once over, he has no disposition to return. Where is the man who has been carried forward on the broad tide of moral and spiritual reform, for the last half century, though never so much against his will, that desires to return to the delusion, superstition and inhumanity from which he has merged? Why he can only look back and wonder that his fathers could have remained so long in darkness.

Thus it will be with the generations to come. They will refer to the unchristian barbarities of our day, and say of us, " How astonishing that our fathers could have conceived it either expedient or necessary to deliberately kill men and women because *they* killed!" Our fathers were instrumental in the execution of their own chil-dren for disobedience;—they strangled men and wo-men for theft, witchcraft and profanity, and we are aston-ished." Will not our children be equally astonished at our perverseness in upholding the *gibbet as a Christian institution*, and our almost total neglect of the millions of young and old, upon whom the doom of poverty has fixed its seal? Examine, then, the several subjects pre-sented in the future pages of this work *carefully*. You do not believe that the sanguinary laws of our fathers were either just, necessary, or Christian; and by inves-tigation, you may come to have just as little faith in the necessity, justice or Christianity of the gallows for *any* crime.

If you are a professed Christian, then I would exhort

you *especially* to consider what we have to offer before you "turn from us and pass away." Remember, that every man, no matter how poor, or sinful, or ignorant, or wretched, is your brother; bound up with you in the same bundle of temporal and eternal interests. Christ died for him as well as for you, and when on earth, he sought after just such to heal and bless them. You believe it to be your duty to labor for their future salvation, that their immortal *souls* may be secure from suffering beyond the grave. But is it not equally your duty to labor for the amelioration of their condition in life, as Christ labored when on earth. "Come, ye blessed of my Father, inherit the kingdom prepared for you from the foundation of the world; *for I was an hungered and ye gave me meat; I was thirsty and ye gave me drink; I was a stranger and ye took me in; naked and ye clothed me; I was sick and ye visited me; I was in prison and ye came unto me Verily I say unto you, inasmuch as ye have done it unto* ONE OF THE LEAST OF THESE *my brethren, ye have done it unto me.*"*

Now, is it possible for you to enter the spiritual kingdom of the Lord Jesus—a kingdom of "righteousness, peace and joy"—and experience its promised blessings, so long as you neglect to "remember in mercy" the weak and perishing ones, whose *bodies* as well as *souls* Christ himself has made it your duty to look after and bless?

Another consideration you must not fail to notice, viz: that *the world must be renovated, if at all, through the influence of the Christian religion.* If Christians fail to labor in the cause of humanity, therefore, the work must stop. I have demonstrated the growth of humanity in the world; but this advancement is *confined mainly to Christian countries*, as is its civilization, and the progress

*Matthew 25: 34—40.

of science, art, and philosophy, and all the activities of the world's life.

I said in a previous chapter, that I desired to encourage the Christian in the labors of humanity, by showing that Christianity is the main-spring in all moral, social and intellectual progress, and advancement in humanity.

Let him take a map of the world, and examine for himself. The nations of the earth, when considered in a religious point, are arranged into two great classes, viz : the *Pagan* and *Christian;* and these two into other two, viz: the first into Pagan and Mohammedan, and the second into Catholic and Protestant. Now, in what countries do we find the progress and growth which I have described in these pages? Where the most intense love of learning? Where the schools and colleges? Where the profound knowledge of science? Where the books, newspapers, post routes, railroads, and other marks of a high form of civilization? And above all, where the growth in humanity, which alone is the truest seal of the highest human progress?

Take a map and trace. The activities and developments of which I have spoken are not in Africa. There, darkness and cruelty still reign predominant. We visit Asia—India, China, and what is the result? Very nearly the same as that of Africa. The people of the "Celestial Empire" boast of their *antiquity.* The Chinese, if we believe the affirmations of their philosophers, were the first and the purest people formed by the gods. They have existed from all eternity, and from all eternity *the same.* They never change. Change, development, with them is weakness.* And the consequence is, the

---

* It is said of a Chinaman, that he chanced to learn to roast a pig, three hundred years ago, by the burning of a house; and to this day, when one of his descendants wishes to roast a pig, he burns a house, not having been able to discover any other method.

grossest superstition and ignorance, and the most dreadful barbarities still prevail among them. During the past year (1855) more than 150,000 "rebels" have been executed in the most dreadful manner, in China. An American, present during one day of slaughter in Canton, writes as follows concerning the dreadful scenes that passed before his eyes:

"As we approached the execution ground many were met with their hands to their nostrils, or with their tails tied round their faces, for the purpose of avoiding the horrid stench, which could literally be "felt" at a considerable distance. The ground was covered with partially dried gore, the result of the past day's work. There are no drains to take the blood away, nor is any substance used to slake it. One man was found digging holes for two crosses, on which, he said, four were to be tied and cut in pieces.

"The execution had been fixed for noon. At half-past eleven, half a dozen men arrived with the knives, preceded by the bearers of rough deal-wood boxes, decorated with bloody sides. These were the coffins. Unconcern was the general appearance of the soldiers and spectators, of whom, altogether, there may have been one hundred and fifty. At a quarter of twelve, the first batch of ten prisoners arrived. speedily followed by the rest in similar quantities.

"Each prisoner (having his hands tied behind his back, and labeled on the tail,) appeared to have been thrust down in a wicker basket, over which his chained legs dangled loosely, the body riding uncomfortably, and marked with a long paper tally, pasted on a slip of bamboo thrust between the prisoner's jacket and his back. These "man-baskets," slung with small cords, were carried on bamboos on the shoulders of two men. As the prisoners arrived, each was made to kneel with his face to the south. In a space of about 20 feet by 12 we counted as many as seventy, ranged in half a dozen rows. At five minutes to twelve a white-button mandarin arrived, and the two to be first cut in pieces were tied to the crosses. While looking at this frightening process the execution commenced, and twenty or thirty must have been headless before we were aware of it. The only sound to be heard was a horrid cheep—cheep—cheep, as the knives fell. One blow was sufficient for each— the head tumbling between the legs of the victim before it. As the sword falls, the blood-gushing trunk springs forward, falls on the breast, and is still for ever.

"In four minutes, the decapitation was complete; and then on the other victims commenced the barbarity, which, to think of only, is sufficiently barbaric. With a short sharp knife a slice was cut out from under each arm. A low, suppressed, fearful groan from each followed the operation of the weapon. Dexterous as butchers, a slice was taken successively by the operators from the calves, the thighs, and then from each breast. We may suppose, we hope, that by this time the sufferers were insensible to pain; but they were not dead. The knife was then stuck into the abdomen, which was ripped up to the breast-bone, and the blade twisted round and round as the heart was separated from its holding. Up to this moment, having once set eyes on the victim under torture, they had become fixed as by fascination; but they could be riveted there no longer. A whirling sensation ran through the brain, and it was with difficulty we could keep ourselves from falling. But this was not all; the lashings were then cut, and the head, being tied by the tail to a limb of the cross, was severed from the body, which was then dismembered of hands and arms, feet and legs, separately. After this the mandarins left the ground, to return, however, with a man and woman; the latter, it was said, the wife of one of the rebel chiefs—the man a leader of some rank. The woman was cut up in the way we have described; for the man, a more horrible punishment was decreed. He was flayed alive. We did not see this, but it was witnessed by the Sergeant of Marines of the United States, J. P. Kennedy—the cry at the first insertion of the knife across the forehead, and the pulling of the flesh over the eyes, being most horrible."

How shocking this description! And the more shocking to the senses of the well-informed Christian, from the fact that he *feels* the enormity, the astounding injustice and folly of such barbarities! We look in vain, then, in the Pagan world for the developments which we have described.

We come next to Turkey, where Mohammed and the Koran have had their day and their influence, and what is the result? Do we discover a love of improvement and learning—a progression in the arts, science, and knowledge, among the Turks? or do they grow in the divine principles of benevolence and humanity? Are they influencing the world of mankind, on these subjects, by their essays, and books—and by missionary effort? Not at all. The Turk loves his belly and his ease, and hates all beyond. The whole country is buried in a dark cloud of ignorance and superstition. There is not a post-route within its borders, and the people are too indolent to establish any. And many of their laws and customs are such as marked the sterner cruelties of the darker ages. No, in no Pagan, in no Mohammedan country, do we discover the developments which we have described.

We have only the Christian nations left. And here they exist. *But they exist no where else on the face of the globe.* Does not this significant fact teach us a lesson with reference to the influence of Christianity in effecting this glorious result? Many men rail at the Christian religion. Here is matter for the contemplation of such.

There is one other significant fact connected with this subject, which I feel it my duty to mention, viz: that the growth in humanity, and the activities of which I have spoken, are confined mainly to Protestant countries. Take the map, and examine again. Visit South and Central America, Mexico and Cuba;—pass over into Spain, Portugal, Italy. In all of these countries Catholicism is the predominant religion; but in none of them do we find an active moral or intellectual development. Here are ignorance, superstition, filth, immorality, crime, cruelty and tyranny; but few schools, newspapers, books, Bibles or colleges. It is for the simple reason, that unmixed Romanism forbids growth. It anathematizes progression, starving and stinting the soul. In the main, it is not Christian. The Inquisition is no Christian institution. To decapitate men, women, and children;—to burn them over a slow fire of green wood;—to draw them asunder, joint by joint, or incarcerate them in gloomy dungeons, is not Christ-like. Still, notwithstanding all these corruptions of Christianity, we find even Catholic countries in advance of the Pagan or Mohammedan.

But it is where the people have had the Bible in their own hands, and studied for themselves the commands of God and the inculcations of a Christian philosophy, that the growth of humanity is untrammeled and has manifested itself in a universal diffusion of knowledge, and a broad and generous desire for the improvement and happiness of the race. In Great Britain and the United States, the inspired word has been circulated without "let or hindrance." Here, Christianity, in a purer and more divine, loving and benevolent form, exists. And *where* it does so exist, no matter in what community, *there* you behold the highest form of civilization on earth—the most profound love of learning—the most humane laws—the largest benevolence, the purest morality, the least crime, and the *greatest amount of happiness.* We are certain of the truth of what we say. Reader, we ask again, are you a *professed Christian?* If so, we repeat, Consider well the claims of what we say in the future pages of this book, before you decide against them ; *for only in Christianity, and the efforts of its supporters, is there hope of the world's renovation.*

CHAPTER IV

ABOLISHMENT OF THE GALLOWS.

The Gallows a Relic of Barbarism—It is Unnecessary and Unchristian—Should be Abolished—It has been regarded the Hand-maid of the Church.—But so was the Pillory, the Stocks, and the Whipping-post—The Charge of "Morbid Sympathy"—It will not apply to the Great and Good who have labored for Reform—The Boy hung in Alexandria, La.—Touching Incidents,

If the reader has perused the preceding pages, he is prepared for what we have to say on the abolishment of the Death Penalty. The gallows we honestly believe to be a relic of barbarism—is not a Christian institution—is the cause of more crime than it cures—is unnecessary—is condemned by the spirit of the Christian religion, and should, therefore, be condemned by every good citizen, and *especially* by every *professed Christian;* and the law that sustains it should be wiped from the statute book of every civilized state and nation under heaven.

"Abolish the gallows!" exclaim thousands of excellent men and women, as they start and raise their hands in astonishment; "what would become of society without the gallows!" "Abolish the gallows!" echoes the minister of God; " the gallows, an instrument sustained by God's own law, and which has been the hand-maid of the Church for long centuries, in the protection of life and property, and so efficacious in preventing the depredations of the robber and assassin! Oh! this will never do—*never!* NEVER!! There would be no safety for honest people!"

(46)

So said our fathers and mothers when the whipping-post, the stocks and the gallows graced every churchyard in the country, and were thought to be as necessary to good order and good government as the pulpit or the Bible. I can assure you, my readers, that the reforms in human punishments, which I have described in the preceding pages, were not effected without an effort. Every inch of ground has been stoutly contested by those who venerate the customs of the fathers. When it was proposed by the humane to abolish the whipping-post, the stocks, and the pillory, many were alarmed at the bare thought of such a change, and said: "These punishments are of divine origin,—how can society exist without them?" And yet these old relics of barbarism have passed away forever, and society is still in existence. No moral earthquake has shaken the foundations of community, and the institutions of Christianity are not *totally* demolished.

Indeed, as we have seen, all rejoice that a better day has dawned, and would not return to the wilderness from which our fathers escaped, for any consideration. Now what we desire is, that our Christian communities should have faith in the divine teachings of their religion, and like the children of Israel, journey still on toward the promised land. Most certainly Christianity predicts the time the gallows shall cease to exist; when every nation, tribe and language, shall unite in one holy and harmonious society, and labor to "*save*, and not to *destroy* men's lives;" when "*violence shall no more be heard in the land;*" when " the knowledge of the Lord shall cover the earth;" when "the wolf shall dwell with the lamb, and the leopard shall lie down with the kid, and the calf and the young lion and the fatling together, and a little child shall lead them." Then "judgment shall dwell in the

wilderness, and righteousness in the fruitful field, **and**
the work of righteousness shall be peace, and the effect
of righteousness *quietness and assurance forever; and all
people shall dwell in peaceable habitations, and in sure
dwellings, and in quiet resting-places.*"

When the fulfilment of this blessed prediction shall be
realized, as it surely will be in the progress of the Christian religion, we think it altogether probable that the
gallows will be known only upon the pages of history,
and as an instrument of the darker ages.

One consideration more, before we enter on the main
argument. Great exertions are made by those who sustain the gallows, and are in favor of a rigid penal code,
to impress the public mind with the idea that those who
advocate a reform have no regard for the public welfare
—no love for good order and good government—are full
of a morbid sympathy for the criminal—but entertaining
no regard for those whom his lawless passions have destroyed—that we are mere " *humanity mongers;*"—and
even say that all we desire is, that *all law* should be abolished, so that robbers and assassins and murderers may
be turned out into the world, to wander up and down the
earth, " like a roaring lion, seeking whom they may
devour."

Now all this is unfair—it is ungenerous—it is posi-
tively *false!* Look at the long list of eminent Christian
men, of modern times, who were so earnestly engaged in
the reform of which I am speaking, and answer, could
they have acted from the motive thus ascribed to them?
Were LAFAYETTE, and Dr. JOHNSON, and Judge BLACK-
STONE, and MONTESQUIEU, and Sir THOMAS MOORE, and
LIVINGSTON, and HOWARD, and FRANKLIN, and Lord
BROUGHAM, and FOX, and PITT, and RUSH, and WILBER-
FORCE, and CHANNING. and RANTOUL, and UPHAM—were

these great and good men regardless of good order and good government? Were they laboring only to save the miserable criminal from merited punishment? Had they no sympathy for society as well as for the offender? Were they disposed to abolish all law, and permit the most desperate villains to run at large? Why, you might as well charge CHRIST HIMSELF with cherishing a "*morbid sympathy,*" for he was their guide. Then consider the character of the Quakers. They, as a sect, have always opposed the gallows. Are they not a pure, peaceable, order-loving and excellent people? Are they disregardful of the public good?

Why, we must have laws—and *penal* laws—so long as there are wicked men to be punished. But it does not, therefore, follow, that we must punish any man, or woman, or child, by KILLING. Have we not strong prisons and bars and bolts enough, and places for solitary confinement, if necessary? Can not the citizens of the great State of Ohio, or any other, guard themselves with all their jails and State prisons and penitentiaries, from the depredations of the few persons who may be disposed to murder? Must we take them from our prisons where they are perfectly secure, and choke the life out of them as a Christian duty, and for fear they may again injure us? A few months since, (Sept., 1855,) the people of Alexandria, La., were engaged in the work of strangling a little boy on the gallows, only ten years old. A secular paper,* in giving an account of the affair, said: " On the day before he was called to face death, some gentlemen visited him and propounded questions to him; but his answers were and could be no other than childish. He was, I believe, only ten years old. The gentlemen told him the sheriff was to hang him the next morning, and asked him

---

* New Orleans Delta.

5

what he thought of it, whether he had made his peace with God, and why he did not pray? His answer was, 'I have been hung many a time.' He was, at the time, amusing himself with some marbles he had in his cell. He was playing all the time in jail, never once thinking that death was soon to claim him as its victim. To show how a child's mind ranges when about to die, I will mention that, when upon the scaffold, he begged to be permitted to pray, which was granted, and then he commenced to cry! O, what a horrible sight it was!"

Now, was *that* act necessary? Was it Christian? Was it humane? Was it not rather barbarous and cowardly? In our view, Christian missionaries need not go to the Sandwich Islands to find heathen customs and barbarities. Pagans would be ashamed of the above deed! I would abolish the gallows, then, not from a morbid sympathy for the criminal—not because we would screen him from punishment—nor because we disregard the security and welfare of society—but for other important reasons, which to us are good and sufficient;—some of which we will now present.

CHAPTER V.

FIRST REASON FOR ABOLISHMENT.

The Gallows an institution of Vengeance—Lynch Law—"String him up," "Stretch his neck," "Burn him," not Christian exclamations—Execution of Colt in New-York—Declarations of Vengeance of Christian Ladies in Cincinnati—All this foreign from the spirit of the Christian Religion, and condemned by it.

The first reason I would offer for the abolishment of the Death Penalty is, *It is founded in a spirit of retaliation. It is a work of vengeance!*

We profess to be a *Christian* people. Retaliation and vengeance are inconsistent with Christianity. Lynch law sometimes prevails in some portions of our country. A man commits a gross outrage, which exasperates the public mind. Vengeance! vengeance! is now the cry. The culprit is seized, and either hung up and strangled, or tied to a stake and burned. Nothing but *revenge* will satisfy the enraged multitude

Now, in this act, you perceive the spirit which first prompted the taking of human life for crime, and which does much towards sustaining the gallows at the present time. How many do we find in every community who advocate the existence of the Death Penalty on this very ground? "The miserable offender of the law," say they, "has outraged society—he isn't fit to live—he has no claims on society for life—his brother's blood should be avenged! String him up, we say—string him up!"

(51)

Bills for the abolishment of the Death Penalty have been rejected in the Legislatures of New-York, Pennsylvania and Ohio, at different times, mainly from the influence of the argument drawn from what was called the *justice* of capital punishment. It was argued that "men who would murder *ought* to be killed;"—they "*deserved* this punishment;"—"hanging was just good enough for them;" while the speakers actually ridiculed the "mock sympathy" that would institute a milder punishment for a man guilty of death. When a magistrate of eminence, in conversation with Mr. Livingston the philanthropist, on this subject, was driven from every other argument, he said very frankly, "I must confess that there is some little feeling of *revenge* at the bottom of my opinion on the subject." "If all other reasoners," adds Mr. Livingston, "were equally candid, there would be less difficulty in establishing true doctrines." "Passion first made revengeful laws, and revenge once incorporated with the system of justice, reproduced its own image, after passion had expired."

When Colt was expected to be executed in New-York, some years since, and the people had assembled in thousands to witness the act, and it was found that a portion of the prison was on fire—a writer, describing the scene, said:

"The hearts of men were filled with murder; they gloated over the thoughts of vengeance, and were rabid to witness a fellow-creature's agony. They complained loudly that he was not to be hung high enough for the crowd to see him. 'What a pity!' exclaimed a woman who stood near me, gazing at the burning tower; '*they will have to give him two hours more to live!*'"

And when a man,* who now lies in jail in this city,

---

* Arrison, the Torpedo Murderer.

charged with a diabolical murder, was taken and brought here, both men and women, even *ladies*—*Christian* ladies, exclaimed, " Hang him !"—" String him up !"—" He deserves to have his neck stretched!" One lady—a most devout member of a most devout Church—went so far as to declare, in her wrath, that "he should be hung by his toes, head downward, that he might die by inches!" the common method being too merciful.

Now, this is the spirit which prompts the work of death, but it is not the spirit of Christ. It is the spirit which nailed him to the cross, but not the spirit which dictated that more than mortal petition, " *Father, forgive them, they know not what they do.*"

I behold the Savior, as he went from place to place blessing the poor—healing the sick—raising up the bowed down—imparting hope to the sinner, and weeping over the frailties and sufferings of humanity; *but no where do I see him giving countenance to an act of vengeance.* On one occasion, when the Samaritans refused to receive him into their city, we read that his disciples said, " Lord, wilt thou that we command fire to come down from heaven and consume them, even as Elias did?" How were they exasperated! But what said Jesus, that calm, and mild, and blessed being? "He turned and rebuked them; and said, Ye know not what manner of spirit ye are of. For the Son of Man is not come to DESTROY MEN'S LIVES, BUT TO SAVE THEM."

"As if he had said," remarks Dr. Adam Clarke, the Methodist commentator, in his paraphrase on this text, " Ye do not consider that the present is a dispensation of *mercy* and *love;* and that the design of God is not to *destroy* sinners, but to give them space to repent, that he may *save them* unto *life eternal.* And ye, my disciples, do not consider that the zeal which you feel springs from

an evil principle within you. Let not the followers of
that Christ who *died for his enemies, think of avenging
themselves on the sinner.*"

Now, these are reasonable and Christian words. The
closing declaration is full of meaning. "Let not the
followers of that Christ who *died for his enemies, think of
avenging themselves on the sinner.*" Did Christ ever avenge
himself on the sinner? Did he ever hang, or burn, or
kill?

"Artists once loved to paint the Savior in the lowly
toil of lowly men; his garments covered with the dust
of common life; his soul sullied by no pollution. But
paint him to your fancy as an *executioner*—legally killing
a man; the halter in his hands, leading Judas to the
scaffold for high treason! You see the relation which
such an act bears to Christianity." You perceive that
in Christ it would not be Christian. And if not Christian in *him*, how can it be in *you* and *I*, who hold up the
hands of the sheriff when he destroys the life of a fellow-
creature?

No, my reader, the true Christian can never avenge
himself on the sinner. And yet, how general, how universal, has been the work of vengeance by the Church.
Look at the slaughter of the inquisition;—the millions
slain by order of the Romish Church! Our law for killing is said to be *humane;* for while it demands the life
of the offender, it requires that he be executed in the
quickest possible manner, and in the way that shall produce the least pain. But it was not thus with our fathers; not thus with the old Church when it was actuated
only by revenge. As we have seen, our fathers not only
killed, but they *tortured,* in a manner the most diabolical;
by burning—by the rack—by pulling out toe and finger
nails, unjointing the limbs—flaying alive, &c., &c.

Christian writers have detailed a long list of modes of killing, as perpetrated by the Church, and which were resorted to only to wreak vengeance on the poor victim, by producing the greatest possible suffering. Amongst these, may be mentioned the following: " Crucifixion—burning—roasting—hanging by the leg or rib—starving —sawing asunder—exposing to wild-beasts—rending asunder by horses drawn opposite ways—burying alive —blowing from the mouth of a cannon—compulsory deprivation of sleep—rolling in a barrel stuck with nails—pressing slowly to death by a weight laid on the breast—casting headlong from a rock—tearing out the bowels, or the heart—pulling to pieces with red-hot pincers—stretching on the rack—breaking on the wheel—squeezing the marrow from the bones by screws or wedges," &c., &c.

Now, is all that *Christian?* Is it not rather *diabolical?* And when men have been put to death from this revengeful, this hellish spirit, have they not been *murdered?* What *is* murder? It is to kill with *malice prepense* or *aforethought.* It matters not whether *one* man or *ten thousand* commit the deed; if we destroy human life with *premeditated vengeance, we murder.* Every man, therefore, who says, " String him up "—" Crucify him "—" Stretch his neck "—" He deserves to be killed," etc., etc., has the spirit of murder in his soul, which is unchristian, and should never be cherished. I again say, The gallows is sustained by this spirit, and should therefore be abolished, for we profess to be Christians.

CHAPTER VI.

SECOND REASON FOR ABOLISHMENT.

EACH CITIZEN'S RESPONSIBILITY.

Each Citizen's responsibility for the acts of the Gallows—Inconsistency of Christians—"Thou shalt not kill"—Killing by Proxy—Dreadful Case of Young Boyington—So long as the Death Penalty remains, can I shake off my Individual Responsibility—I wish to have no part nor lot in the shedding of Human Blood—The Authority of the State to kill—Has it such Authority?—Argument of Rantoul.

Another reason why I labor for the abolishment of the gallows, is, that so long as men are executed in the State of which I am a citizen, *I feel that as a citizen, I with others, am responsible for the act; a sort of particeps crimi·nis—"accessory before the fact."*

"THOU SHALT NOT KILL," is one of the TEN great commandments of the Decalogue. When I listen, it comes as the voice of God, the Great Fountain of all Life, to my soul. "Thou shalt not kill." These words I learned to repeat by heart, when a little child at Sabbath School. "To destroy human life," said my pious teacher, "is the most dreadfully wicked act that was ever committed!" So said my minister; and so said all his Church.

And yet, my Sabbath School teacher, my minister, and all his Church, *would themselves kill;*—not as individuals, but as citizens of the State;—and not with their own hands, but *through the instrumentality of the hangman.*

I look around in society, and I find that very much the same instruction is given in all our Sabbath Schools

(56)

and Churches, concerning the sixth commandment, as when I was a child, whilst the same disposition is manifested, on the part of the people, to violate its requirements. Our Christian fathers and mothers, lawyers, doctors and divines, still say it is very wicked to kill; and yet, each of our thirty-one States, with the few exceptions I have stated in the preceding pages, have enacted laws which absolutely require the death of men, women and children, when guilty of certain offenses. Yea, even if *innocent*, the same demand is made, provided the tribunal before which they are tried, *believes* them to be guilty, and they have no means of establishing their innocence.

Now, for one, I desire not to participate in any such responsibility. A few years since, suspicion was fastened upon a respectable young man, by the name of Boyington, in Louisiana, of having murdered a fellow-lodger at a tavern. He was tried, found guilty, and condemned to death. His letters to his parents from his prison were most touching—and always to the purpose that he knew nothing of the crime for which he was condemned.

When placed on the gallows, he made an able and most moving vindication of himself; again protesting, in the name of God, that innocence which his fellow-men refused to believe. He said he could not die for such a crime, when he was no more guilty than any man in the vast crowd before him. But when informed that he *must* suffer—that there was *no help for him*—he broke wildly loose from those by whom he was surrounded on the scaffold, and rushed in among the multitude, in the most piteous manner crying, in the name of God, for help, and repeating the assurance, with the most dreadful shrieks, that he was innocent. He was soon again secured by the sheriff, dragged back to the scaffold, and in the midst of the most awful cries, and heart-rending calls for mercy, *launched into eternity.*

What followed?—A few months after this terrible scene, the tavern-keeper, on his death-bed, *confessed his own guilt, and proved the innocence of young Boyington!*

But now it was too late. The die had been cast. The innocent victim was slain. His life could not be restored. His poor, heart-broken mother mourned over the event a few weeks, and was laid in the grave beside her unfortunate son.

Now permit me to inquire of my reader : " *Who killed that young man?*" · " Who killed him?" you respond: "Why the sheriff, the hangman." No, my friend, you mistake. The hangman acted simply as an instrument of the government. " Ah, yes," say you, " I see how it is, the *government* killed him. The government made the law declaring that he should be killed; described *how* he should be killed, and *who* should be used as an *instrument* in the work of death. Then the *government* strangled the man, simply using the hands of the sheriff to adjust the knot—place the rope—draw down the cap, and——let him swing." Just so. But then there is another question behind all this, in which *you* and *I* should have been specially interested if we had been citizens of Louisiana at that time, viz: *Who, or what, constitutes the government of a State?* " Who, or what, constitutes the government," you ask. Yes. Suppose you desire to find the government of the State of which you are a citizen, where would you seek for it? "Why," say you, " I should seek it at the capitol of the State, if the Legislature was in session." But would you find it there? Suppose you should enter the Senate-chamber of your State, seat yourself by the side of some leading politician, and tell him your errand. What reply do you think he would make, if an honest and intelligent man? I will tell you. "My dear sir, you have come to the wrong place to find the government of our State. We are merely ' the servants of the people.' We never do anything without 'feeling the public pulse.' The wishes of our constituents, when fully known, are ' law and gospel' with us. You perceive, therefore, that it is not *we* who govern the State, but the *State* that governs us !"

If you should enter the private room of your governor, and counsel him, the same answer would be returned, if the truth were uttered. "Go home to *the people!*" he would exclaim, "if you wish to find the government of our State. They place us in these offices—direct us what to do, and we are particularly careful to see that *their* will is respected, when once fully known, especially when we are made to realize that *they are determined and in earnest.*"

The people, then, are the government of the State. They are responsible for its laws and institutions, while the *officers* of government are only responsible for the *execution* of the laws.

Suppose, now, that when the unfortunate young man, Boyington, mentioned above, was forced upon the gallows a second time, to be strangled, all the time terribly conscious of his own innocence, you and I had been present amid the swaying throng as witnesses of the awful spectacle. When we heard him declaring, in the most heart-rending accents, his innocence—appealing to the multitude for mercy, saying, " Oh, spare me ; for the love of God and my poor mother, spare me! I am not fit to die! I am innocent!"—when we saw and heard all this, I repeat, should we not have felt that we were *participators* in this act; and if the poor man was innocent, our hands were not clean of the awful crime of his murder. Suppose he should have pointed to individuals then present

and have said, "Sir, *you* kill me, and *you*, and *you;—*you,
and such as you are the State;—you have instituted, and
you sustain the law which requires that I should be
killed;—you sanction this work; you pay the court for
condemning, and these men for strangling me!" If he
had made such an appeal, would not every word of it
have been true?

All the more humane and Christian of the multitude
might have declared, "*We* have no sympathy for the
gallows—we have no desire for your death. If *our* prayers could be answered, you would be spared;—we wash
our hands clean of this act." But would this declaration
have changed the responsibility from them to others, inasmuch as they were still citizens of the State, and paid
their money and lent their influence, in making its laws
and maintaining its institutions?

Now, for my own part, I do not wish to occupy a position like this. If a man should murder my own child,
or the dearest friend I have on earth, if once fairly secured in prison, I would never consent to his death.
To kill *him* would only be imitating his own wicked example. It would be of no advantage to me. It would
not restore life to my child or friend. It could not benefit the culprit. It would be simply a work of vengeance,
which the religion I profess utterly forbids. I say again,
I could not, therefore, consent to his death. And yet,
as a citizen of the State, I am made, even against my
own will, to share the responsibilities of every *legalized
murder* the State commits. A large majority of the most
order-loving and Christian portion of the people of
Ohio and other States, are unquestionably opposed to
the Death Penalty. Their humanity rises up against it.
And yet, so long as this law remains on our statute
books, and men are executed, so long will these thou-

sands be under the necessity of participating in the act, and feel responsible for its results.

Another consideration. If an assassin should enter my dwelling at midnight, with the intent to murder, but should miss his aim, and I should succeed in securing him hand and foot with strong cords, I should feel that I had *no right* to proceed and deliberately beat out his brains, even if I possessed a desire to commit so dastard an act. He is secure. He can do me no further injury; and if I should kill him under such circumstances, the State would call it murder, and hold me responsible for the deed, declaring that I had *no authority* to deprive him of life, when he was once secure. And this is true. But then the State would take this same man, and though possessed of means to hold him far more securely than I, would go to work, and after weeks or months of preparation, commit the very deed which, if perpetrated by me, as an individual, it pronounces murder. Now, an important and very interesting question arises, viz: *Whence derives the State its authority for this deed?* Many good and wise men have argued, and not without reason, that it has no authority. Look at the subject a moment. Who constitute the State? Answer: Its citizens, irrespective of numbers, whether ten persons, ten hundred, or ten hundred thousand. Well, it is plain that they can possess no authority in their associated capacity as a State, *but such as is derived from themselves as individuals.* The State cannot say, I have a right to kill *because I am the State*, or because I have the *power;* it can only say, I have a right to kill because the citizens which consti tute this body *have delegated this authority to me.* This being admitted, then, we ask, can any individual delegate to another or others a right *which he himself does not possess?* Reader, you are a citizen of some State, and, therefore, a constituent member of the body-politic. You grant, as an individual, you have no right to beat out the brains of an assassin, whom you have securely bound. Now, can you confer this right upon another man, or ten other men, when you do not yourself possess it? You answer, that the authority is derived from the compact, in which the citizens of the State have mutually agreed to surrender life under certain circumstances. But here the same question returns upon us, Can a man enter any compact by which he can confer upon others authority which he does not himself possess?

God has given me life. I hope I am grateful for this blessing—*but he has given me no control over my life.* I hold it under him. I have no authority to destroy my existence or barter it away. I cannot commit suicide; I cannot sell my life, or dispose of my existence in any possible manner, for God has given me no such authority, but *positively forbidden it.* Now, as I have no right to dispose of my existence, can I, by entering a compact, delegate to others this right?

There is a provision in law, that no man shall burn his own buildings; and, can he authorize another to burn his buildings when he has no such right himself? The law of God declares, "Thou shalt not steal." Can any man who has no right to steal, delegate this right to another? No. All can see, then, that we have no power to give to another or others anything which we ourselves do not possess.

Now, then, suppose that ten men, or an hundred, constitute a colony on some island, or in some new territory, and they assemble to digest and adopt laws by which they are to be governed in their intercourse one with another. Have they any right to enter a compact by which they barter away, or shall forfeit their lives? **If**

I were one of this compact, could I say to others, "Gentlemen, if I do certain things, or leave undone certain things, I will give you my existence? You shall be at liberty, and have the right to, strangle the life out of me? And if either of you are, in like manner, guilty, I shall claim the same right to strangle you?" To my mind it is very plain, that if I entered such a league, I should as really transcend any authority that I possess, as I should to burn my own buildings, or kill the assassin whom I had safely secured.

Says Mr. Rantoul,* "A man holds his life as a tenant at will—not, indeed, of *society*, who did not and cannot give it, or renew it, and have, therefore, no right to take it away—but of that Almighty Being whose gift life is, to whom it belongs, and who alone has a right to reclaim his gift whenever it shall seem good in his sight. A man may not surrender up his life till he is called for. May he, then, make a contract with his neighbor that in such and such case his neighbor shall kill him? Such a contract, if executed, would involve the one party in the guilt of *suicide, and the other in the guilt of murder.*

"If a man may not say to his next neighbor, 'When I have burned your house in the night time, or wrested your purse from you on the high-way, or broken into your house in the night, with an iron crow, to take a morsel of meat for my starving child, do you seize me, shut me up a few weeks, and then bring me out and strangle me; and in like case, if your turn comes first, I will serve you in the same way'—if I could not make this agreement with *one* of my neighbors, would such an agreement between *ten* of us be any more valid or justifiable? No. Nor if the number were a hundred instead

---

* An eminent Boston lawyer, who has labored with much industry for years in the cause of humanity. No man has accomplished more in the softening of the penal codes of the New-England States than Mr. Rantoul.

of ten—or a thousand—or twenty millions, who should form this infernal compact, would this increase of the number of partners vary one hair's breadth the moral character of the transaction? If this execution of the contract be not murder on the one side, and suicide on the other, what precise number of persons must engage in it, in order that what was criminal before may become innocent, not to say virtuous? And upon what hitherto unheard-of principles of morality is an act of murder in an *individual*, or *a small corporation*, converted into an act of *justice* whenever another subscriber has joined the association for mutual sacrifice? It is a familiar fact in the history of mankind, that great corporations will do, and glory in, what the very individuals composing them would shrink from or blush at. But how can the division of the responsibility transform vice into virtue, or diminish the amount of any given crime?"

There is both truth and reason in the foregoing. If it is morally wrong for one man to steal, it is morally wrong for ten—twenty—fifty—a hundred—or a hundred millions, to steal. If it is morally wrong for one man to take human life, when the culprit is securely bound, it is morally wrong for ten, twenty, fifty, a hundred, or a hundred millions, to commit the act. I, therefore, feel that as a citizen, I should use my influence to abolish a law which I fully believe is not valid, and for which I feel that I should not be held responsible, and yet must be, so long as it remains.

Mr. Rantoul says that "great corporations will do, and glory in, what the very individuals composing them would shrink from or blush at." This is true. Let me secure the assassin with manacles and cords, and chain him to a post so that he can not move, hand or foot; and though he had murdered my wife and children, I should blush and be ashamed to cut his throat, or beat out his brains, or strangle him with a halter, now that he is secure and helpless.* Indeed, it would be a murderous and dastardly act. For no consideration would I thus become an executioner. And should I ask another to do an act for me which I would shrink from doing myself with the utmost horror? And this is what I demand of the State when I ask the State to sustain the gallows. It is what the State consents to do, when it places upon its statute books the Death Penalty. It becomes the executioner of those who are securely bound or imprisoned, and for whose further depredations it can have no fears. Thus will great corporations do, and glory in, what the very individuals composing them would shrink from or blush at.

In concluding this chapter, I would remark that some may say that the Bible affords authority for killing, and refer us to " Moses and the Prophets." In reply, I answer, that it was Moses and the Prophets who authorized our fathers to burn the witches, execute for profanity, strangle their children for disobedience, and hang for stealing forty shillings. But was this authority valid? And if so, why is it not still in vogue? Suppose Moses gave this authority to a particular people, existing under

---

* Dr. Rush says : " The power over human life is the sole prerogative of Him who gave it. Human laws are, therefore, in rebellion against this prerogative when they transfer it to human hands." I understand Mr. Rantoul to advance the same doctrine in the above argument;—that is, that human life is in the hands of God alone—that power over it is his sole prerogative, and, therefore, that man has no right to destroy the life of his fellow *under any circumstances.* Many good men have advocated the same doctrine. It is not my design to discuss it in this work, as it is not necessary; but I wish simply to say that, though every man *feels* that the power of life and death is alone in the hands of God, he also *feels* that self-preservation is the first law of his nature, and that if an assassin were cutting his throat, or murdering his wife and children, he would be recreant to the duty which he owes to himself and his family, if he did not protect them to the utmost of his power, even to the sacrifice of the assassin's life.

6

peculiar circumstances, in a dark and rude state of society, can *we* claim the same authority from the same source?

We live under the influence of a "new and better covenant." We are not heathen nor Hebrews, but CHRISTIANS. Show me a single declaration or act of Christ or his apostles that sanctions the gallows—or burning—beheading—strangling—the rack—the wheel, or the taking of human life *in any form, or for any crime*, and I will yield the argument. But till then, you must not condemn me if I love the spirit and commands of my Master more than the inhumanity and barbarity of a darker age.

More on this point when we come to consider the scriptural argument for the gallows.

CHAPTER VII.

THIRD REASON FOR ABOLISHMENT.

IRREMEDIABILITY.

Execution of the Innocent—The evil cannot be remedied—Declaration of Lafayette—Execution of the Innocent during the French Revolution—Dying Protestations of Innocence—Injustice of executing the Innocent—Instance of the Imprisonment of an Innocent Man—Agony which the Innocent must experience in Conviction and Execution—Execution of an Innocent Man in Indiana—Execution of a Poor German—Execution of an Innocent Young Girl—Innocent Man hung in England—Circumstantial Evidence not to be relied on—Positive Evidence not always Certain—Extract from O'Connel of Ireland.

One of the most pressing and cogent reasons with me for the abolishment of the Death Penalty, is the fact that *so long as it remains on our statute books, and is enforced, the* INNOCENT *are liable to be put to death as well as the guilty.*

The great and good Lafayette said, "I shall ask for the abolishment of the Penalty of Death, until I have the infallibility of human judgment demonstrated to me." And he said this because of the awful scenes he had witnessed in consequence of the execution of the innocent. "The punishment of Death has always inspired me with feelings of horror," he exclaimed, "since the execrable use made of it during the former revolution." During that revolution, the innocent and the guilty were made to pour out their blood upon the block indiscriminately. "Oh! spare me; for before God I proclaim my innocence!"—"With the voice of a dying mortal I solemnly declare that I am guiltless!" were protestations for

(67)

which the guillotine tarried not in its work of death. Neither has the gallows in Europe and America. In England more than 10,000 men and women have been executed who protested most sacredly, with their last breath, that they had no knowledge of the crimes for which they were about to suffer. And, in the United States, the number is rising three hundred.

It is true, that even the dying testimony of men is not always to be credited; but, out of so many, is it not altogether probable a large number uttered the truth? Some of them—indeed, a majority—were entitled to credit, for they had become hopeful converts to the Christian religion — were "changed from nature to grace"—fitted for the immortal spheres, and were expecting a world of glory on passing away from this world of sin. So said their spiritual advisers, and so said the Christian Church generally. Hence I repeat, they were entitled to credit *among Christians*. But they were *not* credited. On the contrary, every one of them was strangled;—yes, strangled by the hands of Christians, *in the very midst of their protestations of innocence!*

Now, as I view the subject, to kill a human being for a crime of which he is innocent, is one of the most un just and dreadful deeds that can be perpetrated. He is made to suffer an evil which it is impossible *to remedy*. We can restore *property*, and *liberty*, and even *character*, to the innocent, but we can never restore LIFE. A few years ago, a man in the western part of Massachusetts was convicted of burning a barn, on the positive evidence of a neighbor, and was sentenced to the State prison for six years. But when three years had passed, the very man on whose testimony he was convicted, when on his death bed, confessed his own guilt in the crime; and thus was the innocent man restored to liberty, and to his discon-

An Innocent Man preparing for Execution —Page 69.

solate and wretched family, who had been deprived of
his presence and assistance during these long and painful months and years.* But though *he* was restored,
how could that world of mortification, and anxiety, and
suffering, which he and his family had experienced, be
restored ?

Now, this was sufficiently unjust and dreadful, but it is
as nothing—or as the mere "dust in the balance"—when
compared with the evil perpetrated in executing the innocent. Here, *nothing can be done to remedy the evil.* The
poor victim has gone into eternity. It is now too late.
Think of the long days and nights of suffering of the
doomed man, when in prison awaiting his trial; of his
agony, when the awful word "GUILTY" is pronounced,
and his sentence passed. Think of the days and weeks
of wretchedness which follow;—of his soul on fire with
the conviction of his own innocence, when the world will
not credit his protestations. Think of his grief when
the awful thought comes to his soul, that his own
parents, his wife, his darling children, will *always* believe
him a felon; and must always suffer the disgrace that
will attach to his memory. Think of his agony as his
day of doom approaches, and he takes his last farewell
of wife and children. He is innocent, but *no man believes it*, and he has no means of proving it. He stands
upon the gallows, and still protests his innocence, but in
vain. For weeks and months he has lived on the hope
that a just God would not desert him; that in his Providence the truth would be revealed, and his innocence
proved. But now he is in despair. The fatal noose is

---

* The State, feeling the injustice it had thus inflicted on one of its
citizens, by three years' false imprisonment, made an effort—a very *weak*
effort it was—to compensate him for his labor while in prison. The Legislature magnanimously voted the stipend of $300, as an equivalent for
three years' confinement and hard labor. And this was all.

fixed; the minister has commended him to God, and prayed that He will have mercy on his soul, when *he* feels no mercy;—the cap is drawn down, and the hangman is ready to strike the blow that will send him into eternity, and yet there is no one to testify to his innocence. He *must* die, and die a felon! There is no hope! Great God! what must be the agony of a sensitive soul, conscious of its own purity, under such circumstances! For what would the reader take his place?

THE DROP FALLS! The man dies—dies a murderer. His body is given over for dissection. A knowledge of his execution is heralded to the wide world. But the next month, or week—nay, it may be the *next hour*, (as has many times occurred,) the *facts* in the case are revealed, and the truth of the poor man's protestations verified. But it is now too late—TOO LATE! Who can bring back the life—or even restore the *body*, for a decent, Christian burial? Who can heal the wounds of that broken-hearted widow, or father, or mother; or give an equivalent for the long days, and weeks, and months, of agonized suffering, on the part of the children? Oh, all this is *irreparable*.

And yet, the supporters of the gallows will turn away from this argument, with a mere word, as if the whole matter were of but little or no consequence. Says a minister of the "true Church," "When an innocent man suffers, all that can be said is, that Providence has seen fit to take away, by painful exit, one whom a few more years would have necessarily carried to the tomb." Yes, and he should have added, "The poor wretch should submit to the mandate of Heaven, *without a pang or a murmur!*"

Now, is not that cool? Is it not heartless? *"All that can be said!"* Indeed; suppose that the case were *his own,* or that of *his son* or *daughter,* would he dispose of it in this calm and philosophic manner? Would he not find utterance for other words? And does not that religion which he professes teach him that every man is *his brother,* and that he should feel the same interest in the unjust sufferings of others that he does in his own? Did not Jesus forget his own trials and weep alone for others? And yet here is a Christian minister, high in an evangelical Church, who can dismiss this great question of inhumanity and injustice with the cold answer, that if the innocent victim is doomed to be hung he must make the best of it; *he would have died in a few years anyhow.*

Lafayette was right when he said that he would oppose the Death Penalty until the infallibility of human judgment was demonstrated. The writer of these pages has made this a principle of action for years. It is his motto still. Society had better permit a score of felons to go clear, than to put to death one innocent fellow-creature. For, at best, the murderer cannot escape punishment. The mark of Cain is upon him. "Vengeance is *mine, I* will repay, saith the Lord." "Though hand join in hand, the wicked shall not be unpunished." Man is fallible, but God cannot err. Human tribunals are endowed with only human wisdom, and though governed by motives the most sincere, have often misjudged. Even when the evidence has been *positive* and to the point, they have, in numerous instances, been deceived, and convicted and put to death the innocent. Many cases of this kind have taken place, both in this country and in Europe, a few of which we relate.

EXECUTION OF AN INNOCENT MAN IN INDIANA.

Several years ago, a man residing about seventy miles from Cincinnati, died by poisoning, and suspicions resting on a near neighbor and acquiantance, he was arrested and brought to trial. The wife of the deceased made positive oath that the prisoner at the bar was at her house previous to the sickness of her husband, and administered the poison in a cup of coffee, as she had reason to believe. It was also proven that the prisoner purchased poison in Cincinnati about that time, of the description found in the stomach of the deceased. Thus was conviction of the man's guilt fixed in the minds of the jury. In his defence, the prisoner admitted that he had purchased the poison, but declared that he had purchased it for the woman who swore against him, and who said, when she sent for it, that she wanted to employ it to exterminate rats;—that he gave it into her hand on his return from Cincinnati, and was utterly ignorant of when or how it was administered to her husband. This story, however, availed nothing with the jury. The woman was a *religious* woman, and her story was entitled to credit. The man was accordingly convicted, sentenced and hung. But he always protested his innocence to the hour of his death. A few years passed, and the guilty woman confessed, not long before her death, that *she* was the guilty wretch, and declared that the State had executed an innocent man—one who was utterly ignorant of the circumstances of the murder. What injustice was here! And yet the court and jury sinned ignorantly. The State was in fault, for by sanctioning the Death Penalty it had wantouly thrown away the power to atone for the grievous wrong. If the man had been put to work in the State prison, he could have been discharged when the facts came out;—the State could have compensated him for his services, and done what was in its power to make full reparation for the wrong committed.

The following is another instance, somewhat similar:

EXECUTION OF A POOR GERMAN FOR MURDER.

A few years ago, a poor German came to New-York, and took lodgings where he was allowed to do his cooking in the same room with the family. The husband and wife lived in a perpetual quarrel. One day the German came into the kitchen, with a clasp-knife and a pan of potatoes, and commenced to pare them for his dinner. The quarrelsome couple were in a more violent altercation than usual; but he sat with his back towards them, and, being ignorant of their language, felt in no danger of being involved in their disputes. But the woman, with a sudden and unexpected movement, snatched the knife from his hand, and plunged it into her husband's heart. She had sufficient presence of mind to rush into the street and scream murder. The poor foreigner, in the meanwhile, seeing the wounded man reel, sprang forward to catch him in his arms, and drew out the knife. People from the street crowded in, and found him with the dying man in his arms, the knife in his hand, and blood upon his clothes. The wicked woman swore, in her most positive terms, that he had been fighting with her husband, and had stabbed him with a knife he always carried. The unfortunate German knew too little of English to understand her accusation, or to tell his own story. He was dragged off to prison, and the true state of the case was made known through an interpreter, but it was not believed. Circumstantial evidence was exceedingly strong against the accused, and the real criminal swore that she saw him commit the murder. He was executed, notwithstanding the most persevering efforts of his lawyer, John Anthon, Esq., whose convictions of the man's innocence were so painfully strong that, from that day to this, he has refused

7

to have any connection with a capital case. Some years after this tragic event the woman died, and, on her death-
bed, confessed her agency in the diabolical transaction ;
but her poor victim could receive no benefit from this
tardy repentance.

We could relate many accounts of this description,
where the evidence was positive, had we space. A few
must suffice.

EXECUTION OF AN INNOCENT YOUNG GIRL IN ENGLAND.

In the " Old Bailey (London) Trials" of the last century, there is an account of the conviction and execution of a young girl of seventeen, for stealing a
roll of ribbon, worth three shillings. But one witness
appeared against her, viz: the shop-man. " The prisoner came into my shop," said he, " and bought some ribbon. I saw her secrete this piece also. I personally
knew her, and was on the most friendly and sociable
terms with her. When she left the shop I accompanied
her, and *offered her my arm*, which she accepted. We
chatted together. As we reached the corner of a street
leading to the Bow street office, I turned toward it. She
said she was going in another direction, and bade me
good morning. I said to her, '*No!* you are going with
me! I saw you steal a piece of my ribbon!' She immediately implored me for God's sake to overlook it, and
restored to me the article. I said to her that I had lost
many things in this way, and was resolved to make her
an example—*that I was determined to have her life!*"

How heartless the testimony of this cold-blooded
wretch. He accomplished his designs. His testimony
was *positive*. The court and jury believed his story, convicted the girl and *hung her*. And yet the subsequent
confession of the shop-man revealed the innocence of

the girl, and the enormity of his own sin, in taking this method to hide the fruits of an illicit intercourse with the girl.

From the relation of such facts, the reader will not only come to realize the injustice liable to fall upon the most innocent at any moment, but he will also discover how little implicit credit is to be placed upon even the most positive testimony. It is often said, even by those who sustain the Death Penalty, that a man should never be convicted and hung on *circumstantial* evidence, because of its uncertainty. But we see in all the cases above presented, that *positive* testimony is equally uncertain. The witnesses may be personally interested, and swear falsely to shelter themselves. Does not the reader see that so long as human tribunals are fallible, that they may err, even when most certain that they are correct in the judgment rendered. The following is another instance of the same description:

AN INNOCENT MAN HUNG IN ENGLAND FOR ROBBERY.

A robber in England knocked a traveler from his horse, stabbed him, and took his pocket-book. It was in a turn in the road, and he was hidden by the bushes. He had no sooner accomplished his work than he heard another traveler approaching; but he had injured his ancle and could not escape. He, therefore, secreted himself near the place of the murder. The traveler came up, saw the dying man with the dirk still in his breast. He sprang from his horse, drew out the dirk, and did all in his power to staunch the wound, but in vain. Just at that moment other travelers appeared, and the robber, thinking that he would be discovered, came boldly from his hiding-place, and upon his testimony the innocent man was arrested, and, to his own astonishment, on his person was found the pocket-book of the murdered man. The real thief had slipped it, unperceived, into his pocket, at a moment when all eyes were turned in another direction. The prisoner protested, in the most positive manner, his innocence ; but there were the positive testimony of the witness, the bloody dirk in his hand, as seen by other witnesses, the pocket-book of the murdered man found on his person, and, besides all this, it was shown that he and the deceased were enemies. He was, therefore, convicted, sentenced and hung. In a few months the real murderer was convicted of another crime, and when on the gallows confessed the facts as above related.

Again, *circumstantial* evidence sometimes appears equivalent to positive and certain proof, it is so linked and woven together, and yet there may be no proof in it. Consider the following cases:

A SURGEON CHARGED WITH THE MURDER OF HIS SERVANT.

A gentleman was tried in Dublin on the 24th of May, 1728, charged with the murder of his maid-servant. An opposite neighbor saw him admitted into his house about ten at night, by his servant, who opened the door, holding in her hand a lighted candle in a brazen candlestick. Not long after, the gentleman made an alarm, exclaiming that his servant was murdered. The woman was found a corpse in the kitchen, her head fractured, her neck wounded so as to divide the jugular vein, and her dress steeped in blood. On further search, the inquirer discovered that the prisoner had on a clean shirt, while one freshly stained with blood, and ascertained to be his, was discovered in the recess of a cupboard ; where also was found a silver goblet, bearing the marks of a bloody thumb and finger. The prisoner fainted on being shown the shirt. He was executed.

His defense, on trial, was, that the maid-servant admitted him, as sworn, and went to the kitchen; that he had occasion to call her, but not being answered, went and found her lying on the floor; not knowing her to be dead, and being a surgeon, he proceeded to open a vein in her neck; in moving the body, the blood stained his hands and shirt sleeves. He then thought it best to make an alarm for assistance, but being afraid of the effect which his appearance might produce, he changed his linen, and displaced the silver cup in order to put his bloody shirt out of sight.

This story was deemed incredible. Several years after, a dying penitent confessed to a priest, that he was concealed in the gentleman's house for the purpose of robbing it, at the moment of the gentleman's return; that hearing him enter, he resolved to escape; that the woman saw, and attempted to detain him; that he, fearing detection, knocked her down with the candlestick she had in her hand, and fled, unnoticed, from the premises.

The following case, from a London paper, furnishes the strongest arguments to the friends of abolition of Capital Punishment. At the Surrey Sessions, Mr. Charnoch, who was engaged to defend a prisoner on circumstantial evidence, said such evidence was always dangerous to conviction, and cited the following illustration:

EXECUTION OF A FARMER FOR THE MURDER OF HIS NIECE.

A farmer who was left executor and guardian, was indicted for the wilful murder of his niece. A serious quarrel took place between them, and the farmer was heard to say, that his niece would not live to enjoy her property. Soon after, she was missed. Rumors were quickly spread that she was murdered by her guardian. On being apprehended, blood was found upon his clothes. The judge was persuaded to postpone the trial, and the most strenuous exertions were made to find the niece, but in vain. The prisoner, to save his life, resorted to a step which procured his condemnation and execution within forty-eight hours after his trial. A young lady was produced, exactly resembling the supposed murdered female. Her height, age and complexion and voice were so similar, that the witnesses swore to the identity. An intimation was given that the female was not the niece. By skilful cross-examination, the artifice was detected, and the unfortunate man was hung. The unhappy convict declared his innocence, but was rebuked by the clergyman for his hardihood.

In two years after, the niece made her appearance, and claimed the property. It appeared that, the day after the fatal quarrel, she had eloped with a stranger to whom she was attached, and she had not been heard of till her unexpected return, and that, by mere accident, she had heard of her uncle's execution.*

To show, still further, the fallibility of human judgment, we would state, that when tribunals have hung, even on the *confession* of the parties, they have sometimes erred. The confession, a false one, may have been extracted from the prisoner by hope of reward or pardon. How many thousands, in olden times, confessed to anything suggested by the blood-thirsty priests, in order to save themselves from the horrid tortures of the inquisition.

CONFESSION OF AN INNOCENT MAN IN ENGLAND.

Some years ago, the London *Morning Herald* contained the account of a man who confessed his guilt of a

---

* We take the above instances from a work entitled " Essays on the Punishment of Death." by Rev. Charles Spear, Boston.

certain crime. "Circumstances transpired, which, notwithstanding his confession, led many to doubt his guilt. He at length admitted that he had made up his mind to suffer the punishment, in order to claim, upon conviction, a reward which had been offered, and hand it to his starving wife and children."

Here the wretched man confessed, when he was innocent. But all can see his motive; it was the hope of a reward offered, that he might, by suffering the punishment of the alleged crime, save his wife and children from starvation. What a comment on the *Christianity*, *civilization* and *organization* of society in England. And in America it is the same, as we shall see in the future pages of this work. Shame on our *inhumanity* and our *professions* of the Christian religion! The most ignorant Pagan is less indifferent and unfeeling toward those in distress!

A remarkable case of confession, where the prisoner was innocent, happened in Vermont, in our own country. It has been cited on many occasions, and was narrated as given below, by Rev. W. S. Balch, of New-York city, who was born and educated in the vicinity of the place where the facts occurred. We copy from Mr. Spear's work on Capital Punishment. It will be seen that Bourne confessed to a falsehood in hope of commutation.

BOURNE CONVICTED OF THE MURDER OF HIS BROTHER-IN-LAW.

A case occurred in Manchester, Vermont. Two men, brothers, by the name of Bourne, were convicted of murder of a brother-in-law, named Colvin. While under the sentence of death, one of the brothers *confessed* a participation in the murder. By an act of the Legislature, his punishment was commuted to imprisonment for

life. The other stoutly persisted in asserting his innocence. Great excitement prevailed during and after the
trial; I remember it well. It was near my native town.
But when the confession was made under oath, and published, none longer doubted. Had he declared he did
not assist in the murder, would he have been believed?
The day of execution at length arrived. Hundreds of
people from the hills and vales were gathered around the
gallows, to witness the dying struggles of a poor unfortunate fellow-sinner. The hour had arrived, and the
elder Bourne, still avowing his innocence, wan and weak,
was led forth into the ring, and beneath the horrid engine of death. The sheriff was about to adjust the halter, and draw down the dismal cap, when a cry was heard
from behind the ring—"Stop! stop! For God's sake
stop." All eyes were directed that way, when to the
astonishment of all, the *murdered* Colvin was led into
the ring, presented to the sheriff, recognized by the assembled neighbors, and greeted by Bourne with feelings
better imagined than described; and the people doomed
to return home in disappointment—as some remarked,
" without seeing the *fun* they anticipated."

Had Colvin, (says Mr. Balch,) not been found, for he
was in New Jersey, or had some little hindrance delay-
ed a single hour, an innocent man would have been hur-
ried out of the world as a felon, leaving wife, and children, and friends to lament his untimely death; humanity to weep over the mistakes and weaknesses, and cruelties of human legislation; and judges and juries to re-
proach themselves for taking the fearful responsibility
of destroying a life which they could not restore when
their errors were clearly manifest.

Thus do we have pressed upon our notice, the fallibility of human judgment. How liable are we to be de-

ceived. How many thousands have been acquitted who
were guilty, and condemned who were innocent. Amid
all this uncertainty, and with a knowledge of the tremen-
dous injustice attending the execution of the innocent,
I feel that society has no right to wantonly throw away
its power of atoning for the wrong committed, by de-
priving a human being of that which it has not the
power to bestow. Within the walls of a strong prison,
safely guarded with bars and bolts, he would be secure.
There he could be instructed in heart and mind, by
the aid of books and good men; and, if guilty, be
made to feel the power of a love that could return good
for evil, and blessing for his efforts to destroy. And if,
in the providence of God, it should be revealed that he
was innocent, as we have already said, he could be compensated for his labor—restored to liberty, and so far as
possible, atonement could be made for the wrong committed.

We have already extended our remarks on this subject beyond our original intention, but cannot conclude
them without introducing an eloquent extract from a
speech* made by O'CONNELL, several years ago, before
the London society for the diffusion of information on
the subject of the Death Penalty. He refers to facts
most touching that had come under his own observation.

"He had long been deeply impressed," he said, "with
the conviction that Capital Punishment ought to be utterly abolished. He could not forget that 'vengeance is
mine, saith the Lord, and I will repay it.' Perhaps it
was by the impulse of feeling, and what he conceived to
be humanity, that, in the early part of his life, he was
brought to this conviction; but long, and he might ven-

* Originally published in the *Herald of Peace*, for 1832. We copy from
"Essays on the Death Penalty."

ture to say, great experience in the criminal law—for no advocate, at least in his own country, had the miserable boast which he could make of the frequency of his practice in that branch—that experience had confirmed him in his opinion, that there should not be in man the power of extinguishing life, because the result was irreparable; because the injury could not be compensated which might be done, if the beings were not infallible who inflicted the punishment; (and where should we find such?) and, because, while we thought we were vindicating the law of society, we might be committing the greatest outrage that could be perpetrated upon our fellow-creatures. The honorable and learned gentleman who spoke last, shuddered at the death of even a criminal; but what would his feelings have been had he witnessed, as he had, the execution of the innocent!

"One of the first events which struck him when he was rising into life, was seeing a gentleman who had forsaken society, and thrown himself into a mountain lodge, abandoning the intercourse of men, and wandering about like a troubled spirit, a willing outlaw, and an outcast from the social state. He inquired the cause, and learned that it originated in these circumstances:— Two men got into his bed-room at night, and robbed him, but did not treat him with any brutality. He prosecuted two brothers for the crime; and they being unprepared with any defense, from a consciousness of their innocence, were convicted and executed. Not a fortnight after they had been laid in the grave, in the presence of their father, and amidst the tears of their broken-hearted mother, the gentleman discovered his total mistake!"

Mr. O'Connell said he would mention another instance, of which he had a personal knowledge:

"He defended three brothers who were indicted for

murder; and the judge having a leaning, as was not unusual in such cases, to the side of the crown prosecution, almost compelled the jury to convict. He sat at his window as the men passed by, after receiving sentence. A military guard was placed over them, and it was positively forbidden that any one should have any intercourse with them. He saw their mother, strong in her affections, break through the guard, which was sufficient to resist any male force—he saw her clasp her eldest son, who was but twenty-two years of age—he saw her cling to her second, who was but twenty—and he saw her faint as she clasped the neck of her youngest boy, who was but eighteen. And they were innocent, but were executed

"He mentioned these facts to show with what extreme caution any one should do that which was irrevocable. When we recollected that, in criminal cases, a prisoner was almost shut out from making any defense; and that, in cases of circumstantial evidence, men were convicted, not upon facts, but upon reasonings and deductions;— when we recollected that the criminal law permitted the counsel for the crown to aggravate the impression against the prisoner, and prohibited his counsel from opening his mouth in his defense,—it might be said, without much exaggeration, that such a code was written in letters of blood. Was this England, the first country in the world for the love of liberty, and the encouragement of all the arts which adorn civilization and morality? Was this the country where, if a man had five pounds at stake, he might employ ten or twenty counsel to speak for him as long as they liked; but, when his life was in jeopardy, the law said, 'The counsel against you shall speak in aggravation of the charge; but the lips of your counsel shall be sealed!' Up to the present moment, that horrible state of the law continued.   He was firmly persuaded that if he had been entitled to speak on behalf of those three brothers—feeble as might be his advocacy, perhaps his heart would have aided his judgment and given him an inspiration beyond the natural dulness of his disposition—he felt that he would have made it impossible for any jury to convict.   If the punishment of these three brothers had not been incapable of being recalled, they might have been restored to their family; and the mother, who wept over their grave, might have been borne in decency to her tomb by those over whose premature death she mourned."*

But enough.   Were there no other reason for the abolishment of the Death Penalty, this would be sufficient for us.   Down with the gallows, then.   It can be spared with injury to no one; and so long as it remains, the innocent are not safe.

---

* See *Herald of Peace* for April, May and June.   London: 1832.

CHAPTER VIII.

FOURTH REASON FOR ABOLISHMENT.

THE BIBLE ARGUMENT.

The Death Penalty forbidden by the Christian Scriptures—Authority of the Scriptures above Human Authority—The *Lex talionis* of the Jews—The Law of Love the Christian Law—Touching account of recent Executions—All Christian Codes must Harmonize with the Law of Love—The Old Covenant not binding on Christians.

Another reason why the Punishment of Death should be abolished, especially by all CHRISTIAN *governments, is, that it is positively forbidden by the Christian Scriptures.*

With the writer of these pages, there is no authority superior to the authority of God. His word is our criterion. We never, knowingly, swerve from its divine requirements and teachings. Human speculations, in the presence of the plain teaching of the inspired volume, like mist before the morning sun, dissipate into airy nothingness. "Let God be true, but every man a liar," is the motto by which we are led; and, happily, with reference to the subject under consideration, He is upon the side of clemency. He "will have mercy and not sacrifice."*

"But," answers the objector, "the Bible certainly sanctions the Death Penalty. There is no plainer or more positive declaration than this: 'WHOSO SHEDDETH MAN'S BLOOD, BY MAN SHALL HIS BLOOD BE SHED;' and all know, who know anything of the Bible, that the law

---

* Matthew, 9: 13.

(85)

of Moses demanded the life of the offender for a multitude of sins. ' Breach for breach, eye for eye, tooth for tooth,' is the express declaration of God himself. How, then, can we abolish the Death Punishment, without first abolishing the law of God ; and how can we disregard the law of God with any degree of safety ? Ah, I fear for that community which will thus thoughtlessly or wilfully trample under foot the wise instruction of the Divine Being!"

So said our fathers, both in England and our own country, fifty years ago, when an attempt was made to abolish the stocks, the pillory and the whipping-post, all of which were regarded as divine institutions, and indispensably necessary to the safety of society. So it was thought a hundred years ago, by the most orthodox Christians in Europe and America, when hanging was the penalty for stealing forty shillings; also for idolatry, blasphemy, Sabbath-breaking, abuse of parents, perjury and adultery. All these laws were devoutly believed to be founded on God's law, binding on the Christian, and could not be abolished with any degree of safety. And yet they were abolished, and with no detriment to either morals or religion, and are not now believed, by any sect of Christians living, to be required by the divine law. No well-informed, sane man, no matter what his religion, would consent, for any consideration, to go back to the middle of the last century, and institute its penal code as a substitute for our own. But if the Jewish law is still binding, how can we remit all its punishments *but one ;* and what grounds have we to argue that *this* is binding, —*and to the end of time*—when we admit that all the rest were temporary, and only designed for a previous age? More than this: is not the question at least worthy of our careful consideration, whether, having abolished the entire code of Moses, with the exception of this, with no apparent injury, but with manifest improvement and with no violation of the divine precept, we cannot also give up this?

And this, we repeat, is what the *Christian Scriptures actually demand.* That "breach for breach, eye for eye, tooth for tooth, is the express declaration of God," as the objector says, is, at least, problematical. Christ did not so understand by the demands of the Mosaic dispensation. It was not God, but "them of old time," who said this. "Ye have heard that it hath been said by them of old time . . . . an eye for an eye, and a tooth for a tooth." This was the *lex talionis,* or law of retaliation, incorporated into the code of the early Hebrews and the rule of vengeance by which they were governed. And suppose we admit that God did permit or even *command* the Jews, when in a rude and barbarous state, to institute laws thus sanguinary and bloody, where is the man who can make it appear that they are still binding under the Christian dispensation? On the contrary, there is no truth of the divine word more palpable than the fact, that Christ himself abrogated the very spirit and principle of that old code, and gave the world a new and better covenant in his life, teachings, sufferings and examples.

In the very first sermon he preached, behold how positively and clearly he defined the principles of his own religion, in contradistinction to those of Moses: " Ye have heard that it hath been said, an eye for an eye and a tooth for a tooth; but *I* say unto you, that ye resist not evil; but whosoever shall smite thee on thy right cheek, turn to him the other also. And if any man will sue thee at the law and take away thy coat, let him have thy cloak also."* We cannot suppose that Christ

---

* Matthew 5: 38—40.

designed that this command should be *literally* obeyed; but the *principle* contained in this declaration he did design should be enforced as a new, a better, a more divine law; a law which should abrogate the Mosaic precept and take its place. And I ask my Christian brother or sister, who may peruse these pages, is not its rule the exact opposite of the Levitical law? "I say unto you that ye resist not evil, but whosoever shall smite thee on the one cheek, turn to him the other also." He farther says: "Ye have heard that it hath been said, thou shalt love thy neighbor, and hate thy enemy; but *I* say unto you, love your enemies, bless them that curse you, do good to them that hate you, and pray for them that de-spitefully use and persecute you; that ye may be the children of your Father which is in Heaven; for he maketh his sun to rise on the evil and the good, and sendeth his rain on the just and on the unjust."* How can the man who professes to have been born into the spiritual kingdom of the Master—a kingdom of "right-eousness, peace and joy in the Holy Ghost"—and to be governed by the foregoing instruction, still uphold the killing of men, women and children by "legal strangu-lation?" How would the above declarations of Christ appear as written mottoes for the gallows? "LOVE, THE FULFILLING OF THE LAW," inscribed on the cross-bar of the gibbet! What an inconsistency! Jesus "lived the doctrine which he taught." He returned good for evil and blessing for cursing; and finally died upon the cross for his enemies, closing and sanctioning his labors of love by that more than mortal petition, "Father, forgive them, for they know not what they do!" Oh, blessed Being! the true guide and pattern of all Christians. Here is light communicated from heaven, to illuminate

---

* Matthew, 5: 44—45.

our path of duty. We are not left to our own sagaciousness, but should follow our great examplar. " For even hereunto were ye called : *because Christ also suffered for us, leaving us an example, that we should follow in his steps; who did no sin, neither was guile found in his mouth; who, when he was reviled, reviled not again; when he suffered he threatened not; but committed himself to Him who judgeth righteously.** How divine, how beautiful this instruction ; and how plain it is that, everywhere in the New Testament, LOVE is made the test of the validity of our claims to the Christian character. " By *this* shall all men know that ye are my disciples, *if ye have love.*"† Again, " He that loveth, dwelleth in God and God in him."‡ " For this, thou shalt not commit adultery, *thou shalt not kill;* thou shalt not bear false witness; thou shalt not covet; and if there be any other commandment, it is briefly comprehended in this saying : *thou shalt love thy neighbor as thyself. Love worketh* NO *ill to its neighbor;* therefore, *love is the fulfilling of the law.*"‖ *Above all things,*" says the same apostle, after enumerating various other duties, "*put on* CHARITY," (or love) " *which* is the bond of *perfectness.*"§ In short, the inculcation of this divine principle as the great central element of the Christian religion, is as common in the Gospel as its practical utility is superior. So common and so plain is it, that the wayfaring man, though a fool, need not err. "It is the theme of all the apostolic exhortations, that with which their morality begins and ends, from which all their details and enumerations set out and into which they return."

Is it not, then, evident that if all the relative duties of the Christian are embraced in *one word* and *that word is*

---

* 1 Peter, 2 : 21. † John, 13 : 35. ‡ John, 4: 16.
‖ Romans, 13: 9. § Colossians, 3: 14.

8

LOVE, that he can institute no form of government, nor sanction any modes of punishment, that are founded on vengeance, and that result in the violent destruction of a fellow-creature?

As I write, the daily papers laid on my table give the particulars of two executions which have just taken place, one in Louisville, Ky., and the other in Roxbury, N. C. George Huffner, executed in Louisville, asserted in the most positive manner, till the moment of his exit from time to eternity, his entire innocence of the crime for which he was about to suffer, and left a brief but touching epistle, in which he expressed an ardent hope that the time would come when the people of Louisville and elsewhere, would know that he died an innocent man.

Says the account: "After the clergyman, Rev. Mr. Adams, addressed the people, and exhorted them to preserve decorum, the prisoner stepped forth, and in a firm voice said, that he '*was not guilty of the crime of murder.*' Prayer was then offered up to God by the Rev. Mr. Adams, after which the prisoner desired him to *tell the people that he died in full hope of heaven.* The sheriff adjusted the fatal noose, after covering the victim's head with a cap. He then bade farewell to the ministers and officers around him, and just a moment before being launched into eternity, he earnestly asked if there was any one around 'who believed him innocent.' 'I do,' was heard, and just then the drop fell and all was over.

"Just at that moment, a woman, almost wild with excitement, forced her way to the foot of the scaffold, begging the sheriff to send the body to his unfortunate wife, who was almost crazy with grief and despair. The wish was complied with, and the body sent to her for burial. The sympathies of the community are demanded for this poor woman, who is in extreme destitution, with a small child to support, twenty months old, and is again on the eve of confinement."

Here was a man—a *Christian* man—with a soul all bright with a glorious hope of immortality, whom the Christian people of Kentucky, his brethren, strangled into eternity. Was that act really a Christian act? Was it in harmony with the law of love, the great central principle of the Christian religion?

The other case was somewhat similar. The prisoner's name was Williams. He was greatly distressed and dreadfully alarmed with reference to his future condition, but protesting his innocence, with the most piteous appeals to the last. Every moment he besought the prayers of all Christians around him in his behalf. Says the writer: "The hour arriving for his execution, the sheriff, with a bleeding heart and tear-moistened eye, called for him. Taking Mr. Lyon, (his father's friend and neighbor,) by the hand, and begging him to go with him and pray for him, he proceeded to the gallows, praying all the way, until he arrived in sight of the gallows, when, trembling like a leaf, he gave vent to an expression of feeling which no pen can describe, and which touched the most callous heart. Arriving at the gallows, he sued for the last moment, and begged every Christian on the ground to pray for him.

"It was here that the sheriff read him a brief note, reminding him of future rewards and punishments, of the awfulness of dying with a lie on his lips, and invoking him to say, while he looked eternity in the face, whether he was guilty or innocent of the murder. He replied, that he had 'said all he had to say about it—he was not guilty!' So the prisoner protested his innocence to the last moment. Mounting the scaffold, and forgiving everybody, his soul was launched into eternity."

Yes, but if every Christian duty is embraced in a single word, and that word is *love*, could this act be a Christian act? Would not Christ have had mercy on the poor man? Did he ever condemn to death? Can the law which demanded the death of these wretched men, be in harmony with the Christian precept which requires " good for evil." A law which would secure them in prison—treat them kindly—instruct them in their duty to God and their fellow men—renovate their souls with the spirit of Christianity, and thus cast out the spirit of evil, by a manifestation of goodness, would be Christian; but that which demands "eye for eye, tooth for tooth, and life for life," *never!* NEVER! This belongs to another covenant, and another age. *We* are living in the nineteenth century of the Christian era. We profess to be *Christians.* We are not *Hebrews* nor *Hindoos.* Whom, then, shall we follow, *Christ* or *Moses?* There is such a thing as progression; as " a growing in grace, and in a knowledge of our Lord and Savior, Jesus Christ." Why should we go back four thousand years for our morality, our laws, our religion, and our faith? when Christ is the light that is to lighten every man that cometh into the world, he being " the way, the truth and the life?"

Yet, this is what the majority of Christians are everywhere doing. Christ himself has instructed them that " the law and the prophets were until John; since that time the kingdom of God is preached;"* but giving no heed to this, they forsake the "kingdom of Christ," and going back to " the law and the prophets," and planting themselves on the old covenant, say, "*This is our law, our morality, our Christianity, our faith.*"

It is a fact which no one will attempt to dispute who is at all acquainted with the subject, that every opposer to

* Luke, 16: 16.

progression in humanity and moral purity, has gone to
the "types and shadows" of the Old Testament, to maintain his position. He could obtain no sympathy, no aid
from Christ and his apostles. If a *Christian* would find
a scriptural argument for drunkenness, he must go to
Noah, or the history of the ancient Hebrews. So of
war and the gallows. These practices can find no advocate in Christ or his immediate followers. But even
Christian men believe that they must be sustained, and
they, therefore, appeal to commandments and a code
which existed *two thousand years before Christ,* and which
he clearly abrogated, as we have seen. But where is their
authority for such a course ? What consistency is there
in it? Why not advocate the sacrifice of sheep and goats,
the burning of incense, and the making of offerings of
oil and flour? They were demanded by the law of
Moses, and are as really binding on us under the Christian dispensation, as the Death Penalty. This, then,
we repeat, is a very important reason for the abolishment of the gallows. *It is not sanctioned, but positively
condemned, by the Christian religion.*

And here, so far as the demands of the Bible go, we
might rest the argument. It satisfies me ; for admitting
all the opposer claims for the Levitical code, under the
old dispensation, to be true, it is no more binding on us
than is the penal code of Connecticut colony, which
hung for witchcraft, profanity, idolatry and petty robbery. We are followers of Christ, and not of " them of
old time," and until it can be shown that the New Testament clearly sanctions the Punishment of Death, we may
rest in the assurance that the Bible contains no commands, nor instructions, that demand at our hand the
blood of a fellow creature, no matter what his offenses.

But this disposition of the subject, though satisfactory

to some, will not answer the expectations of all my readers. Many sincerely believe that the Mosaic law is still
binding, and especially the declaration of God to Noah,
"Whoso sheddeth man's blood, by man shall his blood
be shed"—"a declaration," it is contended, "that is expressive of the law of God concerning the murderer. He
must be slain. The command is *universal* and *perpetual*.
From the beginning God made this demand, and it must
run parallel with the existence of man, to the end of
time." So affirm the most able supporters of the Death
Penalty. Let us, then, enter into a more minute and
critical examination of the subject. "Prove *all* things,
and hold fast that which is good," is an apostolic injunction by which we have long been led. It shall be our
motto in the investigation of the question before us.
We begin with the declaration to Noah.

CHAPTER IX.

THE BIBLE ARGUMENT CONTINUED.

COVENANT WITH NOAH.

Is it positive, universal and perpetual?—Accidental killing—Killing in Self-defense, or in defense of one's Country, must be visited with Death - The Executioner must be slain The text restricted to the Murderer; but in what degree of murder shall it be applied—Death Penalty not known till the year of the world 1650—Cain not put to death Lamech not put to death Moses a murderer and not slain - Numerous other cases of the same description God did not himself regard the declaration to Noah - The true rendering and teaching of the text—Opinion of learned men—Evidence conclusive against the continuance of the Gallows.

" *Whoso sheddeth man's blood by man shall his blood be shed.*" Gen. 9: 6.

If the reader has perused the foregoing chapter, he is prepared for what we have to say on this declaration of God to Noah; a declaration which the advocates of the Death Penalty contend is *positive, universal in its application and perpetual to the end of time.* "Can language be more emphatic or universal?" exclaims an ardent defender of the gallows. "Whoso"—that is, *any person whatever*—"sheddeth man's blood"—who kills his fellow creature—"by man *shall* his blood be shed " There is no escape, and no limit as to time, or country, or situation. On the contrary, such were the circumstances under which the declaration was made, that the whole context goes to show that this command was designed to be "perpetual and universal."

Let us admit, for the sake of the argument, that the objector is correct in these premises; and then query.

(95)

"Whoso" signifies, he says, *"any person whatever,"* and to "shed blood" means *"to kill."* The meaning of the text is, then, if applied literally, that *any person whatever who kills, shall himself be killed.* "There is no escape." It follows, then, that the man who destroys life accidentally, or in self-defense, or in defense of his country, *must* be killed, for he kills. "There is no escape." The jury who convict the prisoner of murder, the judge who passes sentence of death on him, and the hangman who closes the scene of blood, all must be killed, for they are all guilty of killing; the judge and jury by proxy, the hangman, personally. The heroes of "seventy six," who fought the battles of the American Revolution, with the Father of his Country at their head, should all to a man have been executed, for they all "shed blood." Notice, the language of the text is "positive" and "without restriction," "extending to *all* who kill." " *Whoso* sheddeth man's blood, by man *shall* his blood be shed." "There is no escape." As says a writer when discanting on this subject: "If this command to Noah requires the death of all who shed blood without exception, then it is clear that the *executioner* should be killed; and when *he* is slain, his slayer must be put to death, and *his* and *his*, and thus the work of slaughter should go on, till the last man becomes his own executioner and crowns, with his corpse, the work of universal carnage."

Here, the objector finds himself in a dilemma, and to escape, says that he would restrict the application of the text to the *murderer.* But, we reply, first, that the moment he restricts the text, that moment he surrenders the ground already assumed, that it is of *"universal* application;" and second, that he has no authority for such restriction, as there is nothing either in the text or context that will warrant it.

But suppose he is permitted to make the restriction and apply the principle contained in the text only in a case of murder; in what degree of murder would he make the application? The penal codes of all our States recognize, at least, two degrees of murder. Killing with *malice prepense*, or aforethought, is murder in the first degree. Killing in the heat of passion, is man-slaughter, or murder in the second degree. Does the objector say that he would apply the principle of the text only in the case of murder·in the first degree? But with what propriety can he make this restriction? If a man rises up in the heat of passion and slays his fellow, does he not just as really shed his blood as if the act were premeditated? and if so, does not the declaration to Noah demand his blood? If he answers in the affirmative, then he must make the penal code of his own State more severe, for no State in our Union, as our laws now stand, demands death for man-slaughter. But why not, if we are Christians, and the declaration, "whoso sheddeth man's blood by man shall his blood be shed," is still binding on us?

From the foregoing considerations, it will be perceived that the declaration cannot be literally and universally applied; and that no Christian nation pretends to live up to such a construction; for it is only in extreme cases, and for the worst form of murder, that we "shed blood."

And when we say that this declaration contains a law which God designed from the beginning to restrain the passions and regulate the conduct of men,—a law to be regarded perpetually to the end of time,—we say what the Scriptures do not sanction—indeed, what *they positively deny*, as we will now show.

9

THE WORLD SIXTEEN CENTURIES WITHOUT THE DEATH PENALTY.

First, the declaration contained in the text under consideration was not given to Noah till the year of the world 1657; and, what is a little remarkable, up to this time the Death Penalty was not known among men, and yet murder had been committed. How will the objector account for this fact, if the law of "life for life" was designed *from the beginning* to restrain men from violence, and proclaimed as an adequate punishment for the crime of murder? *For more than sixteen hundred years* the generations of men had been multiplying in the earth, and had been guilty of slaying each other, and still the law of death was not instituted!

Go back to the first murder ever committed, and how does God himself deal with the wretched homicide? Does he make an application of the principle contained in the declaration to Noah as a punishment for the crime of Cain? Not at all; instead, he positively declares that Cain should not be slain. Let us look at his case.

CASE OF CAIN.

"And Cain talked with Abel his brother: and it came to pass, when they were in the field, that Cain rose up against Abel his brother, and slew him. And the Lord said unto Cain, Where is Abel thy brother? And he said, I know not. Am I my brother's keeper? And he said, what hast thou done? The voice of thy brother's blood crieth unto me from the ground, and now art thou cursed from the earth, which hath opened her mouth to receive thy brother's blood from thy hand. When thou tillest the ground, it shall not henceforth yield unto thee her strength: a fugitive and vagabond shalt thou be in the earth. And Cain said unto the Lord, My punishment is greater than I can bear. Behold thou hast driven me out this day from the face of the earth; and from thy face shall I be hid; and it shall come to pass, that every one that findeth me shall slay me. And the Lord said unto him, therefore whosoever slayeth Cain, vengeance shall be taken on him seven-fold. And the Lord set a mark upon Cain lest any finding him should slay him."*

Here we have the account of the first murder ever committed, the first law ever instituted for the punishment of the offender, and the details of the first trial on record where the criminal was a murderer. The Almighty God was himself the Law-giver and the Judge; the garden of Eden the court-room, and the blood of the slain Abel, crying from the teeming ground, both the accuser and the witness.

And what is the nature of the penalty attached to the awful offense of the wretched man? Was it "blood for blood?" If Capital Punishment is a perpetual institution, divine and universal, why was it not then proclaimed? There was no mistake in the *guilt* of the criminal at the bar. At first, he was inclined to cover his sin with a falsehood. "And the Lord said unto Cain, where is thy brother Abel? and he said, I know not; am I my brother's keeper?" But "God is not mocked." Human tribunals are fallible and may be deceived, but infinite knowledge, *never!*

We may succeed in hiding our crimes from man, but the eye of God penetrates into the very secrets of the soul, and our sin will find us out, and "though hand join in hand, the wicked shall not be unpunished." Cain *was* guilty of murder, and when fully charged with the dreadful crime, he did not longer deny. We ask again,

---

Gen. 4: 8—15.

why did not the Almighty *then* institute the Death Penalty? Why did he not *then* erect the gallows, and himself become the executioner? Do you say that the murder was not an aggravated one; that Cain slew his brother in the heat of passion, and was, therefore, entitled to lenity? But the facts in the case will not warrant such a supposition; on the contrary, they show plain enough that the murder was premeditated and wilful. Look at the preceding account. "Abel was a keeper of sheep, and Cain was a tiller of the ground. And in process of time it came to pass, that Cain brought, of the fruit of the ground, an offering unto the Lord. And Abel, he also brought of the firstlings of his flock, and of the fat thereof. And the Lord had respect unto Abel and to his offering; but unto Cain and his offering he had not respect. And Cain was *very wroth*, and his *countenance fell.* And the Lord said unto Cain, Why art thou wroth? and why is thy countenance fallen? If thou doest well, shalt not thou be accepted? and if thou doest not well, sin lieth at the door."* Here we witness the "wrath" of Cain. His heart was filled with envy, jealousy, and hatred toward his kind and innocent brother; and these passions raged like a sea, unbridled, till the destruction of Abel was the consequence. What a cold-blooded, heartless murder! And yet, God did not slay the murderer! He did not deprive him of *liberty*, even; and instead of hanging him up like a cat on a gibbet, and strangling the life out of him, as we Christians would do in a similar case, *he actually instituted a law* TO SAVE HIM FROM DEATH. Is not this remarkable, if "life for life" is so necessary to restrain the vicious, and so sanctifying in its moral influences! Hear the *sentence* pronounced by God Himself, upon the guilty man. "And now art thou

---

* Genesis, 4 : 2—7.

cursed from the earth which hath opened her mouth to receive thy brother's blood from thy hand. When thou tillest the ground, it shall not henceforth yield unto thee her strength; a fugitive ·and vagabond shalt thou be in the earth."

Here was the doom of Cain. God did not slay *him* because *he* had slain. This would have been a work of retaliation and vengeance. "Thou shalt not kill," is the law of God, and He would not be the first to violate his own precept; but by his dealings with the murderer, he would show all men the sanctity of human life. And thus: "from the ashes of murdered Abel, and from the stamped forehead of Cain, is proclaimed to the *magistrate*, and the *criminal*, to the *murderer* in his bloody purpose, and the *judge* in his fearful decision, '*Thou shalt not kill.*'"

But though God did not slay the murderer, the penalty that he pronounced was a fearful one. He was banished from God and from society. His conscience was full of guilt, and the awful apprehension of being hunted like a wild beast, by his fellow men, was overwhelming in its effect; so that he exclaimed, in the voice of despair, "My punishment is greater than I can bear! Behold, thou hast driven me out this day from the face of the earth, and from thy face shall I be hid; and I shall be a fugitive and a vagabond in the earth; and it shall come to pass, that every one that findeth me shall slay me."

Some contend that the Death Penalty must have been previously instituted, or Cain would not have expressed a fear of being slain. But not so. God has implanted a sort of instinct in man, which causes him to dread the very evils which he inflicts on others. The dishonest man suspects the integrity of all men; the liar confides in no man's word; the thief expects to be robbed, and the murderer to be killed. So with Cain. He was a murderer. The voice of his brother's blood was ever crying from the ground; and he felt that as he had killed without provocation, the hands of all men would be turned against him, and whosoever found him would slay him.

But God said this should not be. "Whosoever slayeth Cain, vengeance shall be taken on him seven fold. And the Lord God set a mark upon Cain, lest any finding him should kill him." What this "mark" was, has given rise to many conjectures. Nothing is said in the context from which we can decide; neither does it matter, so far as the present question is concerned, inasmuch as we are assured that it protected the wretched homicide from destruction. Still we think the explanation, as given by Dr. Shuckford, of England, an eminent Hebrew scholar, very reasonable and beautiful, and so perfectly in harmony with this entire account, that we cannot forbear giving it a place here "The Hebrew word *oth*," says he, "which we translate '*a mark*,' signifies *a sign* or *token*. Thus, Gen. 9: 13, the bow set in the heavens, was to be *leoth, for a sign* or *token* that the world should not again be destroyed by flood; therefore the words, '*and the Lord set a mark upon Cain*,' should be translated, '*and the Lord appointed unto Cain a token or sign*,' to convince him that no person should be permitted to slay him. To have *marked* him would have been the most likely way to have brought all the evils he dreaded upon him; therefore, the Lord gave him some miraculous sign or token that he should not be slain, to the end that he should not despair, but, having time to repent, might return to a gracious God and find mercy."

Here, then, we have the case of Cain. He was guilty of a dreadful murder, arraigned by God himself, convicted and sentenced. His punishment was dreadful, still his life was preserved, and so should be the life of every homicide. He was banished from the face of society, and so should be every homicide. The murderer is guilty of the worst crime that man can commit. His presence is dangerous in any community, and he should, therefore, be safely secured. But he should not be injured. God has given us an example of clemency, in his dealings toward the miserable Cain, which it would be wise in us to follow. He visited him with no act of vengeance, but while he assured him of the certainty of his punishment, he gave him a sign or token, that he should not be slain, "to the end that he might not despair, but, having time to repent, might return to a gracious God, and find forgiveness." What mingling of mercy and justice! And what a beautiful example for legislation in all ages! The reader must see that the argument founded on the case of Cain, when Jehovah himself was both Law-giver and Judge, affords the Death Penalty no aid; neither does it sustain the assertion that the principle contained in the declaration to Noah was of *universal* application; on the contrary, it refutes the idea, as God did not himself regard it.

Coming down from this first offense in the history of man, to the year of the world 500, we find an account of the second murderer, whose case we will briefly consider.

LAMECH, THE SECOND MURDERER.

Lamech is the second murderer of whom we have any account; and it is a little singular that he was a descendant of Cain, and the father of Noah. We are told that after the sentence was pronounced upon Cain, that he " went out from the presence of the Lord, and dwelt in the land of Nod, on the east of Eden." " The Hebrew word *nod*," says an eminent commentator, "signifies the same as *nad* a *vagabond*, and, therefore, should have been rendered, as some contend, "*and Cain went out 'from the presence of the Lord*, (that is, from the spiritual paradise of God in the garden,) *on the coast of Eden, and dwelt a vagabond upon the earth;* and thus the curse pronounced on him in the twelfth verse was accomplished." But notwithstanding the curse that followed him, we are told that his wife accompanied him, that he had sons and daughters—built a city, and that his descendants were prosperous. The account is given in the following language : " And Cain knew his wife, and she conceived and bare Enoch, and he builded a city, and called the name of the city after the name of his son Enoch. And unto Enoch was born Irad ; and Irad begat Mehujael; and Mehujael begat Methusael, and Methusael begat Lamech. And Lamech took unto him two wives; the name of the one was Adah, and the name of the other Zillah." Thus it will be seen that Lamech was a bigamist. " He was the first man," says Dr. A. Clarke, "who dared to reverse the order of God, by introducing *polygamy*." He was also guilty of killing a man ; and notwithstanding both these offenses, was not himself slain. "And Lamech said unto his wives Adah and Zillah, hear my voice; ye wives of Lamech, hearken unto my speech; for I have slain a man to my wounding, and a young man to my hurt."*

" It is supposed that Lamech had slain a man in his own defense, and that his wives, being alarmed lest the friends of the deceased should seek his life in return, to quiet their fears, he makes this speech, in which he endeavors to prove that there was no room for fear on this account; for if the slayer of the wilful murderer,

* Genesis 4 : 23.

Cain, should suffer a seven fold punishment, surely he who should kill Lamech, for having killed a man in self-defense, might expect a seventy-seven fold punishment."

These two are the only accounts of murder on record, previous to the declaration to Noah now under consideration, which was given, as we before said, in the year of the world, 1652, and in neither of these was the life of the offender destroyed.

INSTANCES OF DISREGARD OF THE DECLARATION TO NOAH AFTER IT WAS MADE.

It may be said by the objector, that previously to God's covenant with Noah, no express *law* against the murderer had been instituted, and for this reason he was not visited with death. But what a mistake. Could not a law against murder be instituted, without annexing the penalty of death? Let the reader look carefully at God's dealings with the first murderer, as exhibited in the preceding pages; let him reflect upon the guilt of the wretched man—his arraignment before the bar of offend ed justice—his examination as a criminal—the verdict rendered, and the sentence passed, and answer whether a law was not then and there instituted against the murderer; a law, too, which but echoed the very *instinct* which God had previously written in the *soul* of man, and inscribed on every filament of his nature, standing as a perpetual and eternal *edict*, declaring, " Thou shalt not kill." We grant that no *statute* law had been instituted, no chains forged, or prison reared, or gallows erected. Still, God had instituted a law, annexed the penalty, and punished the offender; and yet, as we have seen, he neither burned, hanged nor drowned him.

But suppose we grant that no express law against the murderer had been instituted previously to the declaration of Noah, and, therefore, the offender was not put to death; this plea cannot be put in against God's disregard of this penalty, *after* he spoke so emphatically and said: " Whoso sheddeth man's blood, by man shall his blood be shed ;" for here, the objector says, is the law of " life for life," instituted by God, and which is to be *perpetual* and *universal.*

But was it a universal law ? After the declaration was made, was *every* man put to death who was guilty of murder ? Did God himself regard it in his dealings with those who killed ? Why, instead of this, we find no intimations of the Death Penalty in the sacred history, for more than *six hundred years* subsequently to God's covenant with Noah. Is not this remarkable, if the law of " life for life " was to be a rule of perpetual and universal application ?

In the year of the world, 2200, we find Isaac and his wife tarrying with Abimelech, the king of the Philistines. To secure them against harm, after Isaac's prevarication, Abimelech charged all his people, saying, " He that toucheth this man or his wife, shall surely be put to death "* And this is the first threatening of the Death Penalty that appears in the Bible.

In the year 2266 Simeon and Levi, sons of the patriarch Jacob, as the sacred word informs us, armed themselves, with each a sword, and fell upon the defenseless and innocent men of a certain city, and slew them all.† And did Jacob, their father, convict them of murder, and command that they, in turn, be slain ? Not at all. He simply reproved them at the time, and when on the bed of death, pronounced the natural consequences of a life of cruelty and vengeance. He called them to him and said, as he spoke to his children in the order of their ages :

---

* Genesis 22: 11.   † Genesis 2: 3.

"Simeon and Levi are brethren. Instruments of cruelty are in their habitation. Oh my soul, come not thou into their secret; unto their assembly, mine honor, be not thou united. For in their anger they slew a man," (the original says, a. *noble* and *honorable* man,) "cursed be their anger, for it was fierce, and their wrath, for it was cruel. I will divide them in Jacob, and scatter them in Israel."* This was all. And it was enough. Simeon and Levi were not slain; still, like Cain, they were punished. They and their posterity were divided and scattered. They attained to no political eminence; but were followed by adversity and a curse, in the future years of their existence.

Now, we must keep in mind that the law of Noah was given to the Hebrews, and that Jacob was a judge or ruler among them. Is it at all probable, then, that this just and devout man could have regarded the declaration to Noah, which we are considering, as a positive command, that all who shed blood should be killed? If he had so understood this instruction, would he not have executed these murderers though they were his sons, or offered some apology for not doing it? Most certainly. But instead of this, we find no intimation in the entire account, that the necessity of such a punishment occurred to him.

Pursuing history still further, in the year 2433, we find even Moses—Moses the man of God, the great law-giver—himself slaying a man. "He looked this way, and that way, and when he saw that there was no man, he slew the Egyptian, and hid him in the sand."† Moses committed this deed with the full knowledge of all that had been said to Noah, and yet God did not visit him with death. He was neither hung nor crucified.

---

* Genesis 49: 2—7.   † Exodus 2: 12.

Coming down further still, we behold Doeg, by order of the blood-thirsty and cruel Saul, wickedly murdering no less than eighty-five innocent and defenseless
priests, together with all the "women and children and
sucklings" of the city, and yet the declaration of God,
"Whoso sheddeth man's blood, by man shall his blood
be shed," was not even mentioned to him.

Again, in the year 3074, Zimri conspired against
Elah, king of Judah, and treacherously "smote and
killed him"* in his own house when drunk, and he, in
turn, was not slain, but reigned as king in place of the
murdered Elah.

Then, coming down further, we find David killing the
Amalekite directly, and the faithful, noble and heroic
Uriah, indirectly, but was not in turn himself destroyed.
But why not, if God had designed the declaration of
Noah as a positive law against the murderer? David was
guilty of a double crime. He had stolen the affections
of the wife of Uriah, in the absence of the latter;—had
become her paramour, and now wished to rid himself of
the husband that he might marry the wife. So he wrote
a letter to Joab, the commander of his soldiers, saying,
"Set ye Uriah in the forefront of the hottest battle, and
retire ye from him that he may be smitten and die."†
This letter was put into the hand of Uriah himself to
carry to Joab, so that the unfortunate man became the
bearer of his own death-warrant. Joab did as he was
directed, and poor Uriah perished by order of the king,
when he was fighting for the honor of that king. What
a diabolical act on the part of David! And yet, though
God himself took this matter in hand, and arraigned the
unfortunate David before his "judgment-seat" through
the instrumentality of Nathan the prophet, he did not

---

* 1 Kings 16 : 9—10.   † 2 Samuel 11 : 15.

command that he be put to death; but pronounced the following sentence upon him: "Thus saith the Lord God of Israel: I anointed thee king over Israel, and I delivered thee out of the hand of Saul. Wherefore hast thou despised the commandment of God, to do evil in his sight? Thou hast killed Uriah the Hittite with the sword, and hast taken his wife to be thy wife, and hast slain him with the sword of the children of Ammon. Now, therefore, the sword shall never depart from thine house; because thou hast despised me. Behold, saith the Lord God, I will raise up evil against thee out of thine own house. . . . . And David said unto Nathan, I have sinned against the Lord. And Nathan said unto David: the Lord hath put away thy sin—*thou shalt not die.*" Here was David's punishment. His life was preserved; but all which was pronounced against him was fulfilled to the very letter.*

And when we come down to the time of Christ, we find the cruel Herod beheading the innocent John in his prison;—Christ himself nailed to the cross;—Saul breathing out wrath and slaughter;—Peter and Stephen cruelly murdered, and yet we have no account that those engaged in this work of blood were themselves slain. Instead of this, Saul the murderer was converted to Christianity, through the power of the Holy Ghost, and afterward became " Paul the apostle to the Gentiles," and the author of thirteen books of the New Testament.

In conclusion, then, we come to ask, can it be that God designed the principle contained in the declaration, " *Whoso* sheddeth man's blood, by man shall his blood be shed," to be *universally* applied? Can we arrive at this result with all these facts before us? Did the Almighty design even that its spirit should enter the moral and

---

* See the entire account, 2 Samuel 12th chapter.

penal codes of nations, and that blood should be poured out for blood, to the end of time? We cannot believe this; and many of the most eminent Christians and biblical scholars of all denominations, who have written on the subject, some of whom believe in the necessity of the Death Penalty, entertain the same views; assuring us that this text does not afford that support to the punishment of death, that Christians so generally ascribe to it, as will more fully appear in what follows.

TWELVE DIFFERENT TRANSLATIONS.

We have not yet done with Noah. All that we have said may appear *plausible* to all, but may not be *satisfactory* to all. For though Noah lived two thousand and five hundred years before Christ, God's declaration to him is the rock on which the Christian plants himself in his defense of the gallows. In the year 1843, the Rev. George B. Cheever, of New York, in his reply to O'Sullivan's masterly production, in favor of the abolishment of the Death Penalty, calls this text in the ninth chapter of Genesis, "the CITADEL *of the argument commanding and sweeping the whole subject.*" Thousands view the text in the same light. Converse with whom we will on the subject, and if he be a Christian in favor of legal strangulation, whether minister or layman, he will be sure to adduce this text; and though he is driven from every other point in the fortress, will retire within the precincts of this with an air of the most perfect confidence that it cannot be taken from him. During the past year we have noticed three published sermons and many essays and articles in religious journals of our land, in favor of the Punishment of Death, and in each, the foundation of the argument was God's declaration to Noah.

Now, we believe the Bible. We believe that it contains a pure and exalted morality; that it inculcates the most ennobling ideas of human duty, of God and the immortal world. There is no man who has a more sacred reverence for this "book of books,"—the greatest gift of God to man—than the author of these pages. But this is not all. We not only entertain a high opinion and strong affection for the Bible, but we strive, above all things, to understand its true teachings. "*Understandest* thou what thou readest?"* is an important injunction, which it would be well for all Christians to keep in mind, in the perusal of the divine word; because a bare reverence for the Scriptures is not enough. They will be of little service to us if we do not comprehend their teachings.

With reference to the text under consideration, we have given several reasons why we cannot believe that God designed the declaration it contains as a law demanding the blood of the offender, and reaching down to the end of time. But there are more and weightier reasons for this conclusion—reasons drawn *from the text itself*. In the first place, let me say that this verse has had *twelve different translations*, all by learned Christian men. Some of these translations favor the Death Penalty, and some oppose it, as we shall see bye-and-bye. But let us put the reasonable question here, whether it is probable that Almighty God would have left a matter of so much importance, resting upon a single line of Hebrew—and that line of Hebrew so ambiguous as that twelve different Christian men, of equal sincerity and learning, give it as many renderings? The Christian says that this text is his "impregnable foundation;" and yet, if he is a Hebrew scholar, he dare not stand up in

---

* Acts 8: 36.

a company of scholars and affirm that he is *sure of its meaning.*

THE TRUE MEANING AND DESIGN OF THE TEXT.

We have now arrived at the proper place in our investigations, to give what we believe to be the true meaning of this declaration. The writer of these pages is not a Calvinist *theologically,* but respecting the intent of this text, his views are perfectly in harmony with those of the great Genevan. Calvin says, that to render it "by man," is a "forced construction;"—that the following is a better translation: "Whoso sheddeth the blood of man, his blood will be shed;" making the rendering, not in the form of a *command,* but *denunciatory,* and describing prophetically what is the *natural* consequence of bloody deeds. The declaration was a general one, and never designed for *literal,* particular and universal application. Christ used nearly the same form of expression and with reference to the same subject, when he reproved the hasty Peter who was about to commit an act of violence, in defense of his Master: "ALL they that take the sword *shall* perish with the sword."* How positive, how *universal,* is the sense of this declaration when understood literally. And yet no one can believe that Christ designed to teach that Capital Punishment should be inflicted with the sword on *all* who use it. He meant only that "a violent life is apt to close with a violent death." Again, John says: "He that killeth with the sword, *must* be killed with the sword."† How emphatic is this expression, and yet, the meaning is, simply, that they who contend in battle, are likely, on both sides, sooner or later, to become sacrifices to their mutual animosities. So of the declaration to Noah. When God spake these

---

* Matthew 26: 57.   † Revelation 13: 10.

words the ark had rested upon the mountain; and Noah and all his family walked forth upon the green earth, for the waters had abated. Then God established his covenant; and gave the precious promise that "summer and winter, seed-time and harvest," should never cease. Then the bow spanned the heavens, as a token which should remain perpetually, of the love and constancy of the Father, and of his declaration that the earth should never again be destroyed by a deluge.

And God said to Noah: "And the fear of you shall be upon every beast of the earth, and upon every fowl of the air; upon all that move upon the earth, and upon all the fishes of the sea; into your hand are they delivered. Every moving thing that liveth shall be meat for you; even as the green herb, have I given you all things. But flesh with the life thereof, which is the blood thereof, shall ye not eat. And surely your blood of your lives will I require. At the hand of every beast will I require it, and at the hand of every man; at the hand of every man's brother will I require the life of man. Whoso sheddeth man's blood, by man shall his blood be shed."

Great stress is usually laid upon the word "*shall*" in this text. "By man SHALL his blood be shed," as if the declaration was *imperative*. But this same auxilliary is employed in this same connection where the meaning cannot be imperative. "*Every moving thing that liveth* SHALL BE *meat for you.*"* Caterpillers, spiders and rattlesnakes " live " and " move;" so that if this text is to be taken in its *literal* and *imperative* sense, all men are doomed to subsist upon these poisonous insects and reptiles. Do you say this instruction was limited to the Hebrews, and designed only to regulate their practices in diet?

---

* See third verse.

then, on the same grounds, we can limit the instruction of the sixth verse to the Hebrews, and say that only they should pour out blood for blood. But this was not the design of the text. " Bloody and deceitful men *shall not* live out half their days."* Here is the same imperative *form;* but the *sense* is not imperative. The instruction is general, and the same as that contained in the declaration to Noah, teaching us that " violence begets violence." Again, it is declared that "the wicked *shall* do wickedly, and none of the wicked *shall* understand."† . If we take this in an imperative sense, then it contains a *command* to sin and not to understand the truth. So in the declaration of Christ to Peter, " They that take the sword, *shall* perish by the sword," the same imperative form occurs, and yet we know the declaration was not imperative. A better rendering would have been, " They that take the sword *will* perish by the sword," which is the sense, as we have seen, in which Calvin gives the phrase " shall be shed," in the declaration to Noah, notwithstanding he was both theoretically and *practically* in favor of Capital Punishment, especially by burning.‡

TESTIMONY OF LEARNED MEN.—TRUE TRANSLATION.

The views we have now taken of this subject are sustained by some of the leading spirits in every age of the Christian Church. Even three hundred years before Christ, we find the Seventy-Two learned Jews of Alexan-

---

* Psalms 55: 7.   † Daniel 12: 10.

‡ The Death Penalty has always been a dreadful instrument of injustice and cruelty in the hands of both political and religious despots. Millions of innocent men and women have been put to death by the Church, for matters of faith. Calvin possessed this power. James Gallet was beheaded by his order, " because he had written," what Calvin deemed "profane letters." Michael Servetus, in his passage through Geneva, in 1553, was arrested, and on Calvin's accusation, was burnt alive because he had attacked, (not men and women,) but *the mystery of the Trinity."* Numerous other similar examples might be adduced, showing how fearful is such a law even in the hands of religious men.

dria, in translating their Hebrew Scriptures into Greek, omitting the words "by man." They gave the text as they understood it, merely as indicating the natural consequences of violence. Now, is it not probable that they understood the teachings of their own Scriptures, as correctly as we at this late day; and as they were probably in favor of the law of "life for life," is it not reasonable to suppose that they would have employed this declaration to support the practice, if they could have done so without violating the text? And yet they have it, when literally rendered, as follows: "Whoso sheddeth man's blood, *for* his blood, (i. e. the blood of the slain,) will have his own shed."

Not only the Septuagint, but Wickliffe and the Vulgate omit the words "by man." The Samaritan version has it: "For the man his blood will be shed." While the Latin version has it: "Whoso sheddeth human blood, his blood will be shed." Martini's Italian version has it: "Whoso sheds human blood, his blood will be shed," not mentioning the instrument by which the bloody work will be accomplished, and like the others, giving the *general* form. "The French Bible in common use, and which is distributed by our Bible societies, has it: 'Who will shed the blood of man *in man*, his blood will be poured out;' making the 'beth-adam' of the Hebrew to refer to the mode of the first life-taking, and not to the agent in the second. Swedenborg also renders it: 'He who sheds the blood of man in man, his blood shall be shed'—placing the comma after 'in man,' as in the French. Paschal quotes it: 'Whoso sheddeth human blood, his blood will be shed;' and adds—'This general prohibition takes from man all power over the life of man.' Cahen, the director of the Hebrew school in Paris, who not long since published a new version of the

Old Testament, also uses the future *indicative*, 'will be shed.'"

A writer in the Democratic *Review*,* gives a learned criticism, showing the obscurity of our common translation, and what has to be *assumed* by the translators to give the text the form and signification with which it is clothed as it comes to us. He says:

"Although the question is one of criticism, it may, however, be made plain enough to the *unlearned*, as well as to the more scholarly reader. What is the literal rendering of the Hebrew of the sixth verse of Genesis, ix? This is the first question. Simply this: ' Shedding blood of man in man his (or its) blood will be shed.' No one will dispute this. Now, in order to convert this into the common English version, three things have to be *assumed* on the strength of some right or authority, which, wherever it may reside, it is very certain does not belong to the Hebrew itself. Namely: 1st. The *participle* ' shedding,' is not only made personal and masculine, but it is confined to the personal and masculine sense, in the words ' whoso sheddeth.' 2nd. The verb, which in the original is the simple future tense, so as to be rendered in Latin *effunditur*, and in English 'will be shed,' must receive an *imperative* sense so as to be read '*shall be shed.*' And 3dly. The expression which is literally 'in man,' in the original, must be made to denote agency, by selecting and assigning to the preposition employed, only one of its various meanings, so as to be converted into 'by man.' It is only after the performance of this triple process that the original Hebrew (of which we have given above a literal rendering) becomes translated, or rather transformed, into the common English reading of our Bible.

---

* March, 1843: page 228.

" Respecting the *future* form of the *verb*, however, we deny most emphatically that our opponents have any right or reason to claim for it any necessary *imperative force.* Do they deny the fact? No. But they say, as there is no third person *imperative* in the Hebrew, the *future* has to be used when it is desired to express that sense. The word *may*, undoubtedly, be so rendered *if we choose*, but it is not necessary to do it so. Because the future form may sometimes be rendered imperatively, must it always be? Are *may* and *must* identical? For one instance of the *imperative*, ten can be pointed to, of the simple and proper future tense. . . . .

" Our position on this point cannot be shaken; no scholar, no candid reasoner, can dispute it—namely, that there is not necessarily anything *imperative* in the use of the Hebrew verb here used, and that it may as well be rendered '*will* be shed,' (denunciatory or declaratory)— or '*may be shed,*' (permissively.) To give it the *imperative* sense, and then claim our obedience as a command, is not only to beg the whole question, but even *imperatively* to clothe in the garb of divine authority, that which is the mere *imposture* of human assumption. The present application of it may be fairly compared to an act of forging a sovereign's signet to a death-warrant."

Le Clerc, who is excellent authority, also tells us that the translation "by man," should have been "*among men.*" " Whoso sheddeth man's blood, his blood will be shed among men." " This is the natural consequence of bloody deeds." He adds: "Homicides suffer a retributive punishment for their crime, whether they fall into the hands of the law, or by the providence of God, they generally perish by some violent death."

Professor T. C. Upham,* of Bowdoin College, Maine,

---

* A Presbyterian or Congregationalist in sentiment.

one of the first Hebrew scholars in the country, says, that "the passage may be read, 'Whoso sheddeth man's blood, by man WILL his blood be shed.'" He adds that the expressions are "obviously not to be understood as a command, authorizing and requiring every one, by his own act, and in his own person, to put to death any and every other individual who has been guilty of murder. Such an interpretation would fill the world with violence and confusion." He also says: "We regard it as merely expressive of a great retributive fact in nature, and in the overruling providence of God, that he who designedly and wickedly takes human life shall, assuredly, in some way or other, meet with severe punishment, and will probably come to a violent end."†

"The mark of Cain is stamped upon murderers, and they are lost and ruined men, even if the civil magistrate does not touch them. All nature frowns upon them; the very stones cry out; some perish by quarrels in the streets; some seek a refuge on the ocean and are drowned; some are put to death by their fellow men from feelings of revenge; some are killed in war; some put themselves to death by violent means; some die of pure remorse and anguish of spirit; and, in one way or other, as sure as there is a God in heaven, who requires the blood they have shed at their hands, they all, sooner or later, come to a miserable end."

Never were truer words than these, or more in harmony with the express declarations of heaven. "God is not mocked; for whatsoever a man soweth *that* shall he also reap." The history of the world from the beginning attests to the truth of this declaration. Many facts that have come under our own observation, and others drawn from history, both sacred and profane, might be given in

† Manual of Peace, page 219.

illustration, had we space. Read the Old Testament history, and mark the course and end of cruel and bloodthirsty kings and others, and you will be astonished to find how large a number died of violent deaths; and, therefore, how true is the declaration, "Whoso sheddeth man's blood, by man will his blood be shed."

In illustration of this general truth, Rev. Mr. Spear, of Boston, in his Essays on the Death Penalty, gives a striking account, taken from some English work, of the murder of an exciseman, on the southern coast of England, "that was barbarously beaten to death in the presence of his wife and children, who were deterred from giving any alarm by two of the gang, who stood over them with a pistol at each of their heads." This was seventy years ago. "The government offered a large reward for the apprehension of the murderers, but no tidings were obtained of them for *twenty-five years*. At about that time the minister of Symington Church was sent for by a man on his death-bed, and this man confessed that he was the thirtieth man of the gang who had murdered Bursey; that he stood watch at the garden wicket, between the house and the road, to give the alarm, if needful, but had no further active hand in the murder ; that the *other twenty-nine had every one died a violent death;*—some by fire, shipwreck, battle, frays with their companions in crimes, or some other means, so that of the whole thirty, no one but himself had a chance to die in their beds or at their homes. At the time of his confession, the writer was in the neighborhood of Symington, and had the facts from the minister who received the dying man's confession."

Such are the proofs we are able to adduce to support the views advanced concerning the true meaning and intent of this declaration to Noah.

We would add here, that many critics entitled to equal credit for learning and piety, with those we have mentioned, translate the words "whoso," referring to *man*, by the term *whatsoever*, referring to the beast; and contend that the declaration is not that the blood of man shall be shed for the crime of killing, but that man shall destroy the beast who kills. Michaelis renders it: " *Whatsoever* sheddeth man's blood, his blood shall be shed." Rev. E. H. Chapin,* in a series of lectures in Boston, a few years ago, on the Death Penalty, takes this view of the passage: " I am inclined to the opinion," says he, " that we find the true meaning of this text in the translation, ' *What-soever* sheddeth man's blood, by man shall *its* blood be shed.' This translation is well authorized and supported. Thus rendered, it extends the sanctity of human life, even to the *beast*, and accords with the context. " And surely your blood of your lives will I require; *at the hand of every man;* at the hand of every man's brother will I require the life of man. *What*soever sheddeth man's blood, by man shall *its* blood be shed, for in the image of God made he man." . . . . " The great idea inculcated here, is the sacredness of the *mysterious principle of life.* Even in the beast it was to be respected; the life thereof, which is the blood, was not to be eaten. But should the beast violate that principle of life in man, by shedding his blood, man was to shed the blood of the beast, in order to demonstrate the sanctity of that which was *made in the image of God.*" But, says God, " at the hand of every man's brother, will *I*," not shall *man*—not shall *a court of justice*—but " will *I* require the life of man."

" The penalty, here," continues Mr. Chapin, "is not with *man*, but with *God*, ... for in the case of man's

---

* An eminent Universalist clergyman of New York city.

murder, not only is the sacred principle of life violated, but the image of God in man is desecrated."

There is reason in this interpretation. God required the life of Abel at the hand of Cain, for Cain had dese-crated the image of God, and violated the principle of life in his brother. Still Cain was not executed, for this was not the kind of requital that God demanded, as it would have been but a repetition of the offense—a desecration of another image, and a violation of another life. The muderer was called to an account, and the Lord settled it with him in his own way. So he does with every one who violates his image in man. " Vengeance is *mine,* saith the Lord, *I* will repay." It is our business to guard the murderer, from committing greater depreda-tion on society. God will see that his punishment is sufficiently severe. Was it not thus with Cain ? In cold blood had he wantonly slain a kind-hearted brother with-out provocation, and behold how he sinks in wretched-ness and ruin, a miserable vagabond and outcast on God's earth. Shunned and forsaken of all men, no won-der he exclaims, " My punishment is greater than I can bear!" Surely " the way of the transgressor *is* hard, and " *there is* NO *rest to the wicked,* saith my God." Men, even *Christians,* are sometimes inclined to contra-dict God, and say that the way of the sinner is easy,: pleasant and delightful ; whilst the path of the virtuous is hard, barren, and cheerless. And so they would visit the criminal with vengeance, declaring that if there were no whips, or prisons, or dungeons, or gibbets, that there would be no *punishment.* Ah! how little such persons confide in the wisdom and positive declarations of Him who knoweth the condition of all hearts, and who hath said, " the wicked are like the troubled sea when it *can-not rest,* whose: waters cast up mire and dirt." Is there

11

no punishment in remorse? Can the murderer run away from his own conscience? Is not his soul like the troubled sea? Has he not kindled the fires of hell within him, which many waters cannot drown? Is his rest upon his pillow sweet, and with a soul overwhelmed in guilt, does he not "flee when no man pursueth?" Why, then, should *Christians* entertain this strong desire to visit the criminal with vengeance, and dabble with their own fingers in his blood, lest he escape a "just recompense of reward?" Cannot they fasten him securely with strong chains and bolts and bars in his stone prison, and trust to Him "who cannot lie," when he affirms that, "though hand join in hand, the wicked *shall not be unpunished?*"

This is the doctrine in which we should educate our children, and which we should teach at the fire-side, in the street, at our place of business, in the pulpit, at the bar, in the halls of legislation, and *everywhere:* that while human life is sacred—while the image of God in man should never be desecrated, even in the murderer, the power over human life being the sole prerogative of Him who gave it—it is impossible for the offender to go unpunished. Let society everywhere be impressed with this undeviating truth—this eternal law of God—that "violence begets violence," while kindness and clemency alone will kill revenge, and melt and subdue the heart—and more will be accomplished in a single year for the suppression of crime, and the purity and safety of society than was effected during the whole reign of Nero the tyrant, with all his dreadful severity and cruelty, his chains, racks, dungeons, gibbets, fires and other engines of torture and destruction.

. Such, then, are our views with reference to this noted passage in Genesis. We cannot deem it a command upon which the penal code of nations should rest, requiring blood for blood to the end of time, even allowing it the common interpretation. It was addressed to no government, but to an individual in the early ages of the world. God did not himself regard it. More than 2200 years of the world's history passed away before it was enforced; and since, in millions of instances, where the offender was guilty of murder, it was not regarded. It may be a warrant for "the avenger of blood," the nearest relative of a murdered man, to kill. This is the most that can be claimed for it. But let any man attempt to obey that custom now, and he would be arrested, convicted, and executed for murder.

THE CODE OF MOSES.

But by this time the reader is impatient to inquire of the writer if he has forgotten that God gave a law to Moses; and if he is not aware that the principle of the declaration, "Whoso sheddeth man's blood, by man shall his blood be shed," was incorporated into that law, and that this law must be still binding on us under the Christian dispensation, for Christ himself said, "Think not that I am come to *destroy* the law or the prophets; I am come not to destroy, but to fulfil. For verily I say unto you, till heaven and earth pass, one jot or one tittle shall in no wise pass from the law till all be fulfilled."*

We are not unaware of the existence of the Levitical code, and are ready to grant that the Death Penalty was clearly embodied in its demands. But our questioner would do well to notice that it required life for other crimes beside that of murder. Let him examine the fol lowing catalogue of offenses, all of which were recognized as capital, and punished with death by the law of Moses, and then answer if every *"jot and tittle"* of that law is still

* Matthew 5: 18.

binding on Christians in the middle of the Nineteenth Century. It was carefully prepared by Mr. Spear of Boston, who in introducing it into his " Essays on the Death Penalty," says : " It is remarkable that no writer with whom we have met has performed this labor. We feel that it will do more to settle the question of its adoption by any civilized community than all other considerations."

CAPITAL OFFENSES IN THE MOSAIC CODE.

Murder, ...	Exodus, xxi.	12
Kidnapping, ...	" "	16
Eating leavened bread during the Passover,	" xii.	15
Suffering an unruly ox to be at liberty, if he kill; the ox also to be stoned, ...	" xxi.	29
Witchcraft, ...	" xxii.	18
Beastiality, the beast put to death,	" "	19
Idolatry, ...	" "	20
Oppression of Widow and Fatherless,	" "	22
Compounding holy ointment, or putting it on any stranger, ...	" "	33
Violation of the Sabbath, ...	" xxxi.	14
Smiting of father or mother, . . .	" xxi.	15
Sodomy.	Lev. xx.	13
Eating the flesh of the sacrifice of peace-offerings with uncleanness, ...	" vii.	20
Eating the fat of offered beasts, . . .	" "	25
Eating any manner of blood, . . .		27
Offering children to Moloch, .	" xx.	2
Eating a sacrifice of peace-offering,	" xix.	8
Screening the idolater, ...	" xx.	4
Going after familiar spirits and wizards,	" "	6
Adultery, [both parties, if female married, and not a bond-maid,] . . .	" "	10
Incest, [three kinds,] . . .	" "	11
Cursing of parents, . . .	" "	9
Unchastity in a priest's daughter, . .	" xxi.	9

Blasphemy, ...	Lev.	xiv.	16
Stranger coming nigh the tabernacle,	Numbers	i.	51
Coming nigh the priest's office, . . .	"	iii.	10
Usurping the sacerdotal functions, . ,	"	iv.	20
Forbearing to keep the passover, if not jour-			
neying, ...	'	ix.	13
Presumption, or despising the word of the Lord,	"	xv.	30
Uncleanness, or defiling the sanctuary of the			
Lord, ...	"	xix.	13
False pretension to the character of a divine			
messenger, ...	Deut.	xiii.	5
Opposition to the decree of the highest judic-			
ial authority, ...	"	xvii.	12
Unchastity before marriage, when charged by			
a husband, . . , . . .	"	xxii.	13

Here is the Levitical catalogue of offenses punishable with death by the law of Moses. To those in our day whose hearts are chastened by the grace of Christ, and who, therefore, pity the sinful, and would "save" and not "destroy men's lives," it looks dark and cruel. The thunderings of Sinai are heard in it—smoke and lightning, and mutterings of wrath are mingled with its fearful demands. And the modes of killing described were equally cruel. *Stoning* and the *sword*—afterward *decapitation, sawing asunder, strangulation* and *crucifixion* were the methods.

We have presented this code, thus in detail, that the objector, especially the *Christian* objector, who is everlastingly harping on the "requisitions of GOD'S LAW," and the necessity of our walking "by the *light* of that law," may know just what it is, what it demands, what amount of *light* there really is in it, and whether it is binding on us upon whom the "SUN of righteousness has arisen with healing in his beams."

Now, if the Christian stickler for the gallows contends

that Christ did not abrogate "one jot or tittle" of the foregoing code, but came to render it positively more binding, then it comes to us *entire*, and we, as the followers of Christ, are under the necessity of taking it to our hearts *as it is*, and of making it the law of the land in which we chance to reside, whether it be in a highly civilized society, or among barbarians. We contend that this is the only alternative. *There is no other.* Do you say that the *criminal* law of Moses was sanctioned by Christ, and is still binding on society? then we say you must take the *entire* law. "He that smiteth father or mother *shall surely be put to death*."* This is the declaration of Moses. Incorporate it into your own penal code, and you must do it if you are a follower of Moses. "He that curseth father or mother *shall surely be put to death*."† So says the Levitical law. "He that stealeth a man and selleth him, or if he be found in his hand, *shall surely be put to death*."‡ This is the demand of the Mosaic code. It also required the life of the offender for kindling a fire, or gathering sticks on the Sabbath. Is not this law, "one jot or tittle" yet abrogated? Then blot out the penal code of your own statute book and inscribe this in its place. "Ye shall not afflict any widow or fatherless child. If thou afflict them in anywise, and they cry at all unto me, I will surely hear their cry, and my wrath shall wax hot, and I will kill you with the sword; and *your* wives shall be widows, and *your* children fatherless."‖ Take care, fellow Christian; you are in danger, if this declaration reaches to our time. How many hard-hearted, cruel men—yea, *Christian* men, if a strict observance of the rites and ceremonies of religion will make them so—are ardent supporters of the gallows

---

* Exodus 21: 15.   †Ibid 21: 17.
‡ Ibid 21: 16.   ‖ Ibid 21: 24—25.

for murder, on the ground that the law of God demands life for life, while they *themselves*, "afflict the widow and fatherless," trample upon their rights, and rob them of their lawful patrimony, and never dream that they have violated the same law, and are, therefore, worthy of the halter. "Thou shalt give life for life, eye for eye, tooth for tooth, hand for hand, foot for foot, burning for burning, wound for wound, stripe for stripe" So said Moses, fifteen hundred years before Christ, and so should the Christian minister, and the Christian Church in the middle of the nineteenth century declare, if not one "jot or tittle" of the Levitical law is abrogated.

Here, then, is the unavoidable position of the man who upholds the Death Penalty; on the ground that the law of Moses sanctioned it. He must take the *entire* law. Go back to Moses, then, if you *will*, fellow Christian, and at the foot of the thundering Sinai, plant yourself on that old code, and plead for the continuance of the gallows, on its authority; but remember that you must use it on other criminals beside the *murderer*. You must write down in your statute book: " Death for him who violates the Sabbath; and for him who profanes the name of God; and for him who afflicts the widow or fatherless; and for him who desecrateth the sanctuary of God; and for him who goeth after any God but the true God ; and for him who communeth with a familiar spirit." Let all this be written down in the penal codes of our States, as it must be, if not " one jot or tittle " of the law is abrogated, and it would probably bring our Christian people, who are so great sticklers for that law, to their senses.

The opposer may say, now, that so much as demands death for the murderer is binding, and no more. But what right have you to say this? By what rule of propriety or reason, can you select from the code of Moses, whatever your whim may choose to dictate, and throw the rest away? Did you not, just now, quote from Christ, "Verily I say unto you, till heaven and earth pass, one jot or one tittle shall in no wise pass from the law till all be fulfilled?" On the same ground that you can dispense with a *part* of the law, we can dispense with the *whole*.

It will be seen by the foregoing catalogue, that the Mosaic code contained thirty-four capital offenses. The opposer strikes off *thirty-three* without hesitation, as not binding, and retains the remaining *one* as binding.

Having presented the demands of the Levitical law, and shown pretty conclusively, we think, that it must be surrendered by the opposer as untenable, not affording any just grounds of argument for the gallows, it becomes necessary, to a full understanding of the subject, that a word of explanation be offered to harmonize what may appear to the casual or thoughtless reader, as a contradiction in the teachings of Christ, concerning the Mosaic law; he declaring on some occasions, that he was "the end of the law," and on others, that he "came not to destroy but to fulfil it."

It may be well to notice here, an error into which many Christians—some of them intelligent Christians— sometimes fall, viz : they not unfrequently confound the declaration to Noah, with the Levitical law, thinking that they are one and the same. This is a mistake. The covenant was made with Noah, as we have seen, in the year of the world 1657; but the decalogue, or ten commandments, and the general laws for the regulation of the Hebrews under Moses, were not given till the year of the world, 2513, or nearly a thousand years after the ark rested upon the mountain, and the bow spanned the heavens, in token of the covenant with every living thing.

To reconcile the apparent contradiction to which we have alluded, it is necessary to understand that the law of Moses was not a unit, embracing but a single design, but was rather threefold in its nature and application, and was divided in the following order, viz: the *Moral*, the *Penal*, and the *Ceremonial;* the first embracing the ten commandments, written on the tables of stone; the second relating to *penal jurisprudence*, or the punishment of crime; and the third relating to the *rites* and *ceremonies* connected with the Jewish worship.

Now, the MORAL LAW of God can never be annulled. It is founded in justice and the nature of things, and can no more be abrogated than the centripetal and centrifugal forces, which regulate the courses of the heavenly bodies. In the decalogue, idolatry, profanity, blasphemy, profanation of the Sabbath, disobedience to parents, destroying human life, the cultivation of revengeful passions, riot, excess, drunkenness, gluttony, slothfulness, superstition, mortifications, self-denials, adultery, theft, cheating, withholding of men's rights, rapine, robbery, murder, perjury, covetousness, and every conceivable wrong and injustice are condemned and forbidden. Not in so many words, it is true, but *really* in the application of the principles involved in the decalogue. And why are they forbidden, and why are the principles involved in the decalogue eternal? Because sin is the worst enemy of man; and because an adherence to the moral law of Him who is infinite in wisdom, will protect man from this subtle enemy, and guard him safely in the ways of virtue, and therefore in the way of happiness. "Thou shalt not kill." "Thou shalt not steal." "Thou shalt not commit adultery." "Thou shalt not bear false witness against thy neighbor." And why not? Because these acts are *in their nature* unjust; and wrong, because they are unjust. Millions of men and women believè that they can violate these moral commandments, and suffer no unhappy consequences. But how false and fallacious this hope. God's law, whether it regulates the material or the spiritual, cannot be violated with impunity. Can a man bury himself in the sea and not drown? or throw himself upon the flames and not burn? Neither can he become a thief, or robber, or drunkard, or liar, or debauchee, and not suffer the wretched consequences.

The moral law of God, then, still remains. It is yet in full force. Christianity abrogates no moral duty, but it defines all duty more clearly, sanctions it, and strengthens its hold upon the affections of the human soul. The commandment, "*Thou shalt not kill,*" was proclaimed anew by Christ, in the declaration, "Thou shalt love thy neighbor as thyself." There is not a principle of moral duty embraced in the decalogue which was not adopted and reiterated again and again by Christ and his apostles.

Now, it was to this fact—the fact that he came not to release men from any moral obligation imposed by the Scriptures, which God had previously given, and also to the fact that all the types and shadows of the ancient law were fulfilled in him—that Christ referred to when he said: "Think not that I am come to destroy the law or the prophets. I am not come to destroy, but to fulfil. For verily I say unto you, till heaven and earth pass, one jot or one tittle shall in no-wise pass from the law till all be fulfilled." Did he mean to include the *penal* and *ceremonial* in this declaration? Not at all. For he immediately adds: "Whosoever, therefore, shall break one of *these least commandments,* and shall teach men so, he shall be called the least in the kingdom of heaven; but whosoever shall do, and teach them, the same shall be called great in the kingdom of heaven. For I say unto you, that except your *righteousness* shall exceed the righteousness of the Scribes and Pharisees, ye shall in no case enter into the kingdom of heaven."

Here he alludes only to the moral law of the Jews, which he sanctions, enforcing every "jot and tittle" of its demands, and concludes the declaration by asserting, that except the righteousness of those to whom he addressed himself, *exceed* the righteousness of those under the law, they could in no case enter into his Gospel or heavenly kingdom—a kingdom of righteousness, peace and joy in the Holy Ghost, which he came to set up and establish in the earth. Thus teaching the superiority of his religion. In his "kingdom," as we have seen, no hatred or revenge could be admitted, but only *love.* "*Love is the fulfilling of the law;*" "Love worketh no ill to his neighbor " Plainly, then, it was concerning the moral law that he made the declaration under consideration.

We have said that the *moral law* of God is founded on fixed principles, and cannot, therefore, be abrogated or changed, but is eternal. But can this be affirmed of the criminal code of any nation or age? Is it immutable? We have seen what was the code of Moses, and how the Hebrews were punished for violating its requirements. If a man was found gathering sticks on Sunday, he was stoned to death. Was that law eternal? The wilful, disobedient son was killed. Was the law that required his death eternal? Not at all. All this may have been best for the rude, uncultivated condition of the early Jews, but not for us living under the noon-day light of the Sun of Righteousness. God did not design the penal code of Moses for us. Our education, habits of thought, customs, means for securing and instructing the criminal, are all far in advance of those of olden time. The command of God to Abraham, was that he should sacrifice his son Isaac. But this command extends neither to the author nor the reader of this book. It was temporary, and ended with Abraham, and the circumstances under which he acted.

So with the penal code of Moses. It was temporary. It demanded of the Hebrews, "eye for eye, tooth for tooth, blow for blow, life for life." But Christ said, as we have seen, (and he uttered these divine words in the very sermon where he made the declaration, "I am not come to *destroy*, but to *fulfil*,") "Ye have heard that it hath been said, an eye for an eye, and a tooth for a tooth; but I say unto you that ye resist not evil; but whosoever shall smite thee on thy right cheek, turn to him the other also. Ye have heard that it hath been said, thou shalt love thy neighbor and hate thy enemy; but I say unto you, love your enemies, bless them that curse you, do good to them that hate you, and pray for them which despitefully use you and persecute you." Here the spirit of retaliation and vengeance of the old law was forever abrogated, and it was the very first work of Christ. According to that law, adultery was a capital crime. Death by stoning was the awful penalty; but did Jesus inflict it when the persecuting Jews endeavored to ensnare him into an act that would condemn the great doctrine of love and good-will which he had taught? By no means. Look at the course of that lowly Being.

"And the Scribes and Pharisees brought unto him a woman taken in adultery; and when they had set her in the midst, they said unto him: Master, this woman was taken in adultery, in the very act. Now, Moses, in the law commanded us that such should be stoned,* but what sayest thou? This they said, tempting him, that they might have to accuse him. But Jesus stooped down, and with his finger wrote on the ground, as tho' he heard them not. So when they continued asking him, he lifted up himself and said unto them: He that is without sin among you, let him first cast a stone at her. And they which heard it, being convicted by their own consciences, went out one by one, *beginning at the eldest*, even unto the last, and Jesus was left alone, and the woman in the midst. When Jesus had lifted up himself and saw none but the woman, he said unto her, Woman, where are those thine accusers? hath no man condemned thee? She said, No man, Lord. And Jesus said unto her: *Neither do I condemn thee; go and sin no more.*" How perfectly in harmony was the dealings of Jesus with this poor, sinful woman, and the spirit of his divine precepts. He had abrogated the law of Moses in his sermon on the mount, and taught kindness for those who were out of the way; and now, by his own act he condemns that law, and shows the miserable offender pity and forgiveness. But would he have done this if the Mosaic law was designed for *all time?*

Is the reader still in doubt respecting the abrogation of the judicial and ceremonial law of Moses by Christ? If so, we would refer him to Paul, who seemed to understand the nature of the question perfectly. He says to the Hebrews: "The days come, saith the Lord, when I will make a *new covenant* with the house of Israel, and

---

* The Jewish method of stoning, according to the Rabbins, was as follows: The culprit, half naked, the hands tied behind the back, was placed on a scaffold, ten or twelve feet high. The witnesses who stood with her pushed her off with great force; if she was killed by the fall there was nothing further done; but if she was not, one of the witnesses took up a very large stone, and dashed it upon her breast, which, generally, was the *coup de grace*, or finishing touch.—DR. ADAM CLARKE.

with the house of Judah; not according to the covenant which I made with their fathers, in the day when I took them by the hand and led them out of the land of Egypt; because they continued not in my covenant, and I regarded them not, saith the Lord. For this is the covenant that I will make with the house of Israel, after those days, saith the Lord: I will *put my laws into their minds, and write them in their hearts; and I will be to them a God and they shall be to me a people . for I will be merciful to their unrighteousness, and their sins and their iniquities will I remember no more.* In that he saith a *new* covenant, he hath made the first old. *Now that which decayeth and waxeth old is ready to vanish away.*"* "For the priesthood being changed, there *is made, of necessity, a change also of the law.* For there is verily a *disannulling of the commandment going before for the weakness and unprofitableness thereof.*"† Christ, also, affirmed, saying: " The law and the prophets were *until John; since that time the kingdom of God is preached.*"‡ And to make assurance doubly sure, we would say that Calmet, whose learning and orthodoxy, no one will question, remarks that, " The law of Moses is superseded or abrogated by the Gospel. Since the death of the Messiah, the LEGAL *ceremonies are of no longer obligation.*" He also says: " When we say that the Gospel has rescued us from the yoke of the law, we understand only the appointments of the ceremonial and judicial law; not those moral precepts, whose obligation is indispensable, and whose observation is much more perfect, and extensive, enforced, under the law of grace, than it was under the old law."||

Thus have we seen that there are no instructions or

---

* Hebrews 8 : 8—13.   † Hebrews 7.   ‡ Luke 16: 16.
|| Dictionary of the Bible, page 611.

commandments IN ALL THE BIBLE, that stand in the way
of the abolishment of the Death Penalty. The judicial
law of Moses, like all criminal enactments, and political
institutions, was designed for a particular people, in a
particular age, and was, therefore, temporary, and not to
be compared with "the good things to come," under the
Gospel dispensation. It passed away when Christianity
was introduced. Jesus was the " end of the law ;" and
he, by his teachings and examples, not only abrogated
and condemned the law of Moses, and utterly forbid all
retaliation and vengeance toward those who are out of
the way, but, as we have seen. actually demanded of his
followers, kindness and mercy toward them. And think
of it as we may, my brother in Christ, this is what the
"law of Jesus " requires of *you*, if you have entered his
kingdom, and are, therefore, confessedly, a subject of his
government. His religion is a religion of LOVE. All
the priests, and ordinances, and types, and symbols of the
Law and the Prophets were fulfilled in him. " The
Lord thy God will raise up unto thee a prophet from the
midst of thee, of thy brethren like unto me ; *unto him ye
shall hearken*." Jesus came, pronounced the censure of
condemnation on the retaliatory spirit and vengeance of
the old covenant, and summed up and enforced all moral
duty in two great commandments: "Thou shalt love
the Lord thy God with all thy heart, with all thy soul,
and with all thy mind; this is the first and great commandment ; and the second is like unto it : *Thou shalt
love* THY NEIGHBOR AS THYSELF. On these two commandments, hang *all the law and the prophets*." His religion, we repeat, then, is emphatically a RELIGION OF
LOVE. If we love our fellow men as we love ourselves,
how can we strangle the life out of them, or stone or
crucify them? Let the spirit of the law of love be car-

ried out in penal enactments, and we should have no more use for the gibbet or hangman. And this is not all. If we entertained a *Christian* love for the criminal, we should not only not kill him, not only do him no injustice or violence, but our benevolence would prompt us to do him all the good in our power. If he is dangerous when at liberty, he must be confined; but when once secured, and wholly in our power, all unkindness and vengeance are forbidden, and we must labor for the instruction and reformation of the man. Go to Christ, contemplate his acts toward the sinful, and you will find that the obligations of his benevolence are not merely *prohibitory*—directing us to avoid " working ill " to another—but *mandatory*, requiring us to do him good.* Many a Christian possesses love enough for the criminal, to cause him to refrain from doing him actual violence, but not enough to " return good for evil." But to abstain from injustice or violence is not enough. The wretched sinner is our brother. He is weak, ignorant, it may be, at all events, unfortunate. To be Christ-like, we must not " destroy," but " save " him. "LOVE is the fulfilling of the law." But how can we save him if we strangle him while in his sins ?

> "Think gently of the erring !
> Lord let us not forget,
> However darkly stained by sin,
> He is a brother yet.
> Heir of the same inheritance !
> Child of the self-same God,
> He hath stumbled in the path,
> *We* have in darkness trod.

---

* This subject is more fully discussed in this volume under the head of "THE PRISON."

Speak gently to him, brother,
 Thou yet may'st lead him back
With holy words and tones of love
 From misery's thorny track.
Forget not thou hast often sinned,
 And sinful yet must be;
Deal gently with the erring one,
 As God has dealt with thee.

OBJECTIONS DRAWN FROM THE CHRISTIAN SCRIPTURES.

1. It is objected to the ground we have taken in the foregoing, that the Christian Scriptures themselves favor the gallows. Paul said: "Let every soul be subject unto the higher powers. For there is no power but of God; the powers that be are ordained of God. Whosoever, therefore, resisteth the power, resisteth the ordinance of God; and they that resist shall receive to themselves damnation. For rulers are not a terror to good works but to the evil. Wilt thou, then, not be afraid of the power? Do that which is good, and thou shalt have praise of the same; for he is the minister of God to thee for good. But if thou do that which is evil, be afraid; for he beareth not the sword in vain; for he is the minister of God, a revenger to execute wrath upon him that doeth evil.

Render, therefore, to all their dues; tribute to whom tribute is due, custom to whom custom, fear to whom fear, honor to whom honor. Owe no man anything, but love one another."* The instruction of the above is simply this: Let every man be obedient to the laws of the civil government under which the providence of God has cast his lot. The very design of the civil government is to secure the order, harmony, defense and happiness of society, and

---

* Romans 13: 1—8.

also the rights and liberty of individuals. No nation or people can exist without government of some kind; nor can it exist with any degree of security, if individuals to any considerable extent trample upon the laws. No greater curse can befall a nation than sedition and anarchy. Christianity gives no lenity to lawlessness, a fact plainly evident from the foregoing address of Paul to the Christians in Rome.

In order to a more full understanding, not only of the nature, but the design of this instruction at that partienlar juncture, and to that particular people, it should be known that the Jews had a deeply rooted aversion to any government but their own, and had previously manifested an uneasy and seditious spirit at Rome; so that by an edict of the Emperor Claudius they had been banished from the city. Paul was anxious, not only to instruct the Christians there in the duty of obedience to the civil government, but to assure the Romans themselves that they need not fear insurrection or sedition from them, for their religion positively forbid lawlessness, and enforced obedience to " the powers that be."

But no one should ever infer from this that Christianity, in any other way, sanctioned and upheld the cruel, extravagant, and unjust laws of the Romans at that time. It is one thing to be "subject" to a law, and quite another and a different thing to approbate the law itself with our judgment. We should always endeavor to enforce and obey the laws we have, whether they are in harmony with our individual sense of justice and expediency, or not, for the reason before mentioned, viz: the necessity of government and the curse of rebellion. But this does not preclude another duty, which we owe to ourselves and to our country, of equal importance, and that is to labor for the repeal of all unjust and unchristian laws, and the enactment of those in harmony with benevolence, and the true interests and happiness of society.

It is recorded that when John Hancock* was governor of the Commonwealth of Massachusetts seventy-five years ago, one "Rachael Whall was hung in Boston for highway robbery. Her offense consisted in twitching from the hand of another female, a bonnet, worth, perhaps, seventy-five cents, and running off with it. *The most urgent applications for her pardon were unsuccessful.*" "I mention this," says the writer, "not to the disparagement of the governor. He doubtless acted from a sense of duty, thinking it *best for the community that the laws of the land, however frightfully severe, while they were laws, should be executed.*"

Now, this man acted, whether wisely or not, from a sense of the importance of the principle involved in the instruction of Paul, above mentioned. "Be obedient to the powers that be," said governor Hancock. They were obedient, and this young girl was executed on Boston common, for robbing to the amount of seventy-five cents. No man will say that the law which demanded the death of that girl for this crime, was a *Christian* law, or that Christianity forbid its repeal; on the contrary, Christianity demands its repeal.

"Edward Vaile Brown was hung in Boston, fifty years ago, for burglary, committed in the house of Captain Osias Goodwin, in Charter street, and stealing therefrom sundry articles."

"Within the same period, a girl of seventeen was hung in London, for stealing a silver cream pitcher."

"Long after the commencement of the present century, *eight separate capital convictions are recorded* on the

* John Hancock was governor of Massachusetts from 1780 to 1785.

books of the court of the Old Bailey, London, *as one day's job* of a single tribunal, the culprits being all boys and girls between the ages of *ten* and *sixteen*, and their offenses petty thefts."

No one will have the hardihood to contend that the laws which were in force in our country and England, fifty years ago, were in harmony with the benevolence and justice of the Christian religion; or that the instruction of Paul, now under consideration, prohibited a reform. Neither can it be shown that it prohibited a reform in the government or laws of Rome in the days of the apostle.

The truth is, Christ had himself, previously, plainly abrogated the principle of "blood for blood," as we have clearly shown, again and again, in this volume, and given the law of LOVE as the basis of all penal enactments. And if the reader will take the trouble of referring to the connection in which the foregoing is found, he will there find that Paul enforces the Christian principle in the very verses that follow after what we have quoted. After exhorting the Christians to be "subject unto the higher powers," he says: "He that *loveth* another fulfilleth the law; for *this*, thou shalt not commit adultery; THOU SHALT NOT KILL; thou shalt not steal; thou shalt not bear false witness; thou shalt not covet; and if there be any other commandment it is briefly comprehended in this saying, viz: *thou shalt love thy neighbor as thyself*. LOVE WORKETH NO ILL TO HIS NEIGHBOR. THEREFORE LOVE IS THE FULFILLING OF THE LAW."*

All must perceive that the principle enforced here, is perfectly in harmony with the declarations of Christ, already examined, and directly opposed to the sanguinary and terribly cruel laws and customs which prevailed in

---

* Romans 13: 8—10.

Rome at that time. So that while Paul exhorted obe-
dienee to the "powers" that existed, he presented the
great moral principle of the Gospel, divine and beautiful,
as the foundation of all human law. "Thou shalt love
thy neighbor as thyself." "Love worketh _no_ ill."
"Love is the fulfilling of the law." Now, let this principle prevail, and it is impossible for the law which requires
"eye for eye, tooth for tooth, blood for blood," to exist.
And the reason why nearly all our States are still disgraced with the gallows, is simply this: we are followers
of Moses, and not of Christ.

But it may be said here, that Paul declared that those
in authority "bear not the _sword_ in vain;" and that he
designed to sanction the Death Penalty, as he employed
this phrase in connection with the declaration, "execute
wrath upon him that doeth evil." In answer to this, we
reply, first, that the language is not in the form of appro-
bation, but it is the simple statement of a fact; and second,
that the word "sword" was put, not as figurative of the
executioner, but as an emblem of _power_ and _authority_,
without reference to any special office.* Thus is the entire passage in Romans, which is so often quoted to sustain the code of Moses, shown to be, not only not opposed to the views presented in this volume, but entirely
in harmony with them.

2. Again, it is objected, that Paul said, "If I be an
offender, or have committed anything worthy of death, I
refuse not to die; but if there be none of these things
whereof these accuse me, no man may deliver me unto
them."† . In this, it is said Paul did not condemn the
Death Penalty, but rather sanctioned it by declaring his
readiness to die, if they could convict him of having
violated their laws. We answer, Paul was under trial

---

* See Cruden; also Calmet.   † Acts 25:11.

where his life was at stake; not for killing a man, but for other and minor offenses charged on him. Now, if it can be shown that he sanctioned Capital Punishment for *murder*, (the crime for which *we* kill,) because he said he refused not to die if he was proven guilty, it can also be shown that he sanctioned it for the offenses brought against him on that occasion, viz: preaching a new religion, and denouncing the unjust and malevolent sentiments and laws of the Jews; for he said he refused not to die if they *could fix upon him their charges.* The truth is, the sentiment of this text was uttered without reference to either the justice or injustice of Capital Punishment. It is simply the language of a man conscious of his innocence, and with no desire to save his life by subterfuges. The question was not, whether Capital Punishment was lawful, but whether it was lawful *upon him.* He says, I refuse not to die if *I am an offender.* But I am no offender, and therefore you have no right to kill me, even if the laws by which you do your bloody work are lawful and just. This is the substance of Paul's declaration. If it sanctions the Death Penalty *at all*, it sanctions it for all the heralds of the Gospel who have the courage to proclaim the truth of God, in the face of error and superstition, for this was the head and front of the apostle's offending.

3. Once more. Christ was crucified between two thieves. One of them confessed that his punishment was just. Now, because Christ did not then and there speak out and oppose the Death Penalty, and protest against the punishment of these men as unlawful and unjust, it is *inferred* that he sanctioned Capital Punishment. This is a small peg on which to hang men and women, we are aware, but as slight as it may appear to some who may peruse these pages, it has been employed

by many learned divines and others, as a principal argument on which to base the gallows. But what folly. The account does not affirm that those put to death with Christ were *murderers*, but only *thieves*. If then, Christ, by his silence on that occasion, sanctioned Capital Punishment *at all*, he sanctioned it for *theft*. But will the sticklers for the Death Penalty in our day hang for theft? Nor is this all. If Christ, by his silence, approved the punishment of the thieves, he also approved of his own punishment, for "as a sheep before his shearers is dumb, so he opened not his mouth" to assert his own innocence. He also approved of that particular mode of death, viz : *crucifixion;* but will the supporters of the Death Penalty, in our time, go in for "the cross and nails," for all who are worthy of death? The truth is, it was not so much the work of Christ to condemn *particular* institutions, as to advance great truths, scattering them like seed, here and there, and relying on the natural course of things to secure the desired harvest. The Gospel he compared to "leaven which a woman took and hid in meal till the whole was leavened." The principles of religion, like the leaven, work silently, but certainly, in the hearts of men and communities, assimilating the desires and sentiments of the world to their own nature. When hanging upon the cross it was no time nor place for him to condemn the cruel laws of the Jews. It would have availed nothing; and, besides, he had previously, in the most plain and positive manner, condemned and abrogated their judicial covenant, and instituted another, more divine and ennobling. If the malefactors who suffered with him were worthy of death for *theft*, how much more deserving of this punishment were the guilty murderers of the innocent Jesus; and yet that blessed "Lamb of God" did not pronounce upon these wicked men *any* pun-

ishment, much less the punishment of death. Instead
of this, the last accents that fell from his lips, were in a
prayer to God for the forgiveness of those who were nail-
ing him to the cross. " FATHER, FORGIVE THEM, THEY
KNOW NOT WHAT THEY DO!" Well has it been said, that
" Socrates died like a philosopher, but Jesus Christ like
a God!" How can men gaze upon that blessed being,
when thus suspended upon the cross in the awful agonies of death, and listen to this more than mortal petition for the forgiveness of his own murderers—so in harmony with all his teachings, and a whole life of love and
compassion, and still contend that he sanctioned the
Death Penalty, *because he failed to denounce it at this
dreadful hour.* Surely, if they have no better evidence
than this, that Christianity sanctions the gallows, their
cause stands on a precarious foundation

The foregoing are the most prominent objections
drawn from the Christian Scriptures, in favor of Capital
Punishment, which have come to our notice. The reader will perceive that when examined in the light of reason,
and other portions of the divine word, they afford the
gallows no support. Thus is the Bible taken from the
hands of those who support the Death Penalty, and employed as an instrument of abolishment. "Let God be
true, but every man a liar.

CHAPTER X.

THE DEATH PENALTY IS NOT NECESSARY.

The Death Penalty not necessary to Personal or Social Security—Protection in life and property is what the good citizen asks—We have strong Prisons in every State in which to confine men of base passions—The Murderer is not secured by the present Law—Difficulty to convict—Facts from the Criminal Records in the United States and England—There is a repugnance to taking Human Life—If not convicted the Murderer returns to Society—With the Penalty of Imprisonment for Life he would be secured,

WE have now seen that the Christian Scriptures are not in favor of, but are positively opposed to the Death Penalty; and that for various other reasons which we have adduced, it should be abolished by all Christian communities and nations. Another important reason we have for abolishment is, that IT IS UTTERLY UNNECESSARY TO PERSONAL OR SOCIAL PROTECTION.

What every good citizen desires is security. When traveling, whether it be by railroad or steamboat—in carriage or on foot—in the open country or crowded city—and when at home, about his lawful business, or reposing in slumber at night, he wishes to be protected, not from prowling, blood-thirsty beasts, but from men— the robber and assassin. Now a special object of penal law is to protect him; and what he asks is *the* law which will the most certainly secure this result. The Death Penalty is on the statute book of his State. The gallows drinks the blood of its victim every now and then. Still he does not feel secure. The law is not enough. Pistols and dirks are at his side, under his pillow or in his pocket. But, notwithstanding, he possesses great confidence in the moral power of sanguinary laws; so he exclaims : "Annihilate the gallows as a terror to evil doers —abolish all killing for crime, and thus say to a desperado that he may do his worst and he can escape the halter—and would not the result be an overwhelming increase of crime? Would not blood run like water, and all sense of individual and social security be banished?" This, he says, is the main question with him when considering the subject. It is the *utility* of the gallows. Just convince him that by abolishing the Death Penalty you do not lessen restraint and multiply crime—or, in other words, convince him that the gallows is not *absolutely necessary to the protection of society*—and he will gladly consent to a change.

If the reader occupies this position, we would respectfully invite his careful attention to the following thoughts and facts touching the subject, for we are not without hope that we shall be able to convince him not only that the law which requires the death of the offender affords no more security than imprisonment for life, but such is its practical operation, that it is positively *less effectual* in this respect than the latter penalty.

He desires to feel that society is protected from the depredations of the assassin. Now we can imagine conditions of communities where the necessity of killing the offender might be pleaded to secure such protection. Take, for instance, Moses and the Israelites, when in the wilderness, journeying from Egypt to the promised land, at the very time that the law of death was instituted. Where were their jails or prisons, and other means for securing the murderer against the possibility of escape? Or take the condition of our brothers, fathers, or husbands in California during the first year of emigration and effort for gold. There we behold thousands of men in a new, wilderness country, surrounded by savages, without even the form of civil government. No courts, judges, sheriffs, police, nor jails, and no *means* of self-protection. If the assassin was caught and convicted where were the strong prison, the iron bars and bolts and trustworthy keepers to hold him securely? In such a cóndition of society, the *necessity* of "summary justice" and the punishment of death might be argued with some show of propriety. But with the people of Ohio, Kentucky, Indiana, and other States where "law and order" prevail, the case is widely different. Here there are well organized governments, with a court and jail in every county, and police regulations in every town; so that the assassin or murderer can rarely escape detection after committing a crime, and if detected can be secured. If, in Ohio, our laws demanded imprisonment for life for the crime of murder, and the offender should be safely lodged in our penitentiary, would he not be secure? That institution is one of the most substantial edifices and faithfully guarded prisons in the world. It contains workshops for the criminal by day, and cells, constructed of stone and iron, for his safe keeping by night; the whole of which is under the watchful care of the most vigilant keepers. We again ask, if the murderer is not safe when once confined within the walls of that prison. Take the case of Arrison,* if you will. He is thought to be one of the most desperate men living. I appeal to my fellow citizens to know if they would entertain the least fear of his breaking through the walls, or

---

* W. H. Arrison, now confined in the Cincinnati jail, charged wi h the murder of Allison and his wife, at the Medical College in t is City, during the summer of 1854, with a torpedo, a dreadful instrument which exploded and tore them in pieces on opening the box that contained it.

bars and bolts of that prison, and again returning upon society to engage in another work of blood, provided he were once placed there for life?

"Ah," says the objector, "we should have no apprehension of the man's breaking prison, but there are other means of escape. Influential friends, or money, sometimes possess a potent power. Prison doors will open at their nod. In plain words, we should fear the pardoning power." Then take the pardoning power from the Governor, where it is now lodged, and vest it in twelve men who shall constitute a court to examine and decide upon all appeals for pardons and commutations, subject to certain restrictions in the crime of murder.

I ask again, if this provision were instituted concerning the pardoning power, and the murderer were secure in the penitentiary, would not the people of Ohio feel that his depredations on society were at an end? You say you would have him executed, not because the Bible demands his life, nor yet from a spirit of retaliation to avenge the outrage he has committed against society, but simply as a matter of *expediency*, to render your own safety more certain. But are you not just as secure by his confinement in prison as by his execution? It is possible, we grant, that he may break away and escape: but not probable; and this possibility we must risk as we should were his destiny to be decided by us in our individual, instead of our social capacity. Suppose a robber should enter your house and attempt your life: he strikes at your heart with his glittering dagger. The first law of your nature is self-preservation or protection. Either your life or the life of an assassin must be destroyed; and no matter how powerfully your feelings may revolt at the thought of killing a man, you are not long in deciding it to be your duty to defend yourself to the extent of your power. If you kill under such circumstances, you are justified. Why? Because you are driven by *actual necessity* to commit the act in order to preserve your own existence. And this is all that can justify you, or delegate to you the right to kill the man. No Christian will justify the taking of human life *by an individual* in self-defense, on any other ground. Suppose it is a mere child who attempts to rob and murder you—one whom you are certain you can seize and bind securely—but, instead, you kill him; will society justify the act? Or, further, having bound him with cords so that he can move neither hand nor foot, and thus relieved yourself of all fear of farther injury, you take a club and deliberately beat out his brains; would society justify the act? Certainly not. Why not? Plainly because the deed is not committed in *self-defense*. You are safe. He cannot injure you. The officers of justice can take him into custody, and place him beyond the possibility of again outraging society.

I am now writing for the minds and hearts of *Christians*, as well as others. Is the reader a Christian? If so, permit me to ask, would you thus deliberately kill the murderer after you had securely bound him? Would it be necessary? What would you think of your neighbor—a brother in Christ—a member of the same Church —for instance, the pastor of your society, and your spiritual teacher—if, having surprised a robber in his house, and securely bound him to a post with manacles, cords and chains, should call you and other members of his flock to see him cut his throat, or strangle him with a halter? Would you not be astonished beyond measure? And if he should commit the deed, would not the whole Church, yea, the whole community, be struck dumb with horror? "This man is secure," you would exclaim, "why do you kill him?" And your astonishment would not be lessened at the answer of your clerical executioner: "I know he is secure; I feel safe. There is not one chance in a thousand for him to escape. But then escape is *possible*. He *may* break these chains and cords and in jure somebody. It is best for us to be *positively* secure; therefore, I kill him."

We venture to assert that no *individual* can be found, Christian or infidel, base enough to commit so cowardly and damning a deed. And any man who should present such a *reason* for the act, would be regarded as a madman or a consummate villain. And yet this is precisely the principle on which *society* acts, when it has safely secured the offender within stone walls, with bars and bolts, and then chokes the life out of him, on the ground of *self-security*. If the Christian minister should commit an act of this character, as described above, the State would take him, convict him of murder, treat his plea of *self-protection* with derision, and hang him—his own Church assisting in the work—not as individuals, but as members of the body-politic, through the hangman.*

But if the act is morally wrong in an *individual*, how can it be morally right *in the State*. If the act, when committed by a Christian minister, is shocking to the moral sense of the Church, why should it not be, when perpetrated by the State, inasmuch as the State is professedly Christian? And further: if the State treats the plea of the individual who kills the bound man for *self-protection*, with derision, with what propriety can it make this a reason for its own acts of blood? Look at the strength of the State and its means of self-security.

---

* See the sixth chapter of this work, under the head of *Individual Responsibility*.

Look at its strong prisons, its chains, its cells, its dungeons, its strong police force, and its hundreds of thousands of citizens to assist in maintaining the supremacy of the law and prevent an escape. Yet it ridicules the plea of an *individual*, when he kills in *self-defense*, while it leads out from its iron and stone cells, its victims, sometimes little boys, and weak emaciated women, and chokes the life out of them, *because it is unsafe to let them live.** They may escape from prison, and kill or injure somebody.

The reader must perceive, then, that the argument in favor of the gallows, drawn from *necessity*, and based on *self-protection*, possesses but little force, and is hardly entitled to consideration. If we should kill criminals, simply because they are dangerous to society—if this is the *only* ground on which we defend the gallows, then, to be consistent, we should employ it against the lunatic; for it is as dangerous to society for him to have his freedom, and probably more so, than for the murderer. It is not uncommon for madmen to commit acts of the most dreadful violence. Yet where is the man, especially the *Christian*, who would dream of killing this unfortunate class of our fellow-creatures *from necessity*, on the ground of *self-protection*. Every humane heart would revolt at the thought. Even if at liberty and roaming at large, there are but few who would refuse to risk any injury they might do, rather than to put them to death. For

---

* A little boy, but *ten* years of age, was hung in Alexandria, La., in Sept. last, (1855.) See page 49 of this work. In 1854, a woman was executed in New York State, weak and feeble, leaving an infant, which had its birth in her cell. And now, as we write, the secular papers before us contain an account of the death of a woman, who was soon to be executed in New Hampshire. She was delivered of a child a few months ago in her cell, and the authorities were waiting for her to gain sufficient strength to be killed, when death by consumption terminated her miserable existence. Was it necessary to strangle these wretched creatures in *self-defense*?

all such, the State provides an asylum—a place of confinement—where they are not only kept securely, but by humane and judicious treatment, are often entirely restored, and, with sane minds, permitted to return again to their friends and to the blessings of social life. Now, when safely lodged within the walls of an asylum, the lunatic is neither feared nor dreaded by society at large. Confidence is reposed in the strength of the institution and in the caution and vigilance of those in whose charge it is placed. So should it be, and so might it be, with the murderer. He is a *moral* lunatic; perhaps more really so, in many cases, than the world imagines, or will believe. To turn him loose upon society would be a dangerous act. This should not be; justice does not demand it. Let him be safely lodged in the penitentiary and kept in durance. Let him be treated with kindness and humanity, but effectually confined, and society would no longer experience apprehensions of insecurity from the simple fact that the man was living. For, tho' living, he would be so really separated from the world by stone and iron—so utterly banished from society, and so securely guarded—as that he would be dead to the world, and the world dead to him.

The plea of self-protection, then, is a false one. Not only is it false, but it is mischievous. "It is terrible," says one "in the hands of a people's tyrant, or of a tyrannous people. Self-protection, says the despot, and the heads of the noble, brave and good, roll before him in ghastly heaps. Self-protection, says the demagogue, and the guillotine moves its iron jaws, and the streets are red with blood. Self-protection, says the injured man, and anticipates the law, becoming for himself judge and executioner. Self-protection, says the mutineer, dead men tell no tales, and the ocean bubbles red above his comrades.   Believe me, this principle of self-protection that relies on blood, is a dangerous, two-edged principle.   Self-protection may be secured without blood-shed.   We may obey God's law without inflicting Capital Punishment. There is a higher dictate than that of revenge.   There is a nobler end for punishment than the infliction of pain. There is a more binding code than the law of Moses.   It is found in the spirit and precepts of Jesus Christ."

We have said that if the murderer was safely confined within the walls of the penitentiary, society would feel secure.   We come now to add, that if the penalty for murder was imprisonment for life, instead of hanging, murderers *would be secured;* but, as the law now stands upon the statute books of nearly all our States, eight out of ten guilty of murder *escape*, not from *prison*, but they escape *conviction*, and are returned again loose upon society.   Thus does the law of death *defeat the very object for which the class we are now considering would retain it.*   They would retain it, in order to take the offender from society and put him beyond the power of again trampling upon its laws.   But instead of this, it stands directly in the way of securing this result.   It screens the murderer from all punishment, and positively snatches him from the hand of justice, and sends him back into the world, all reeking with the blood of his murdered victim, to prey again upon society, and, it may be, to enact over again the same dreadful deed of which he is guilty.   Thus, is the present law the most *unsafe*, for the simple reason that IT IS IMPOSSIBLE TO ENFORCE IT ECCEPT IN RARE CASES.   But this is an important point in our investigations, and must be made the subject of a chapter by itself.

CHAPTER XI.

SIXTH REASON FOR ABOLISHMENT.

THE DEATH PENALTY DIFFICULT TO ENFORCE.

Scruples of Jurors—Loth to convict—The condition of Criminal Jurisprudence in Ohio, as presented by a Cincinnati Editor—The cause of Laxity on the part of Jurors to convict—The Gallows stands in the way of Justice—It facilitates the escape of the Guilty—Folly of instituting Laws which cannot be enforced—Criminal Jurisprudence in Hamilton County, Ohio, for fifteen years—Large number of Murders—But one hung—How it worked in England—France.

The Death Penalty cannot be enforced only in rare cases. IT FACILITATES THE ESCAPE OF THE GUILTY *in many instances, which is another important reason for abolishment.*
The truth is, the Death Penalty is so far behind public sentiment, and so revolting to the humanity of every morally sensitive heart, that most persons refuse to act as jurymen in capital cases, from "conscientious scruples," while those who consent, will not convict, unless in the most certain cases of guilt. If the least thread of evidence is elicited in behalf of the offender, they will hang upon it, and acquit him through its instrumentality, and thus he escapes *all punishment*, though guilty. Look at the history of criminal jurisprudence in Ohio, Indiana, Pennsylvania, New York, New England, *anywhere* in any Christian country on the face of the earth, where the gallows still exists, and the fact of which we speak is demonstrated to a certainty. While I write, a

(154)

leading daily journal* of Cincinnati is placed before me, the editor of which, a warm supporter of the gallows, utters his complaints against this condition of things, and threatens Lynch law in the following strain, if matters are not speedily amended:

"It does seem as if it were impossible to procure anything like justice in 'capital cases,' as they are called in this State. Murder is alarmingly frequent, yet we hear of no instance where the murderer expiates his or her guilt. Judging by the past, and the history of our jurisprudence, there is no crime that can be committed with such impunity from punishment in Ohio, as that of murder, the most wilful of all crimes. It matters not how atrocious are the circumstances attending it, or the conclusive character of the evidence that points out the criminal, there is always some loop-hole by which the penalty is evaded. When juries do their duty in the premises, and render an honest verdict, some legal technicality is raised, by which the prisoner is enabled to escape. The extraordinary laxity in the administration of our laws for murder, exceeds that of any other State in the Union, with the exception of California. Look into our own county jail, for instance, and see what a farce and mockery are the attempts which have been made for years here to execute the law in those cases where the punishment is death. It is high time that public opinion became aroused to this matter, and that some steps were taken by which the clogs that now retard the wheels of justice were removed. Human life is too sacred a thing to allow the legal barriers and safeguards that protect it

---

* The *Commercial.* The editor's indignation was aroused by the report just received from Piqua, Ohio, that a man and woman, (Jane Elizabeth Riggen and James Mowrey,) guilty of murder, in that county, and who had *confessed* their guilt, had been discharged through some legal technicality. If the law had been imprisonment for life, conviction would undoubtedly have been the result. *Ohio will not hang a woman.*

to be broken down. There should be even a greater certainty of punishment to him who unlawfully takes life, than for any other offense; but in our State the certainty has got pretty much all on the other side—in favor of an escape. If we do not have a reform pretty soon, it would not surprise us to see 'Judge Lynch' erect his summary court and proceed to execute that justice upon murderous malefactors that the regular tribunals will not afford."

All that is here uttered with reference to the difficulty experienced in convicting the guilty in Ohio, is true; and because it is true, and comes from one who has great confidence in the efficacy of legal strangulation, we copy it.

In the recent trial of the notorious Arrison, in Cincinnati, three days were spent in empanelling a jury. Upwards of three hundred persons were excused from serving, on the ground of "conscientious scruples " We were told by a gentleman of intelligence, who was summoned as a juror in that case, that if he had served, he would not have convicted the prisoner of murder in the first degree, *no matter what the nature of the evidence against him,* simply because he could not consent to be an instrument in destroying human life. In the case of Mrs. Riggen, of Miami county, alluded to in the note preceding, nearly two weeks were expended in empanelling a jury; hundreds being pronounced by the court as unfit to serve, in consequence of their scruples of conscience on the subject of the Death Penalty, before twelve could be found who were willing to convict. The same repugnance exists throughout our State, and in every State to a greater or less extent, and is becoming every year, more and more real; so that it has come to be quite generally understood that no jury will jeopardize the life of a fellow creature by conviction, if there is the least possible chance to save him. Almost always there are some of the jury whose *hearts* revolt at pronouncing the word "GUILTY," however strongly their *judgments* may sanction the justness of such a decision, and they refuse to return such a verdict, not because they are not convinced of the offender's criminality, but because the punishment to follow the verdict is so shocking to humanity, and they are so fearful of convicting the innocent, that they shrink from the responsibility, and say "NOT GUILTY," when in every instance, if the penalty were imprisonment for life, they would return a verdict of guilty, and thus secure the offender from further depredations. Such is the repugnance, we repeat, which very generally exists in society, against sending a fellow-being to the scaffold. Some sneer at it—pronounce it a "morbid sympathy,"—a "childish, silly repugnance" —and curse jurymen for a set of chicken-hearted fools, who "themselves deserve to have their necks stretched,"* for their indifference to the public welfare. But all this does not disprove the fact that the repugnance of which we speak *is a reality*. It does not eradicate it from the human soul. Men *do* shudder and they *will* shudder at violating the shrine of human life. The feeling is natural. God has implanted it in every breast, and it grows with the growth of humanity, and strengthens more and more in the soul which is chastened by the principles of a pure and holy religion. And we may rest assured of this fact, viz : that so long as our communities progress in benevolence and intelligence, *our present law cannot be enforced*, as I before said, *only in rare cases*.

Men ask for a continuance of the gallows that " *society may be protected*." But is society protected by this institution? Let the editor referred to above, answer. " It

seems as if it were impossible," he says, "to procure anything like justice in capital cases in this State. Murder
is alarmingly frequent," (notwithstanding the existence of
the Death Penalty,) "*yet we hear of no instance where the
offender expiates his or her guilt.* No crime can be committed with such impunity of punishment in Ohio, as murder.
*There is always some loop-hole by which the penalty is
evaded.* When jurors do their duty in the premises, and
render an honest verdict, some legal technicality is
raised by which *the prisoner is enabled to escape.*" All
this is true. Is not the gallows, then, a glorious protection to society in Ohio? Why, instead of this, *it is
the very instrument that protects the offender, and affords
him a free pass back into society.* Wipe the Death Penalty from our statute books, and place instead imprisonment for life, and our fellow townsmen will no longer
have cause to complain of the "laxity" of our judicial
tribunals; the "impunity" with which the crime of murder is committed; the "loop-holes" of the law, and the
"farce and mockery" everywhere perceptible in the execution of the law. "It is high time," he says, "that public opinion became aroused to this matter, and that some
steps were taken by which the clogs that now retard the
wheels of justice were removed." This is precisely our
opinion. But by investigation* he will find that the
only "clog that retards the wheels of justice," with reference to the murderer, is the gallows. Pull down this

---

* In justice to the gentleman mentioned here, whose talents and motives we respect, we should say, that probably he is becoming convinced
of the impotency of our law as it now stands, for he closes the article referred to, as follows: "While we are in favor of the law in relation to
murder as it now stands on the statute book, yet, if it be true, as many
believe, that in consequence of the conscientious convictions of thousands of people against the Death Penalty, that the present condition of
things is owing, it would be best to have the criminal law changed. It
is a subject that well demands the attention of legislators, who should see
where the fault lies, and apply the remedy, if it is in their power."

old relic of barbarism, and place in its stead *a law that can be enforced*, and there will be no longer complaint about the slow and uncertain movement of the wheels of justice." "Human life is too sacred a thing," he says, "to allow the legal *barriers* and *safeguards* that protect it, to be broken down." But all the "legal barriers and safeguards" we have to protect human life in Ohio, are the gibbet and the hangman; and these, as we have seen, are already "broken down." They exist only on the statute books as a mere *threat*. Every murderer within our borders, is told that if he kills he shall be hung; but he has come to know that this is a mere bug-bear, and that the probability is that instead of being hung if caught, he shall be tried and *discharged*. He has no fear of the gallows. In traveling in a neighboring State a few years since, we tarried a short time at a tavern kept by a widow lady, who had a young negro servant about the house and stable, a mischievous, malicious little urchin, who was full of his pranks, and was anything but obedient to the wishes of his mistress. The good landlady had instituted a government in her domestic affairs, but, unfortunately, it was a government whose "barriers and safeguards," like those of our State with reference to the crime of murder, consisted principally of *threats—awful* threats, which she never dreamed of enforcing. "Here, Tom!" she would exclaim at the top of her voice, "where have you been? Did I not tell you not to leave the house, but to stay here and wait on the gentlemen? Now, you go away again, and I'll tie you up by your two thumbs and *skin you*, you see if I don't." Ten times in a day did she make this *threat*. But it was *only* a threat. Tom came to understand by it that it was merely a bug-bear, and to treat it accordingly. He knew he should not be skinned. He never was skinned in his life, though he had been *threatened* with this penalty a thousand times ; and with a snap of his fingers, a shrill whistle, and shrewd grimace, he would be off to his pranks again.

How unwise in a family, how much more unwise in a State, to institute laws which cannot be enforced, and which, therefore, can claim no respect from the party to be governed. Gambling has been a penitentiary offense in Ohio, for several years, but has it ever been enforced in a single instance? The penalty for murder in the first degree in Ohio, is death by hanging. In Hamilton county* alone, within the last fifteen years, *hundreds of murders, of all descriptions and every degree of violence and atrocity, have been committed,* BUT WITH A SINGLE EXCEP-TION, *this penalty has never been enforced upon the murderer in our county during all these years.* Here is a fact which should astonish the sticklers for the gallows, and bring them to a sense of the true nature of this question. Why has not the murderer been executed in Hamilton county? Was it because he could not be *arrested?* Not at all. But because when arrested he could not be *convicted;* or if convicted, the moral sympathy of the

---

* Hamilton County embraces Cincinnati. Within the last fifteen years, at least five hundred murders have either been perpetrated, or *attempted,* in this county. Of course we do not mean that all these crimes would come under the head of premeditated murder. We include in this number, shooting and stabbing in fights and rows, on the streets, in houses of ill-fame, in bar-rooms, on steamboats, indeed, every form and degree of murder. The author of these pages kept a minute of the violent deaths perpetrated in our city, during the years 1852—3, (Lecount was hung in the beginning of 1853,) and the number in these two years reached to 198. Some have doubted the statement, when publicly made, of five hundred violent deaths in Cincinnati in the time given, and asked us for the authority on which it is based. The above is our authority. If in two years there were nearly two hundred, in the remaining thirteen years it is probable there were, at least, three hundred. But not half of those guilty of perpetrating these offenses were arrested. Out of all arrested during the fifteen years, probably forty-five, or three a year, were tried for murder in the first degree, the penalty of which is death. *One* was hung. Where are the remaining *forty-four!*

public, and the opinion which so generally prevails of the utter inutility of the gallows, have sought for and found a "loop-hole" for the culprit.* In some instances they have been pardoned; in others, sentence has been commuted from hanging to imprisonment.

Now, in every instance where the offender was not convicted, he returned again to society. How unsafe, then, is our present law?—unsafe because of the *uncertainty of its infliction.* Says an eminent lawyer, speaking on this subject: "No one who is acquainted with the history of criminal jurisprudence in this country, can doubt but hundreds of guilty ones have been acquitted, and sent back to the haunts of vice, for the simple reason that jurors would not convict in consequence of the *severity* attached to their crimes, it being death."

Another jurist of New York, equally eminent, says: "None who ever attended our criminal courts in capital cases can have failed to notice the operation of the principle here referred to, in a manner the most subversive of the ends of justice, and the most dangerous to the security of the community. None will question the truth here presented, and none can compute the number of criminals who have been let loose upon society, free of all penalty, and emboldened and hardened by a first *impunity*, nor form any conception of the amount of evil which had its origin in this cause, in casting upon the adminis-

---

* James Summons, now in our jail, where he has been for the last four years, has been three times tried for his life on the same offense ; twice convicted of the most atrocious murder, *once sentenced and the day of execution fixed.* Two years have passed since the law demanded his death, but he still lives. He has cost the State more than $15,000. If the penalty for his crime had been the penitentiary for life, he would long since have been an inmate of that institution, and put to some useful employment, which is his proper place. The case of Arrison is very nearly similar. He should now be diligently at work in our State prison. Cannot the public perceive that it is the gallows which facilitates the escape of these men?

tration of the law an *uncertainty* in the last degree prejudicial to all the policy of penal justice."

Again he remarks : " There can be no criminal lawyer in this State, of any extended practice or observation, by whom the remark, that the *uncertainty* of conviction for capital offenses has grown almost into a proverb, will not be received as a truism. Juries will always be powerfully swayed in judgment as well as feeling, by the horror of shedding blood, which the laws of God have too deeply planted in the hearts of all to be eradicated, however it may be weakened by the influence of any laws of man. In the clearest cases it is constantly seen that they will not convict. They will violate their oaths under a thousand pleas of technical deficiencies or imperfections of evidence, however immaterial."*

The feeling that exists on this subject is seen, as we have already intimated, in the reluctance with which many consent to act as jurymen. We have already mentioned several instances occurring in our State, illustrative of this fact. Many more might be adduced.

On the trial of Howard, in Dover, New Hampshire, some years ago, seven hundred persons were excused or set aside, before a panel was made up.

In the case of Shelby, of Kentucky, on his trial, the jury could not agree, and were discharged; six or eight of them, and the Judge, were hung in effigy. Afterward, in attempting his second trial, nearly every man in the county, who was competent to sit as a juror, was summoned, but the panel could not be filled.

In Kleim's case, in New York, after the panel was exhausted, it was necessary to summon talismen, and nearly a whole day was spent in filling up the jury. So in the case of Gordon, in Rhode Island. It was said

---

*O'Sullivan's report to the Legislature of New York in 1843.

that "not a man in the city of Providence, would consent to sit on his trial."*

These are extreme cases, we grant, but the feeling of reluctance, and the sentiment which gives it birth, prevail, to a greater or less extent, in all communities. They are pronounced by some to be an indication of weakness, and condemned as a hurtful evil, preventing the execution of law and facilitating the escape of the criminal. Hence we are called upon to stifle all such feelings—to trample our foolish whims and opinions in the dust, and lend our influence to assist in making the law we have, potent, by making its execution *certain*.

But we reply, this was the same argument used by our stern old fathers a century ago, in Connecticut and Massachusetts, when their fellow men manifested some slight signs of aversion to the law that would crop the ears, scourge the backs, and bore the tongues of men for being Quakers; yea, that would shut them in jails, banish them out of the colony, sell them as slaves, and hang them on gibbets, simply for worshipping God after the dictates of their own consciences. Those who cherished a little spark of humanity and ventured to say, "is not this punishment too severe?" or "is it necessary?" or, "is it Christian?" were pronounced "weak-minded," and were told that they harbored sentiments that were exceedingly injurious both to religion and the State. A magistrate of Boston, less than one hundred years ago, rendered his name everlastingly odious to all men of the "sterner stuff," by humanely giving back to his victim, a part of the ear he had officially shorn off, that the mutilated member might be restored and made whole. Yes, in criminal jurisprudence, *humanity* was everywhere deemed a weakness and a damning evil.

---

* From Rev. W. Y. Emmet's Thoughts on the Death Penalty.

So in theology; pity for the damned was a mark of fee-bleness in mind and faith. Even for a woman to weep over the endless burnings of her own (non-elect) infant child in the flames of hell, was deemed childish and wrong. But the natural feelings and affections of the human soul would, at times, burst out from the iron shackles of a stern and unrelenting creed, and assert their claims in startling tones of sympathy and denunciation. Hence exclaimed Dr. Edwards, in rebuking this spirit: "What has more especially given offense to many, and raised a loud cry against the doings of some preachers, as though their conduct was intolerable, is their fright-euing innocent children with talk of hell-fire and eternal damnation. But do not these people *believe*, in common with the whole country, that they are by nature children of wrath and *heirs of hell?* And that every one, whether he be young or old, is exposed every moment to eternal destruction, and wrath of Almighty God? This complaint and cry, then, about frightening little children, *betrays a great deal of weakness* and inconsideration."*

But did the stern rebuke of the Church, or the united influence of creeds and the clergy stifle and put out the fires of tender affection, which God himself had kindled upon the altar of every mother's breast for the child she bears, and that pillows upon her breast? Oh no! It has exerted its supremacy;—it has saved the object of its affection and solicitude—it has made it an angel of light and crowned it with immortal glory. Nothing short would satisfy the longings of the affectionate mother for the happiness of her offspring. So with the sentiments that prevailed with reference to the criminal. They were stern and cruel. But humanity, enstamped upon the souls of God's creatures, directed

* Jonathan Edwards of Connecticut, in 1750.

by intelligence and a more divine religion, has asserted its claims. It has grown in the human heart, till now it manifests reluctance to destroy the life of a fellow creature for *any* crime, and asks, "Is it necessary to kill this brother? Can we not put him to a better use? Is the act Christian?" And this is called "*weakness.*" And we are admonished to stand right up to the demands of the law, and choke men, and women, and children, with strong nerves and willing hands, without waiting to inquire into the necessity or expediency of the act. But would men have us go back to the days of heathen barbarity? Would they have us kill simply because our fathers killed, or out of a spirit of revenge? This will never do. Rather let us keep our eyes fixed upon Christ, the glorious star of Bethlehem—have faith in *his* law as the best and safest, and follow "upward and onward" in the light of benevolence and justice. God forbid that we should leave the "light of life," and go back into the "darkness of death!" Men will *not* go back. This is evident. The march of the intellect and the heart is forward. Hence, we repeat, the Death Penalty *cannot be enforced*, in most of our States, only in rare cases.

How unwise, how impolitic, to retain a law which involves interests so important, with which the public mind has no sympathy, and which, therefore, cannot be executed; for so long as it cannot be executed, it defeats the very object it is designed to effect. The principal object of the gallows is to protect society against the assassin. But, instead of this, as we have seen, it stands directly in the way of such protection in consequence of the difficulty to convict the offender; and if not convicted, he is *liberated;* whereas, if the penalty were imprisonment for life, juries would convict—all reasonable minds would approve the law—public sympathy would

beat in its favor—it would be effective, for all law is
trebly strong which comports with the moral sympathy
of the community—the offender would be secured, and
thus society would be protected.

HOW IT WORKS IN ENGLAND.

The wise men of England and France have seen the
operation of the principle involved here, and have gradually softened their penal codes to keep pace with the
growth of humanity and intelligence, till, instead of
having nearly two hundred offenses punishable with
death, upon their statute books, there is but one crime for
which they actually kill at the present time.

Says an English writer: "Such was the effect of the
Death Penalty on the public mind, that the leading juries
of the country looked on perjury as an *amiable weakness*, and even valued themselves on an act which shakes
purity and justice to the very center." Though *sworn*
to return a verdict "according to the law and the tes-
timeny," they did not scruple to falsify their oaths and
go counter to the law and the testimony, to save the life
of the offender.

Lord Suffield, in a speech to Parliament, on this
subject, in 1834, said that he "held in his hand a list
of *five hundred and fifty-five* perjured verdicts, delivered
at the Old Bailey in fifteen years, beginning with 1814
and ending with 1829, for the single offense of stealing
from dwellings, the value of the goods stolen being in
these cases *sworn to be above* forty shillings, the penalty of
which was death." How did the jurors save the offenders? As follows. They were under the necessity of
pronouncing them *guilty*, but at the same time they returned the *value* of the amount stolen *less than forty shil-*

lings. No matter what was *sworn* to be the amount stolen, this was invariably the verdict.

A woman was proven to have stolen a ten pound note —that or nothing. The jury found her guilty of stealing *thirty-nine shillings.* A man was convicted of stealing a pocket-book containing bank notes to the amount of eighty pounds, and drafts to the amount of twenty; the verdict was, "guilty of stealing *thirty-nine shillings."* The same verdict was given in the case of a woman convicted of stealing, *on her own confession,* gold coins, to the amount of sixty-three shillings, and other money to the amount of forty-four—to wit: "*stealing thirty-nine shillings."* Even the judges sympathized with the condition of the offender, and often suggested to the jury what verdict to return. In one case, a man had stolen a valuable watch. Lord Mansfield, feeling anxious to save his life, directed the jury to bring in its value at ten pence. "Ten pence! my lord," exclaimed the anxious owner, "why the very fashion of it cost me fifty shillings." "Perhaps so," replied his lordship, "but we cannot hang a man for fashion's sake;" and the verdict was returned as directed.

"Some years since,"says the *London Morning Herald,* "a man was tried at Carnovan for forgery, to a large amount, on the Bank of England. The evidence was as satisfactory to the guilt of the prisoner as possible, and brought the charge clearly home to him. The jury, however, acquitted him. The next day the same individual was tried on another indictment for forgery. Although the evidence in this case was as conclusive as in the former one, the jury acquitted the prisoner. The Judge (Chief Baron Richards,) in addressing the prisoner, expressed himself in these remarkable words: "Prisoner at the bar—although you have been acquitted by a jury of your countrymen of the crime of forgery, I am as convinced of your guilt, as that two and two make four." A short time after the conclusion of the sessions, I met with one of the jurymen, and expressed to him my surprise at the acquittal of the man who had been tried for forgery. He immediately answered me in the following words: "Neither my fellow jurymen nor myself had the least doubt of the prisoner's guilt; but we were unwilling to bring in the verdict of guilty, because we were aware that the prisoner would have been punished with death —a penalty which we conceived to be too severe for the offense."

Such was the feeling against Capital Punishment in England. And the consequence was, that during nine years, out of eight hundred and eight committed on capital offenses, no less than three hundred and thirty-four, or nearly one-half, were acquitted. While of five hundred and fifty-eight persons committed on charges *not* capital, only fifty-seven, or a little more than one-tenth, were acquitted. England perceived the unfavorable operation of a law so stringent; that it was unsafe, and, therefore, impolitic. She, therefore, raised the capital indictment to *sixty shillings,* instead of forty. But this would not answer. Juries simply put the amount stolen to fifty-nine shillings, instead of thirty-nine, thus saving the offender. She then wiped all such laws from her statute books, and to her surprise discovered from actual experience that this act of clemency did not increase, but actually lessened the amount of crime. For now villians could be secured.

HOW IT WORKS IN FRANCE.

The experience of France corresponds with that of England. Speaking of French juries, M. C. Lucas, an eminent French jurist, says: "There is scarcely a list, at the present day, which does not contain men who experience a conscientious, and almost invincible repugnance, to send one of their fellow beings to the scaffold."

In 1832, an alteration in the penal law of France empowered juries to state, in their verdicts of guilty, that the crime was committed *under extenuating circumstances.* When this is done in capital cases, the punishment is commuted to a milder penalty. Now mark the result: In a single year, (1834,) out of one hundred and thirty-six verdicts of guilty in capital indictments, one hundred and eleven had the qualifying clause in them which saved the offender's life. Only twenty-five out of the hundred and thirty-six, were sentenced to be executed, and six of these received a commutation of punishment. So that only nineteen, less than *one-seventh,* of the whole number, suffered the extreme penalty of the law.

Suppose, now, that this were the law in Ohio, or Kentucky, Indiana or New-York, how many verdicts of guilty, in capital cases, would be returned without the extenuating clause to save the offender's life? Judging from "what we know," every man is ready to answer, *" not one "* For all this corresponds precisely with the history of criminal jurisprudence in our own country, as the criminal records of Ohio, New-England, New-York, Pennsylvania, and all the southern and western States, will testify.

For instance, the only crime punishable with death in Pennsylvania, is wilful murder. Now, from the year 1795 to the year 1845, there were one hundred and eleven persons brought before the court for the city and county of Philadelphia, charged with this offense. Of these, only ten were convicted. The remaining one hundred and one were acquitted, and returned to society.

15

How effectual is the gallows in the protection of society in Philadelphia!

But look again. Man-slaughter, robbery, arson, rape, and highway robbery are *not* punishable with death in Pennsylvania. During the time stated above, viz : from the year 1795, to the year 1845, five hundred persons were brought before the same court, charged with these crimes. Of these three hundred and forty-four were convicted, and only one hundred and fifty-six acquitted. How great the difference, and how much more certain of conviction. Is there not good reason for believing that if the penalty for murder had been imprisonment for life, instead of the gallows, a much larger number of those charged with this crime would have been convicted, and thus secured ?

From all this we must see that the Death Penalty in our country, is unsafe, impolitic, of no utility, and is not necessary to individual or social protection, but is the direct and positive means of the escape of tens of thousands of guilty men and women, and should, therefore, be abolished.

CHAPTER XII

SEVENTH REASON FOR ABOLISHMENT.

EXECUTIONS. DELETERIOUS AS EXAMPLES.

The Gallows believed to be indispensable as a Preventive against Crime—Is a terror to Evil-Doers—This is an Error—The reverse is true—Facts adduced in Proof—The Gallows is hidden from the Public in fifteen States—Lecount's Execution—Certainty of Punishment more salutary than Severity—Opinion of Jurists—How it worked in England and other Countries—Interesting Incidents—Testimony of Rantoul and Livingston—Proofs Conclusive.

In this stage of our investigations, the objector is disposed to remind us of what he deems a very important fact in connection with this question, viz: that the gallows is indispensable as a *preventive* against crime. It is an example of "terror to evil doers"—a dreadful "warning to the offender," and thus a safeguard to society.

This is the opinion, we are aware, which has almost universally prevailed from time immemorial. But what a mistake! As strange as it may appear to those who have given the subject but little investigation, *just the reverse of this is true, as the history of crime in any and all countries will testify. Hanging, as an example, is not beneficial. It will not deter men from crime. It is no warning to the offender, but its tendency is to debase, and harden the heart; to fan the flame of hatred, and to multiply murderers instead of diminishing the number, and, for this reason, should be abolished.*

(171)

If executions are so moral in their tendency, and so necessary as examples, why hide the gallows from the multitude? Why kill the offender *privately*, in the jail or jail-yard, shutting out and positively forbidding the presence of any but a favored few, who are permitted to be present, by cards of invitation? Twenty years ago, a private execution was unknown. Men, and women, and children, were strangled in the open streets and fields, where the example could be witnessed by from five thousand to fifty thousand persons. Now, fifteen of our thirty-two States have decreed that all executions shall be utterly hidden from public view; none can be admitted but a select few, such as clergymen, judges, lawyers, and newspaper reporters. Three years ago, a man was hung in the jail-yard of Cincinnati. Not for twelve long years had an *example* of killing, to prevent the crime of murder, been presented in Hamilton county, and deeds of blood were becoming uncommonly prevalent. "Somebody *must* be strangled as a terror to evil-doers, or blood will run like water." So said the ministers of God; so said the dignified judges, and especially loafing, profane and drunken policemen and constables. Lecount* was accordingly fixed upon as the man to be executed as an *example;* not because he was guilty of any aggravated crime, but because he had been, previously, two years in the State prison—had no money, but few friends,

---

* Henry Lecount was executed for killing a man equally as quarrelsome and dangerous as himself, in a drunken fight. Strictly, the deed was man-slaughter. The man whom he killed had been intimate with Lecount's wife during his absence; boasted at the time of the fight of what he had done, and swore that he would continue his visits in spite of Lecount. With *gentlemen,* this would have been deemed a sufficient provocation for shooting the offender; and if prosecuted, a discharge would have been the result. Lecount was hung, while "Jim Summons," who was guilty of a most diabolical murder, and who was then in jail under sentence of death, simply looked on, swearing that he "should not be hung, for the old man," (his father,) "is rich." He was right—and is still living.

and could as well be spared from *society* as not, though his poor old mother, and brothers and sisters, were overwhelmed with grief and sorrow at the awful event.

Hearing that this unfortunate man desired to see me on the morning of his execution, I went to the jail-yard, and asked to be admitted, but was refused, the keeper at the gate declaring that his orders were positive, to admit none but those who brought cards of invitation. The yard is surrounded by a high and strong wall, but the sheriff, to prevent the possibility of any one seeing from the windows, and tops of the surrounding buildings and trees, had taken the precaution to erect a house, sufficiently large to accommodate the spectators, *over the gallows.* Thus it was entirely hidden from those without. Though early in the morning, when we were there, hundreds had collected around the yard, and in the streets, and on the tops of buildings, in hopes to catch a glimpse of the scene within, or hear the creaking of the gallows, or listen to some parting words of the doomed man. They were a ragged, drunken, profane, cut-throat appearing crew, of all nations and colors—men, women and children, peering through the crevices in the wall—smoking, chewing, drinking and cracking jokes, or each other's heads. Mothers, with their babes at the breast, seemed as intently interested as any persons present. Why not admit *these,* thought I, as well as ministers, judges, lawyers and reporters, as I gazed upon the scene before me? Do they not as really need the *example?* A noisy, drunken loafer, surrounded by a throng of ragamuffins, was at the gate, contending for his right to be let in to see the show. He swore that he had traveled one hundred miles "to see the fellow swing," and that "no man had a better right to a peep at the gallows!" Why not gratify this man's curiosity, especially when the main object of the hanging was to terrify evil-doers? Perhaps the effect would be salutary upon his heart!

Why, the very men who, of all others, need the "example" as a "warning," are denied, by the law itself, the benefit of the example. They are ever ready to perform their part. "Evil doers" are the persons, of all others, to exhibit themselves at a hanging. They are eager to witness the dying struggles of a fellow creature. But the State says peremptorily, they *shall not witness them.* How inconsistent. First it declares the necessity of hanging as an *example,* and then it builds a house over the gallows, lest the "evil-doer" should *witness* the example. We ask again, why all this privacy? this hiding the gallows from public view? this strangling of men and women in the dark and in a corner? *if executions are so salutary in their influence, and so necessary as a terror to evil-doers!*

The truth is, the observing, thinking part of the community, especially jurists, have come to know that public executions have no salutary effect as "examples," but tend to make criminals, rather than reform those already made. Vengeance never softens, but always hardens. "Satan cannot cast out satan." "The spirit of God" alone will accomplish this work. It is not by the influence of a revengeful or bloody act, that an unholy passion is allayed. If you would have men remorseless, familiarize them with blood. Put them in the slaughter-house or army. A wretch who was executed in Exeter, England, on being removed from the bar after the sentence of death had been passed upon him, exclaimed to the bystanders: "I have killed plenty of men to please the king, and why should I not kill one to please myself?" Another soldier, taken up for wantonly shooting a man at Lestwithiel in 1814, in witnessing the horror and agitation of the peaceful townsmen, very coolly observed: "Here is a pretty fuss about killing *one* man; why I've seen *thousands* killed. It's nothing!" Executioners, however "chicken-hearted," when introduced to the awful duties of their avocation, have found themselves at home, after a little practice. A writer in witnessing the strangling of seven men in Portugal some years since, merely for "entertaining constitutional principles," describes the scene as follows:

"*One at a time* ascended the platform, up a broad flight of steps, accompanied by two priests, as in the procession, and was immediately placed on the seat, with his back to an upright post. The hangman, a miserable wretch, walking with a crutch, then secured the legs, the arms and body of the unhappy man, with cords; and placing a short cord round his neck and round the post, he put the hood over the face, and then, going behind the post, introduced a short, thick stick, and giving it four or five turns, produced strangulation. The body was then untied, and laid at a convenient distance, and another brought up from the foot of the scaffold, until the whole had suffered. The youngest, or least criminal, was executed first; and, as each occupied fifteen to twenty minutes, the last had to endure, for at least two hours, the horrid sight of the sufferings of his fellow prisoners. The mind can scarcely imagine a more dreadful state of mental suffering. When the whole were strangled, *the hangman wiped his face, and, seating himself in the fatal seat, coolly smoked a segar, regaled himself with a bottle of wine*, and then, placing a block of wood under the neck, proceeded to cut off the heads, from which the blood flowed copiously in streams from the platform; then, collecting the cords, and coolly wiping the hatchet and knife, on one of the white dresses, he left the platform, first throwing the heads and bodies in a heap, over the iron grating below. The fire was kindled, and in a few minutes the whole was in a blaze. By six o'clock, the whole was burnt to ashes, when a gang of galley-slaves, with irons on their legs, took the ashes in hand-barrows, and threw them into the Tagus."

Here was a man who was constantly witnessing the "examples" of executions, and behold what an unfeeling wretch he became. With how little compunction of conscience could he have murdered any man. When the guillotine was freely used during the reign of terror in France, children, instead of becoming fearful of its name, introduced the practice into their very plays, and amused themselves with guillotining cats, dogs and chickens, to supply the place of the executions which had become less frequent. Here is the direct and certain influence of sanguinary punishments. They have never produced a deep and solemn impression on the mind, and awakened within it kindly feelings and emotions, but directly the reverse. In proof of which I will adduce a few out of many cases that have occurred both in this country and Europe.

INFLUENCE OF HANGING IN OUR OWN COUNTRY.

The last man executed in the State of Maine, was Safer, who was hung in Augusta, in the year 1834. Thousands came from far and near to witness the death struggles of the man. Word was circulated just before the hour of execution, that he was to be reprieved, when hundreds were filled with the most dreadful rage, and swore that he should be hung at all events. Drunkenness, profanity and fighting were the order of the day. Never before nor since, was Augusta so disgraced with rowdyism and crime. A large body of police were brought into service, "and the very jail which had just been emptied of a murderer, threw open its doors to receive those who came to profit by the *solemn example of an execution.** No less than seven men were placed in the very cell from which Safer had just been taken to the gallows.*"

"On the day of Lechler's execution in Pennsylvania, some years ago, the usual scenes of vice and brutality were witnessed, and crime flourished rankly on its favorite soil, the execution ground. Twenty-eight offenders of various grades were committed to Lancaster jail that night, and many others escaped, or the jail would have been overflowed. One of the spectators on his way home murdered another, and was arrested, and *his limbs confined with the same irons which had scarcely been laid aside long enough by Lechler to get cold.*

"After the execution of Lechler, in Pennsylvania, had gratified the people about York and Lancaster, with the spectacle of his death, and produced its proper complement of homicide and other crimes, a poor wretch was condemned to die in another part of the State, where the people had not been indulged with such a spectacle. They collected by thousands—tens of thousands. The victim was brought out—all the eyes in the living mass that surrounded the gibbet were fixed on his countenance, and they waited, with strong desire, the expected signal for launching him into eternity. There was a delay. They grew impatient. It was prolonged, and they were outrageous. Cries, like those which precede the tardy rising of the curtain in a theater, were heard. Impatient for the delight they expected in seeing a fellow-creature

---

* Report of a Committee of the Legislature of Maine in 1835, on a new bill with reference to Capital Punishment.

die, they raised a ferocious cry. But when it was at last announced that a reprieve had left them no hope of witnessing his agonies, their fury knew no bounds; and the poor maniac, (for it was discovered that he was insane,) was with difficulty snatched by the officers of justice, from the fate which the most violent among them seemed determined to inflict."*

Thomas Barrett was executed in Worcester, Massachusetts, on the 3d of October, for rape and murder, and on the 14th another murder was committed within a few rods of the gallows, and not long after a rape in the same county, and only a few miles from Worcester; and within four months, four cases of capital crime, and two of homicide, not capital, were committed within less than a day's journey from the place of Barrett's execution.

Several years ago a man by the name of Strang was hung in Albany, New York. A man by the name of Kelly went from Otsego to Albany, a distance of seventy miles, for the *sole* purpose of seeing Strang executed, On his return, he seemed entirely engrossed by the exhibition he had witnessed. He talked of nothing else on the road and at the public houses where they stopped for refreshment.

A man lived in Kelly's house, by the name of Spafford, with whom he had had some little difficulty. In less than a fortnight after Strang was hung, an altercation occurred between Kelly and Spafford, when Kelly seized a loaded gun, and shot Spafford through the heart. For this offense he was tried, convicted, and executed. There was not a particle of evidence that Kelly was insane at the time he perpetrated the horrid act. Here was a case where the spectator hastened to commit the same

---

* From the "Expediency of Abolishing the Punishment of Death," by Livingston.

offense, and *with the same weapon*, for which he had just seen the terrible punishment of death inflicted.

On the evening of the day on which Kelly was hung, a man by the name of Cooke, in the neighborhood of Cooperstown, who was present at the execution, committed suicide *by hanging*. Now, may not the philosophical inquirer be permitted to indulge the conjecture that the public execution of Strang, instead of tending to preserve life, led to the destruction of three other lives?

Every where the same effects are produced by such public exhibitions, designed as examples to deter men from crime.

Not long since, a man by the name of Smith was hung in Paris, Kentucky, for the murder of his father.

The editor of the *Paris Citizen*, in speaking of the event, says:

"This was the third execution in our county within the last thirteen months, and it has convinced us more fully, not only of the inutility but of the positive evils of public executions. The effect upon the public mind, or rather upon a large portion of those who had collected to witness the solemn scene, seemed to be the reverse of that which would naturally be expected. Instead of producing a subdued, solemn, and thoughtful state of feeling, it seemed to be the occasion of drinking, merriment, and riot. We have rarely seen our streets filled with a crowd so noisy and unconcerned, and we are informed that just as the unhappy convict was about to be launched into eternity, a rabbit, starting up, was followed by the shouts and hallooing of half the company assembled around the gallows. The number present to witness the terrible scene was not large. Much the greater proportion of our thoughtful and respectable citizens stayed away as from a spectacle painful and unsuited to their taste."

Yes, and we may add, that this class not only stayed away themselves, but kept their negroes away, having become convinced that examples of this kind produce no salutary effect upon the mind of even the negro, but, if anything, render him more perverse and brutal. This seems the uniform testimony of observing gentlemen with whom we have conversed in and around Paris. They have come to regard the influence of executions, to be just the reverse of what was once universally believed to be indispensable as a warning to the offender.

We, have described the appearance of the multitude around the jail in Cincinnati, at the execution of Lecount. This man was hung, as we have said, for an "example to evil doers." The execution was on Friday. On the following Saturday night, in the lower part of the city, one man was stabbed, in a bloody affray, and another was shot; and on the following Sunday night, a brutal murder was perpetrated in a more central portion of the city, on the body of a man who was beaten to death with clubs. Within two weeks, there were *seven* attempts at murder. *It is literally true that there was more crime committed in Cincinnati, during the three months following that execution, than ever before or since for the same length of time.*

We do not assert that the execution of Lecount was the *cause* of this state of things: but we do assert that the example of his execution, was no "warning to evil doers," and that the moral condition of our city was not at all improved by this example. The same can be said of every execution which has ever taken place in Ohio.

Two men were hung in Columbus some years since, and "the occasion was one of hilarity, obscene jesting, coarse ribaldly, drunkenness and crime." Pickpockets were present in abundance, and men were cursing, fighting, and thieving, at the very moment of the hanging.

"Nearly fifty years ago, a mulatto boy, about 16 years old, was convicted of burglary, at Paris, Kentucky, and sentenced to be hung. The day of execution turned out to be a very cold, wintry day; but, notwithstanding the inclemency of the weather and bad state of the roads, a great crowd of men, women and children of almost every shade of color and of character, assembled about the gallows at an early hour, remaining in the cold for a long time. At last the sheriff arrived, with the culprit riding on his coffin in a two-horse wagon. Stopping under the gallows tree, a venerable and worthy Presbyterian divine (John Lyle,) got into the wagon, and sung and prayed for him; at the conclusion of which, the sheriff adjusted the rope, drew the cap over the culprit's face, and hallooed to those in front of the horses, 'Clear the way—clear the way,' three or four times. Just then a voice was heard in the distance: 'Stop the execution ! a reprieve ! a reprieve !' A man was seen on horseback pressing through the crowd, and when in reach of the sheriff, handed him a paper; who, after opening it, handed it to the minister. The clergyman uncovered the boy's face, called his attention to the reading of the paper, and then read aloud ; on which the people showed evident signs of dissatisfaction and disappointment. The preacher then appealed to the boy; reminding him of how he had been snatched from death's door through the instrumentality of the Governor ; and exhorted him always to be a good boy; but he was interrupted by the tumultuous uproar of the rabble, who with oaths were expressing their disappointment. To a young man standing near him, the minister said: 'Oh, young man, young man, how can you give utterance to such profanity on an occasion so solemn! *Are you not glad that the Govern-or has reprieved this poor boy?*' 'No,' said he, 'I wish the Governor was in h—l.' 'O, fie, fie!' exclaimed the man of God, and left the ground. The young man contin-ued his profane harangue: 'Here,' said he, 'are hundreds of us, who have been shivering and suffering in the cold for hours, expecting to see that d——d rascal hung, and now the Governor has set him at liberty and cheated us out of the fun. D—n him, I wish both he and the nigger were in h—l!' a sentiment which appeared to be popular with the crowd. By this time the boy was turned loose, and when he leaped from the wagon to the ground, an old colored woman (said to be his mother,) caught him by the arm and said: ' Bill, Bill, did you see dat dam old prince, (the negro wagoner) jest gwoing to drive de cart from under you and hang you?' 'Yes, I seed de dam old rascal; but neber mine, I'll gib him h—l for dat yet.' This raised a shout among the row-dies, and the crowd dispersed."

I should not omit to state here that this boy was hung a year or two after this, in South Carolina. His name was Bill Hardy.* How salutary the effect of the gallows!

But we turn from all other scenes of this description, which have transpired in our country, to mention one of a diabolical character, that has just occurred in our neighboring state, Illinois.

A man by the name of A. F. Monroe, was convicted of the murder of his father-in-law, at a special term of the Cole county court, and was sentenced to be hung, on the 15th of February.† On that day, a large crowd came

---

*This account was furnished for this work by Mr. Jesse Kennedy, an aged gentleman of veracity, who has resided near Paris from infancy, and was perfectly acquainted with the facts at the time they transpired.

†February 15, 1856.

in from the country round about, to witness the "example" about to be presented by the State as a *preventive* to crime. Fathers and mothers came by thousands, bringing their children, large and small, male and female, that they might have the benefit of its "salutary influence." But behold, on arriving at the place of punishment, they found that the rumor which had reached them at their homes, of a respite from the Governor, was true. The day of execution had been deferred till the 15th of May. For this slight cause, the crowd in their rage, broke through the wall of the jail, took out the culprit, and like a set of infuriated demons, *murdered him with their own hands.*

The following particulars of this dreadful deed, we extract from the (Illinois) *State Register.* They are from the pen of one who was an eye-witness to the shocking scene:

"The crowds continued to pour into Charleston all that day and the next—men, women and children—in all kinds of conveyances, and from all parts of the country. By 11 o'clock, on Friday, there were at least 5,000 persons in town, who came, as they said, "to see the fun!"

"At 12 o'clock, M., the crowd began moving toward the Court House, led on by a man named Cunningham, a brother-in-law of the prisoner, who harangued the crowd, saying he was willing to postpone the execution for a short time, but that the people of Coles could attend to their own affairs without the interference of the Governor.

"After the speech of Cunningham, a man named McNary was called upon, who said, speaking of the prisoner: 'Take him out, G—d d—m him, take him out, and hang him.'

"After the speeches of the above named man and

others, the Court House bell commenced ringing, which seemed to be a signal for an attack on the jail.

" The mob, inflamed and excited by the harangues they had heard, rushed *en masse* to the jail yard, where, yelling like demons let loose from the infernal regions, they began to make an attack on the north side of the jail. Some ten or fifteen minutes after they had commenced the attack, the sheriff made his appearance, and addressed the mob for about two minutes, commanding them to desist, but made no appeal to the spectators to assist him in enforcing the law. The sheriff then disappeared, and made no further effort either to resist the mob or to protect the prisoner.

"The mob were about two hours in making a breach in the wall of the jail. I think not more than ten or twelve men did the actual work, but they were encouraged by a large portion of the crowd, who used every means to keep up the excitement. During all this time were heard the sounds of fife and drum, amid the demoniac yells of the multitude.

" When the breach was made large enough, the prisoner was dragged through, badly bruised and insensible, amid the deafening shouts of the mob, who immediately moved with him toward the square, the fife and drum in the meantime sounding. The crowd pressed around, and it would have been impossible to know the position of the prisoner, had it not been designated by one who carried a long staff.

" The mob then proceeded to the public square, with the evident intention of there hanging the prisoner, and thus completing their hellish transaction; but about this time I noticed a prominent citizen edge his way through the crowd, with the intention, as I supposed, of addressing the mob, but in this I was disappointed;

however, the mass commenced moving from the square, and the cry immediately arose, 'To the woods, to the woods.'

" Immediately the mass moved with the prisoner toward the woods. After proceeding about half a mile southwest of the square, another halt was made, and those most active pressed the crowd back and succeeded in making a ring, in which some six or seven held the prisoner. In the middle of the ring was a tree, against which a ladder was placed, on which a man ascended with an axe and trimmed off the smaller branches; the rope was now made fast to the tree, and all things appeared ready for the blackest outrage which has at any time been perpetrated by any people, much less those who have claims to civilization. .

"During all this time the prisoner appeared insensible of what was going on, being unable to sustain himself alone. He appeared like a man who had taken poisonous drugs, which had taken effect upon him; he did not seem to heed the crowd, but would occasionally laugh in a wild and insane manner.

"Again the cry was raised, ' Take him back to jail, 'Will you hang a dead man?' but some demon's voice was heard saying, 'You G—d d——d cowards, are you afraid to hang him after bringing him here.' The prisoner was now placed in a wagon under the rope—and again the mob hesitated. It seemed that no one could be found blood-thirsty enough to adjust the rope to his neck. Finally a tool in the hands of others, by the name of Thomas Fleming, placed the rope around the prisoner's neck, while others held him up. The wagon was pulled away and the awful deed accomplished—the victim, as he hung, not making the least struggle."

Here, again, is the "salutary" and "restraining" in-
16

fluence of the gallows. What a "terror" it proved to evil-doers! How it softened passion and allayed anger; and what a chastening and sanctifying influence this scene must have produced on the minds of children and youth! It may be said, that "if the *State* had executed Munroe, the people would not have been enraged!" And what does this show but that they came to the place of execution with murder in their hearts. The State had resolved that the man should die. They had anticipated the work of death at that particular juncture, and had reflected upon it, until *murder grew in their hearts*, and nothing short of a full realization of their anticipations would satisfy them. "String him up!" "String him up!" was the brutal cry. The governor said it had been "but a few days since the man was convicted. Wait till the middle of May." But they could not wait. Their souls panted for his blood. They were eager to drink it. So, assuming the responsibility, they *themselves became murderers*. They killed Munroe with *malice prepense*. The example of the State fanned up the flames of hell in their bosom, and every man engaged in that dreadful work, is as really deserving the gallows, as the miserable wretch whom their revenge strangled.* Now, if the penalty of murder had been imprisonment for life, in Illinois, it is probable that Munroe, on conviction, would have been sent to the penitentiary, and put to work; that the people would have kept about their business, without once dream-

---

* From all accounts, they were the greatest aggressors. Munroe killed his enemy in revenge. The mob killed him in revenge. But Munroe contended with a single man, who had an opportunity of defending himself, and who said at one time during the fight, when the by-standers proposed to separate them: "Let us alone; let me kill him." When the mob came to murder Munroe, a hundred of them engaged in the work. They pulled the man, half dead, through a crevice in the wall, mangled his limbs, and when he had no more sense than an idiot, strangled the life out of him. The deed committed by him was revengeful; that committed by them, was revengeful, cowardly and malignant.

ing of revenging themselves on the wretch, and that thus the community would have been saved the curse of this shocking tragedy, the evil effects of which will be visible for years.

INFLUENCE OF EXECUTIONS IN ENGLAND.

The influence of public executions has been the same in England as in this country. We have a mass of facts gathered from various English writers, on this subject, all going to show the wretched effects of sanguinary laws, the most of which we omit for the want of space.

"Every execution," says Dr. Lushington, in Parliament, "brings an additional candidate for the hangman." "Wo to society," exclaims Lepelletier, in his report to the national assembly, "if in that multitude which gazes eagerly on an execution, is found one of those beings predisposed to crime by the perverseness of their propensities! His instinct, like that of wild beasts, awaits, perhaps, only the sight of blood, to awake—and already his heart is hardened to murder, the moment he is quitting the spot wet with blood which the sword of the law has shed."*

Mr. Wakefield, who was long connected with the Newgate prison, London, says: "When I first entered Newgate, I had not a doubt of the efficacy of public executions, as deterring from crime. By degrees I came firmly to believe the contrary. *Newgate is the very best place to form a sound opinion on the subject; that is, my opinion as deduced from facts in the case.*"

The editor of the *London Morning Herald*, a man who has given this subject more thought and attention, perhaps, than any other man in England, said: "Frequency of executions, in any country, is generally followed by a

---

* Spear's Essays on the Death Penalty.

proportionate increase of crime, violence and blood. When the Legislature lightly estimates human life, the people are apt to undervalue it."

Says Dr. Dodd: "We constantly hear of crimes not less heinous than those for which the criminal suffers, *being perpetrated at the place and moment of an execution.*' The Doctor himself afterward committed a capital crime, and was executed. And one of the same jurors who convicted Dodd, was executed on the same gallows for the same offense, within a few months afterward. And Fauntelry, who was executed for the same offense, says: " I first conceived the design of committing it, returning from an execution."

· In an account of the execution of two persons in London, no less than FORTY ARRESTS *were made* FOR THE SAME CRIME. What a blessed influence hanging must have produced on the motley crew in attendance! " A pick-pocket being asked by the chaplain of Newgate, how he could venture on such a deed, at such a time, very frankly replied: ' Executions are the best harvests I and my companions have, for when the eyes of the spectators are fixed above, their pockets were unprotected below.' "

"The Rev. Mr. Roberts, of Bristol, England, presents the astounding fact, that he conversed with one hundred and sixty-seven convicts under sentence of death, *one hundred and sixty-four of whom* HAD WITNESSED EXECUTIONS "

T. F. Buxton, the well-known philanthrophist, said, in a speech in the British Parliament: " It is notorious that executions very rarely take place without being the occasion on which new crimes are committed. "At an execution in York, England, in 1844, and at a still later one in London, pick-pockets were detected plying their trade at the very foot of the gallows."

"A speaker at a missionary meeting in England, in 1845, said he began the day at an execution at the Old Bailey, and, continued he, to be convinced of the moral effects of hanging, you should have watched the mob : *all that is licentious, and filthy and abominable, is done under the very gallows tree.*"

· "An Irishman, found guilty of issuing forged bank-notes, was executed, and his body delivered to his family. While the widow was lamenting over the corpse, a young man came to her, to purchase some forged notes. As soon as she knew his business, forgetting at once both her grief and the cause of it, she raised up the dead body of her husband, and pulled from under it a parcel of the very paper, for the circulation of which he had forfeited his life. At that moment an alarm was given of the approach of the police ; and, not knowing where else to conceal the notes, she thrust them into the mouth of the corpse, and there the officers found them."*

It is also related of a thief who was hung in England, in 1827, that on being taken from the gallows, he was sent to the dissecting-room, where experiments in gal-vanism were tried on him, during which the professor was absent for a few moments from the room, and when he returned he found the culprit resuscitated, sitting upright on the table, and looking wistfully round. On his promising to leave that part of the country he re-leased him. Only a few months after, he perceived by the papers that this same man was to *be hung a second time, for a similar offense;* and he became so interested in the case, that he journeyed fifty miles to see him. In conversation he asked him how he could possibly venture to commit a theft, when he had already been hung for a

---

* Livingston makes this statement on the authority of an English gen-tleman, who related it at a public meeting in Southampton, England.

similar crime   "Oh," he replied, "I care nothing for the gallows.   The truth is, I love to steal, and so I run the risk!   When you came into your room and found me sitting up and looking round, *I was just deciding on what I could steal from you of the most value, and with the least chance of detection.*"

This story may be regarded as too improbable to credit· But it is well vouched.   Many instances, somewhat similar, and equally incredible, are on record.   Mr. Rantoul relates that at the execution of the notorious pirate, Gibbs, a few years ago, in New-York, a witness was present, who declared positively that he had seen him hung on a former occasion, for the same crime, at some port in South America.   He insisted that he recognized him beyond the possibility of mistake, by certain peculiar marks of identity; and when we consider the not unfrequent cases which have occurred, of resuscitation after hanging—(a distinguished physician now in New-York, states that he has, in the course of his life, taken part in three such cases)—the story is not incredible.   At any rate, there are numerous cases known, in which criminals, who have narrowly escaped death for an attempted crime, have made its repetition the first object of their newly acquired liberty."

The following account of a conversation, said to have taken place between a convict about to be hung for coining, and a clergyman in England, is from the Essays of Mr. Spear, on the Death Penalty:

"Have you often seen an execution?"

"Yes."

"Did not it frighten you?"

"No; why should it?"

"Did it not make you think that the same would happen to yourself?"

"Not a bit."

"What did you think, then?"

"Think? why I thought it was a d—d shame."

" Now, when you have been going to run a great risk of being caught and hanged, did the thought never come into your head, that it would be as well to avoid the risk?"

" Never."

" Not when you remembered having seen men hanged for the same thing?"

"Oh, I never remembered anything about it; and if I had, what difference would that make? We must all take our chance. I never thought it would fall on me, and don't think it ever will."

"But if it should?"

"Why, then, I hope I shall suffer like a man—where's the use of snivelling?"

From all these facts it will be perceived that men misconceive the true philosophy of sanguinary punishments, when they argue that they exert a salutary influence by restraining men from the committal of crime. The opinions of keepers of prisons, lawyers, judges, and all men intimately connected with criminal jurisprudence, both in America and Europe, have undergone a wonderful change on this subject, since the introduction and test of milder and more humane laws. · Even at the present day, when bar-rooms and liquor shops have become less common, and temperance more prevalent, a hanging is, of all places, the most notoriously drunken, obscene, noisy, fighting and immoral. Every newspaper in the land testifies to the truth of this declaration. Scarcely an account of an execution has reached us from any portion of our country, for the last ten years, but has contained a description of attendant rowdyism and crime, as the legitimate fruits of the occasion. The law of death, as administered even by Judge Lynch, is not a sufficient "terror to evil-doers," to prevent them from the most dreadful acts of vengeance. During the past year, in California, sixty-eight men have been hung in the most summary manner, by Lynch law, and yet no less than five hundred and thirty-nine murders have been committed, some of them of the most atrocious character, in the very neighborhood, and, in some instances, *on the very day of the execution!* At no time previous, for the last fifty years, have laws so terrible prevailed, and their execution been so determined and vindictive, and yet in no part of our country has crime been so prevalent. And this is the history of all countries. Cruel and vindictive laws produce cruel and vindictive people. The State should, therefore, ever be cautious of her *examples.*

"The executioner," says O'Sullivan, "is the indirect cause of more murders and more deaths, than he either punishes or avenges. He is, in effect, a sort of public teacher, both of the doctrine and practice of murder; and in the school over which he presides, are but too many apt scholars for his instructions to prove unavailing. 'Sow an execution and reap a crop of murders,' is an old proverb, but it is one whose meaning is as true as it is terrible." During the reign of Henry VIII of England, the penal laws of that country were dreadfully severe. Hume bears record that seventy-two thousand *'great and petty thieves,"* were executed, for *robbery alone;* and under Elizabeth, his successor, "rogues were still trussed up apace." So that, during her administration, nineteen thousand were strangled; and yet, *there never was a time in all the history of England when crime was so rife.* In nearly every town and village, were **men** "strung up." Frequently were they hung in trees, where they were left for days as a "terror to evil-doers," and yet all this had no effect to deter the offender. "Sure, and it's nothing to be hung, when one is used to it," exclaimed an Irishman, when going to the gallows; "and don't the half of us expect this will be our end! so what matters it whether the gallows claims its own this year or next?"

17

CHAPTER XIII.

EIGHTH REASON FOR ABOLISHMENT.

RESULT OF EXPERIENCE FAVORABLE.

Men ask for Practical Proof—States and Countries have made a trial of Abolishment—Result favorable —Trial in Maine—No Executions in twenty-two years — Compared with other States -Vermont Massachusetts —Michigan—Wisconsin —Effects of the softening of Penal Codes in England and other Countries -Effects of Abolishment in Tuscany—Tuscany compared with Rome—Effects of Abolishment in Belgium —Also in Bombay and Russia—Result decidedly in favor of Abolishment.

Many persons will trust to nothing short of *experience*. They ask for practical, positive proof. " Society is bad enough," they say, "with the gallows; how do we know that it would not be worse without it? Has any State or country tried the experiment of abolishment long enough to determine fairly its moral effect?" We answer, yes. But if it had not, that fact should deter no Christian State or country from following where Christianity and humanity, as well as a wise policy, direct. The time was, in our country, as we have seen, when theft was punished with hanging. Many were fearful of the experiment of abolishment; but at last it was tried, and the result was favorable. So has it been with the crime of murder. In every country where abolishment for this crime has been tested, *the effect has been* TO LESSEN CRIME. So that society is positively less safe with the Death Penalty than without it, *even if the law is rigidly enforced.* What an argument is here in favor of abolishment! Let me now appeal to facts in proof of this statement.

(194)

EFFECT OF ABOLISHMENT IN OUR OWN COUNTRY.

As we have seen during the progress of this work, bloody codes have never had the effect to deter men from crime. To many minds whose only idea of punishment is vengeance, this fact is incredible. Nevertheless it is so. When Massachusetts Colony executed men and women for stealing forty shillings, robbery, burglary and shop-lifting, one would suppose that so dreadful a punishment would have totally prevented this description of crime. But not so; *it was more frequent than now*, in proportion to the population. The softening of the penal code had not the effect to *increase*, but rather to *decrease* the offense. The same result has followed the abolishment of the gallows for murder, wherever a trial has been tested.

MAINE. Here for the last fifteen years, the Death Penalty has been *virtually* abolished.* And what is the result? Just what we have said. In no part of our country has the crime of murder been so rare. Only three persons have been guilty of this foul deed, since the change in the law. It is true, that the progress of temperance, and, therefore, of civilization, in that State— the closing of liquor shops and bar rooms—have had a favorable influence in banishing crime, especially the most aggravated classes of crime, from among the people. All know that "intemperance is the hand-maid of vice." Still, the favorable aspect of society, so far as relates to this question, must not be attributed to this cause. The present law for murder went into force more than ten years previous to the existence of the liquor law; and not for *more than twenty-two years has a man or woman been executed in that State; and during this time but five murders have been perpetrated.* Now,

* See the note at the bottom of the 31st page of this work.

compare Maine with any State in the Union, of the same population, where the gallows still remains, and notice how favorable is the result to abolishment. Take Kentucky, for instance. There have been three executions, at different times, within the last thirteen months, in the town of Paris alone, in that State; and, during the past year, as many as ten murders have been committed within the limits of the State.† As many on an average, for the last twenty-two years, *would amount to two hundred and twenty.* The population of Maine, in 1850, was 583,169, and that of Kentucky, 982,405.

A comparison with Ohio or Indiana would exhibit nearly the same result. As we have shown, *five hundred* murders‡ have been either perpetrated or attempted, in Hamilton county, Ohio, alone, in the last fifteen years. We have no means of ascertaining the history of crime in Indiana, beyond the past year. During the past year (1855) eleven murders were perpetrated in that State. Two months since, three men were hung at once in Lafayette. Since that event, two cases of homicide have occurred in Indiana. The population of Ohio in 1850, was 1,980,329, and that of Indiana, 988,416.

A comparison, even in New-England States, shows a result favorable to Maine. New-Hampshire, with a population of only 317,976, has employed the gallows on several occasions, within the last twenty years; while the number of murders within her borders, has *more than trebled that in Maine.* So in Connecticut, with a population of a little more than half of that in Maine, men have been executed in various parts of the State, from time to time; a majority of her population being decidedly

---

† Those killed in Louisville during the election excitement, in the fall of 1855, are not included.

‡ See note at the bottom of the 160th page of this work.

in favor of hard and stringent laws, and yet murders are *far more frequent in that State than in Maine.* Three months ago, no less than three dreadful murders were perpetrated within a short distance of New-Haven.

Thus is it seen that after a trial of fifteen years, without the aid of the gallows as a "terror to evil doers," it is found that the inhabitants of Maine not only live without the fear of having their throats cut at night by bloody assassins, as was anticipated by timid men and women, when the gallows was abolished, but *they positively occupy the safest spot, as to aggravated crime, on the American continent.*

VERMONT modified her law four years ago, with reference to the Death Penalty, and made it very similar to that of Maine. The result has proved most satisfactory. Crime has not increased; on the contrary it has evidently diminished.

MASSACHUSETTS enacted a similar law, in 1852, with the same happy results. She has no disposition to go back to the usages of a more barbarous age. Her next step will be an advance one. We regret to record, however, that John H. Clifford, the Governor of the State in 1853, saw fit to issue his warrant for the hanging of a man who was convicted of murder, soon after the modified law took effect. The condemned man worked out his year in the penitentiary according to the law. He was as constant, faithful and orderly as any man in the prison, but the Govenor had the *power* to strangle him; he conceived it to be his *duty* to strangle him, and so the man was strangled. The act was *privately* perpetrated in the little jailyard at Taunton, Bristol county. No one, with the exception of the Governor, and a few whose views and sympathies belong to a past age, regarded this deed as either Christian or necessary. Life and property were rendered no more secure, nor were the manners and habits of the people improved.

In those States where the gallows has been absolutely abolished, the result has proved equally satisfactory. These are Rhode Island, Michigan and Wisconsin.

RHODE ISLAND has had an experience of six years, during which time the population of the State has considerably increased, while there has been no increase of crime —especially of aggravated crime.

MICHIGAN was the first State in the Union to abolish the Death Penalty. She made the change in 1847, and as reports have been every where circulated that an increase of crime was the result, and that the people of the State were much dissatisfied with the law and wished it abolished, I deem it necessary to present the facts in the case somewhat in detail. The reader may rely on the correctness of the statements which follow, as they are from official reports.

In 1851, such was the report abroad, with reference to the practical working of the new law in Michigan, that the Secretary of State saw fit to make a statement, in which it was shown that crimes of violence had actually *decreased* after the abolishment of the Death Penalty. He gave the facts as follows, with reference to the number of convictions for murder and manslaughter in the State, from 1847 to 1851.

In 1847, for manslaughter,.........................1
In 1848, for murder in the First Degree, ...4
In "   "   "   Second " 1
In 1849,   "   "   First   " 1
In "   "   "   Second " 9
In 1850, *no convictions for murder or manslaughter.*

To the question whether murder had been more frequent

since the law was changed, he replied at length in the negative, giving the statistics as follows:

COMPARATIVE TABLE,

Exhibiting the number of Indictments found in Michigan during the years 1841 to 1850, inclusive, for murder, manslaughter, and for assault with intent to kill—as taken from the Attorney General's Official Report.

	1841.	1842.	1843.	1844.	1845.	1846.	Total.	1847.	1848.	1849.	1850.	Total.
Murder,	4	1	5	2	1	3	16	0	4	1	0	5
Manslaughter,	0	0	1	0	0	0	1	1	1	9	0	11
Accessories,	2	0	1	0	0	0	2	0	0	0	0	0
Assault, with intent to kill,	11	12	12	7	9	12	63	10	9	13	8	40
Total of homicidal assaults,	16	13	19	9	10	15	82	11	14	23	8	56

"The reader will bear in mind that during the period included in this table, the population of Michigan was rapidly increasing, partly by emigration of the degraded poor of Europe, and that many counties which in '41 and '42 were a wilderness, were filled with an adventurous, hardy and excitable population in '49 and '50· This official statement, therefore shows a most gratifying *decrease* of crime in Michigan, while it had been *increasing* in other States, where Capital Punishment was most frequently and certainly inflicted."

It is true, that in 1852, in consequence of the fact that one or two murders were perpetrated by returned Mexican soldiers, who had become familiar with blood while abroad, it was conceived by certain persons whose sympathies for the institution of the gallows were unyielding, that crime was "alarmingly on the increase," and a memorial was sent from the Grand Jury of Wayne

* We are indebted to the "Prisoner's Friend," a valuable monthly Magazine, edited and published by Rev. C. Spear, of Boston, for the facts recorded above

County, Michigan, to the Legislature of that State, praying for the restoration of that old relic of barbarism.   It
is also true, that that fact was employed in the Legislature of Massachusetts, New-York, Ohio and probably
in other States, as an argument against abolishment in
those States.

We recollect that in lecturing upon the subject of the
Death Penalty in 1852 and '53 we were met with this
statement on every hand: "Michigan has abolished
Capital Punishment; and, after a trial of years, has determined on reinstating the gallows." But what were the
facts concerning this memorial? Let a man* of integrity,
an old and respected resident of Michigan, answer. He
saw by the eastern papers how this piece of intelligence
was received and employed by those favoring the Death
Penalty in New-York and elsewhere; so he writes to the
editor of an eastern publication, as follows:

"Know all men, that said memorial was born in the
city of Detroit, in sight of Rev. Dr. Duffield's church,
the Doctor being the great advocate for hanging in the
State. It was recommended to that same Grand Jury
by the Judge of the County Court of Wayne, he being a
member of Dr. Duffield's church, and strongly in favor
of drawing the halter to make men virtuous and orderly.
The memorial was signed by *but fifteen* of the twenty-four
jurors, and ushered into existence *in the darkest spot of
our State.* It was nursed through a short and feeble
life, by Dr. Duffield and others, but soon died, without
a relative to mourn its loss, and was buried, to be brought
forth by somebody in New-York city and other places,
to answer a bad cause.

* Rev. J. Stebbins. We have other communications and documents,
substantiating the above statement; but deem it unnecessary to offer
them here.

"But it will never do. In Michigan a resurrection of such a dead body would be more offensive than the dissecting-rooms of a medical college, and not half as useful.

"This was the *only* memorial presented to our Legislature during the entire session; and this, together with Dr. Duffield's sermon in favor of hanging, was smothered with remonstrances, and never even got out of the hands of the committee to whom it was referred, they finding NO CAUSE FOR ACTION. Thus ended the affair now brought up to influence legislation in favor of hanging in the great State of New-York. Shame! shame!

"Since the days of that memorial we have had a Convention and made a new Constitution. In the Convention it was thought advisable to *let hanging entirely alone*. Nor is this all. In Detroit there is now, and has been for two years, a daily press fearlessly exposing every attempt from abroad to support the gallows. And what is a significant fact, this press is the *people's*, a penny paper, and has the largest circulation of any paper in Detroit."

This was the last we heard of the efforts of Michigan to reinstate the gallows. The present law works admirably. A letter is before us from one* long resident in that State, and for two years chaplain in the Michigan Penitentiary, in answer to enquiries put by us, in which the writer says: "There never was a time since Michigan was a State when its morals were so pure as now— never a time when the State was so secure from the robber or assassin. In my opinion it would be impossible to abolish the present law. Its practical working is admirable. Outlaws are brought to justice. They are convicted, and, consequently, secured, without effort; and

---

* Rev. J. Billings.

the people consider themselves as safe from the murderer when in the Penitentiary as they would were he in the tomb.   There he is, a living example to all evil doers; and experience has proved that he is no more dangerous or disorderly than other convicts."

WISCONSIN.   The Death Penalty was abolished several years ago in this State, and generally the practical operation of the present law has been favorable.   Not so many murders have been committed by *fifty per cent*, in that State, in ratio to the number of inhabitants, as in some portions of Ohio or Kentucky, where the gallows is still in vogue.   There are men, however, in Wisconsin, who have great confidence in the moral power of legal strangulation.   They look upon the murderer with feelings of savage revenge.   Their hearts pant for blood.   They say—"hang him;" innocent or guilty, "crucify him! crucify him!"   This spirit is rife in Janesville, Wisconsin, so that not long since, a mob arose and seized a man when being conveyed from the jail to the court room, under trial for murder in that county, and as the State had declared that it would not kill him, because he had killed, they took the responsibility to perform this heroic deed themselves.   Amid horrid oaths and the most impious imprecations, they trussed him up to the limb of a tree and choked the life out of him.

Now, some persons, both in and out of the State of Wisconsin, attribute this lawless deed to the want of the gallows in that State ; and say the Death Penalty must be reinstated, as if blood was never known to be shed where the gallows was in vogue.   But how narrow is the vision of such men, and how limited their knowledge of the real facts in the case !   Let them reflect.   Are there no mobs or murders where Capital Punishment exists?   Let them look to Louisville, Cincinnati, Philadelphia,

New-York, California, or nearer home, to Illinois.* In all these cities and States the Death Penalty still exists. And yet how frequent are the most dreadful crimes perpetrated. In California not only the gallows is erected, but everywhere Judge Lynch presides at the trial of the offender and convicts and executes in the most summary manner. According to the statistics of crime just published in that State, no less than 68 persons were put to death in this way, during 1855, and yet crime has not at all lessened under this severity. On the contrary, it has increased. In 1854 there were but 390 homicides. In 1855, under this lawless and desperate code, there were 538.

In Wisconsin, there may have been an increase of crime, during the last year; but this is no certain proof that the cause of this condition was the inefficiency of the present law. The result of a single year is no positive test in a case like this. The circumstances showing an apparent permanent change for the worse or better, may be accidental. For instance, during the years 1845, '46 and '47 there was but *one* trial for a capital offense in Massachusetts. But in the single year 1848, there were *seven—twenty-one times as many* as in the three previous years, a result not paralleled nor even approached in the case of Wisconsin. And this apparent change occurred in Massachusetts without any change in the Penal Code of that state. Now if Massachusetts had abolished the Death Penalty at the beginning of 1848 what an argument this circumstance would have afforded the friends of the gallows in favor of its restoration.

Such is the result of abolishment in our own country. We sum it up by saying, that *in every state of our Union where the Death Penalty is either practically or really abol-*

---

* In Charleston, Coles county, Illinois, a dreadful murder was perpetrated by a mob, similar to that in Wisconsin three months ago. See pages 182—6 of this work, where the particulars are described.

ished, there is LESS *crime of an atrocious character, than in those States where it still exists.* The feeling of security is not, therefore, diminished in consequence of abolishment. The law is more in harmony with public sentiment. The officers of justice are less embarrassed and more prompt in their duties; the guilty can be convicted, and when convicted are secured and punished. Let the gallows be abolished in every State, and the same result would follow.

EFFECT OF ABOLISHMENT IN EUROPE.

"When one casts his eye upon the history of crime and punishment in modern Europe," says Rantoul, "the phenomenon which first attracts his notice is the prodigality with which the Death Penalty was formerly dispensed, and the prodigious advance which has been made by a milder system of repressive policy during the eighteenth and the first quarter of the nineteenth centuries; and still more remarkably, during the last thirty years. As this mitigation of punishment has been tried in every part of christendom, if any evil consequences had followed from it, some one would have been able to point them out, and to tell us when, where, how, and how long the mischief manifested itself. Yet among more than two hundred authors upon this subject, whose writings I have examined, I have never found but two who have seriously attempted to exhibit the evils which these successive meliorations of the law must have occasioned, if those wise men against whose indignant remonstrances these changes were effected were right in their prognostications."

. It is immaterial what countries we select as tests in our investigations, for everywhere we shall find the results subtantially the same, viz.: in favor of mild and humane laws. We will begin with

ENGLAND AND WALES.—The advance of crime was never so rapid as in the latter part of the reign of George III. In 1814, the committals in England and Wales were 6,390, 'and in 1817 they were 13,932. They had more than doubled in three years! And yet more crimes were condemned as capital during the reign of George III. than in the reigns of all the Plantagenets, Tudors, and Stuarts combined, as stern and hard as they were. But thirty years ago or more, through the instrumentality of humane men, Great Britain began to soften her penal code; and it was discovered that no sooner was the Penalty of Death repealed for any given crime than that crime was at once arrested in its progress, while all other crimes continued to advance the same as before. For instance; the Death Penalty for coining was repealed May 23d, 1832; for horse stealing, sheep stealing, cattle stealing, larceny in dwellings, (of £5,) in July, 1832; forgery, 15th Aug. 1832; and house breaking, 14th Aug. 1833. For these offenses, in the four years ending with 1831, there had been condemned to death 3,786 persons, of whom 66 were executed.

Now for these offenses, during the time mentioned in the table below, the *commitments* were as follows:

In three years.	Commitments.	Executions.
1827, 1828, 1829,	4,622	96
1830, 1831, 1832,	4,724	23
1833, 1834, 1835,	4,292	2

In this class, the commitments *fell* 432, or about *nine* per cent., in the *three* years following the repeal. But look at the result for those crimes where the Death Penalty still remained:

In three years.	Commitments.	Executions.
1827, 1828, 1829,	1,705	108
1830, 1831, 1832.	2,236	120
1833, 1834, 1835,	2,247	102

Here the commitments *rose* 542, or about *thirty-two* **per** cent, in defiance of the gallows, in *six* years.

The result shown above proved the same with reference to *every* crime. For instance, mitigation of the Death Penalty, for assaults on females, commenced in 1835. During the four years ending Dec. 1834, there were 14 executions and 520 committals. During the next four years, ending Dec. 1838, there were 4 executed and 528 committals. To have borne the same proportion to the increased population, the last number should have been 551 instead of 528. Again, mitigation for arson commenced in 1837. During the two years ending in Dec. 1836, there were 9 executed and 148 committals; while during the two years following mitigation, ending Dec. 1838, there were *no* executions and but 86 committals.

But though Great Britain has demonstrated in its history, the fact, upon the one hand, that sanguinary laws always make men bloody and cruel, and upon the other, that, clemency on the part of the legislator always inspires humanity among the citizens, yet it has never cherished sufficient faith in the moral power of clemency to *wholly* abandon the use of the gallows. This event will come to pass in a few years. We have presented the above simply to show the validity of the *philosophy* of humanity advocated in this work, and on which the results which we present are based.

We now turn to an examination of the effects of the law in those countries in Europe where the Death Penalty is absolutely abolished for *every* crime.

TUSCANY.—"Here we find the most satisfactory proofs of the practical advantages resulting from the abolishment of Capital Punishment. The grand duke, Leopold, ascended the throne in 1765, and, governed by the enlightened counsels of Beccaria, he commenced a general reform of the penal code. After showing that 'the proper objects of punishment' are 'the redress of injury' and 'the correction of the delinquent,' and that he ought to be 'regarded as a child of the state,' and that his 'amendment ought never to be abandoned in despair,' he goes on to decree in the following language:

" *We have resolved to abolish, and by the present law do abolish, forever, the punishment of death*, which shall not be inflicted on any criminal, present or refusing to appear, or even confessing his crime, or being convicted of any of those crimes which in the laws prior to these we now promulgate, and which we will have to be absolutely and entirely abolished, were styled capital.

"Let us now look at the effects of this experiment. M. Berenger, in his report to the French Chamber of Deputies, in 1830, says the punishment of death was abolished during a period of twenty-five years in Tuscany, 'and the mildness of the penal legislation had so improved the character of the people there, that there was a time when the prisons of the Grand Duchy were found entirely empty. Behold enough to prove sufficiently that the abolition of the punishment of death is capable of producing the most salutary effects.' Mr. Livingston says, 'that in Tuscany, where murder was not punished with death, only five had been committed in twenty years; while in Rome, where that punishment is inflicted with great pomp and parade, *sixty murders* were committed in the short space of three months in the city and vicinity."*

But it is asked by the friends of the Death Penalty, if the milder code was attended with such beneficial results

---

* We take the above from Mr. Spear's valuable work on Capital Punishment. What he says is correct as other documents in our possession abundantly testify.

in Tuscany, why was the punishment of death afterwards restored? Simply because an enlightened and humane sovereign was succeeded by a foreign conqueror and despot. All despotism is based on the power of the ruler to *destroy*; hence all despots have been the most decided friends of cruel and bloody laws. The mild code of Leopold was abolished and the guillotine restored by the conquests under Napoleon, a man who never studied the philosophy of clemency, but deluged all Europe in blood. What better could have been expected? The heart of a lamb is not found under the skin of a tiger. After his reign terminated and the power of his government was lost in Tuscany, the Death Penalty was again abolished, and on the day of abolishment the people showed their joy by "rushing *en masse* for the guillotine, not to put it in operation, but to commit it to the flames, and the bells rung a merry peal."

RUSSIA.—In Russia the punishment of death is never inflicted. The Empress Elizabeth ascended the throne in 1741. At that time she pledged herself never to destroy human life for crime; a pledge which was faithfully kept during her entire reign. Catharine followed . her example, and Nicholas governed by the same humane principle. And what has been the result after a trial of more than *one hundred years*, during which the Death Penalty has been inflicted in that immense realm containing 62,000,000 of people only on two occasions? Why, the most satisfactory. *The least number of murders are perpetrated in Russia of any country on the globe of the same population.* Count De Segur made this declaration on his return from that country in 1791 saying that Catharine herself had several times said to him : " *We must punish crime without imitating it; the punishment of death is rarely anything but a useless barbarity.*"

Is it not singular that enlightened England and France have not, even yet, opened their eyes to the truth of this important fact? So satisfactory has been the trial of abolishment, in Russia, that the reform has been carried into Finland.

"Experience demonstrates," said Elizabeth, "that the frequent repetition of Capital Punishment never yet made men better. If, therefore, I can show that, in the ordinary state of society, the death of a citizen is neither useful nor necessary, I shall have pleaded the cause of humanity with success."

"By her mildness and clemency," said Catharine, "she did more to exalt the nation, and gave the fathers of her country a more excellent pattern, than that of all the pomps of war, victory and devastation." Well did a Russian writer exclaim :—

"Blush! ye countries of a longer civilization, that Russia should teach you the celestial principle of reforming depraved morals, not by the sanguinary execution or inexorable justice, but by the mild and divine precepts of heavenly mercy."*

BELGIUM.—We have full and accurate tables of crime in Belgium both before and after abolishment, but our limits will not permit us to give them in detail. The result there, however, after a trial of years, has been most satisfactory. The Penal Code was once exceedingly severe and executions common in that country, and, as a necessary consequence, crime was rife. With the decrease of executions, as in other countries, crime diminished. Thus in nineteen years, ending with 1814, there were 533 executions, 399 of which were for murder, or 21 *per annum;* the law was then softened, and for the next fifteen years there were 72 executions and but

---

* Spear's Essays on Capital Punishment.

18

114 murders, or only 8 *per annum.* Capital Punishment was then entirely abolished, and for the next five years there were *no* executions and but 20 murders, or *only four per annum.* How remarkable the change, and how hard to credit with many; and yet it is the very result which a true philosophy warrants, as we show in our next chapter.

BOMBAY. It is thought by many that the gallows may be safely dispensed with in a highly civilized community, but is indispensable in countries with a rude and ignorant population. Experience has taught, however that strangling or beheading, burning or crucifying men or women, is just as unnecessary and impolitic with one people as with another, while the moral influence is equally pernicious. Bombay is an Island in British India. It was obtained by the Portuguese in 1530 from an Indian chief and was ceded to Great Britain in 1661. Its population is nearly 200,000 of whom 120,000 are Hindoos, 40,000 Mohammedans, 12,000 native Christians, 15,000 Parsees and only about 5,000 English. And yet among this mixed and ignorant population, of Hindoos, Mohammedans and Parsees,—in the midst of heathen darkness, with but scarcely a ray of Christian light, it was found by actual experiment that killing for crime was utterly useless. On this point we have abundant testimony, but a single statement must suffice. It is taken from the farewell charge of Sir James Mackintosh to the Grand Jury of the Supreme Court of Bombay, July 20, 1811. He says:

" Since my arrival here, in May, 1804, the punishment of death has not been inflicted by this court. Now, the population subject to our jurisdiction, either locally or personally, cannot be less than two hundred thousand persons. Whether any evil consequence has yet arisen from so unusual (and in British dominions unexampled) a circumstance, as the disuse of Capital Punishment, for so long a period as seven years, or among a population so considerable, is a question which you are entitled to ask, and to which I have the means of affording you a satisfactory answer.

"From May, 1756, to May, 1763, (seven years,) the capital convictions amounted to one hundred and forty-one, and the executions were forty-seven. The annual average of persons who suffered death was almost seven, and the annual average of capital crimes ascertained to have been perpetrated, was nearly twenty:

"For the last fifty years the population has more than doubled, and yet from May, 1804, to May, 1811, though we had no capital execution, there have been but *six* convictions for murder. Murders in the former period *with executions* were, therefore, nearly as *three* to *one* to those of the latter, in which no Capital Punishment was inflicted.

"This small experiment has, therefore, been made without any diminution of the security of the lives and property of men. Two hundred thousand men have been governed for seven years without a capital punishment, and without any increase of crimes. If any experience has been acquired, it has been safely and innocently gained."

Here, then, are the results of abolishment. To whatever country we turn our attention we find the same favorable response. Are not these facts significant? Let not our States, then, longer be "faithless, but believing." Cicero said, many centuries ago, "Away with the executioner and the execution, and the very name of its engine! Not merely from the limbs but from the very thoughts, the eyes, the ears of Roman citizens." Shall American Christians of the nineteenth century say less with reference to American citizens?

CHAPTER XIV.

NINTH REASON FOR ABOLISHMENT.

THE PHILOSOPHY OF HUMANITY FAVORABLE.

Validity of our Philosophy doubted—Kindness in the government of Home and the Family—A State or Nation a Family—Want of faith in Goodness to overcome Evil—The Philosophy of Christianity and Humanity harmonious—Saying of the French Sage—Example of the State—Conversation of the Monk and the Executioner—Influence of bloody Examples—Sacredness of Human Life should be enforced—Early training of Children—The Quakers free from Crime—Children of Newgate Criminals.

THE facts which we present in the preceding chapter, will astonish many persons who have given the subject but little attention, or whose education has been such that their prejudices are wholly enlisted on the side of stern and inflexible laws for criminals. Some will doubt the validity of the philosophy upon which the reform we advocate is based, and say *it is impossible* that a mild and lenient government should possess the power to prevent crime, that is found in a stern and uncompromising administration of justice. Even fathers and mothers who have long since learned the *necessity* of love and kindness in the government of home and the family, and who are certain from daily observation that those children are the most disobedient and cruel, who are educated under the most stern and cruel authority, will doubt the philosophy upon which they base all their hopes in domestic discipline, when they come to apply it to the government of a state or nation and say, "*we dare not trust it!*" But what is a state or nation but a family? And we may be certain that whatever principles will exert a

(212)

healthful moral influence on the minds and hearts of our children, will exert the same influence on the minds and hearts of men and women, who are but children of a larger growth. The philosophy of humanity is in harmony with the philosophy of Christianity, and is, therefore, in favor of abolishment. Every principle begets its like. "The *grace* of God that bringeth salvation to all men hath appeared, *teaching* us that denying ungodliness and worldly lusts we should live soberly, righteously and godly in this present world."* God's grace or love will produce this effect, but wrath, hatred, never. "The *goodness* of God leadeth thee to repentance;"† not his vengeance. Christ was once charged with casting out devils by Beelzebub the prince of devils; but he denied the possibility of such a thing by showing that Satan, could not cast out Satan, or in other words, that evil could not allay or destroy evil, but only the Spirit of God—or goodness. Hence the injunction: "Be not overcome of evil, *but overcome evil with* GOOD;"‡ which is the only principle which can overcome evil.

Now, in the philosophy of these Christian declarations will be found an explanation of the seeming mystery connected with the facts recorded in the last chapter, with reference to the effects of clemency. Cruelty and retaliation fan up the fires of hell in the soul, while forbearance and gentleness allay them and awaken only thoughts of repentance and aspirations for a more virtuous and holy life. The lesson of the French sage is a true one; " *Une loi rigoureuse produit des crimes*"—harsh laws, beget crimes; and said Bentham: "If the legislator be desirous to inspire humanity amongst the citizens, let him set the *example;* let him show the utmost respect for the life of man. Sanguinary laws have a tendency

---

* Tit. ii : 11.   † Rom. ii : 4   ‡ Rom. xii : 21.

to render man cruel, either by fear, by imitation, or by revenge. But laws dictated by mildness humanize the manners of a nation and the spirit of government."

Douglass Jerrold, in his "Lessons of Life," gives a conversation between a *monk* and a *hangman* in Paris, as follows:

"Ho! hold you there, Father—'*example.*' 'Tis a brave *example* to throttle a man in the public streets, on the gibbet. Why, I know the faces of my audience as well as Dominique did. I can show you a hundred who never fail at the gallows' foot to come and gather *good* 'example.' Do you think, most holy Father, that the mob of Paris come to a hanging as to a sermon—to amend their lives at a gibbet? No: many come as they would take an extra dram! it gives their blood a fillip—stirs them for an hour or two; many to see a fellow man act a scene which they must one day undergo; many come as to puppets and ballet-singers at the Point Neuf; but for *example*, why, father, as I am an honest executioner, I have, in my day, done my office *upon twenty*, all of whom were constant visitors, of years standing, at my morning levees around the gallows, to witness the jerk and the struggle. *That* was the *effect* of a 'good *example*' Father!"

Here is exhibited the philosophy of sanguinary punishments; as an example, they harden and demoralize the soul, and prepare men for deeds of revenge and blood. When the state kills, it authorizes and sanctions the work of death. Naturally, man has a horror of taking human life. His instincts revolt at it, and his frame shudders at the thought of it. It is not the old and experienced soldier who trembles at the blood and carnage of the battle field, but the man whose sympathies have not been blunted by these dreadful exhibitions. Let the men, women and, children of any community become familiar with the work of death as sanctioned by the state in the execution of offenders, and their horror of bloodshed will gradually but certainly diminish, and they themselves will kill if they have what they deem sufficient provocation. The state has set the *example*. Duelling, bloody affrays and murders, are fostered and sustained by the gallows. This is wrong. The state, in its dignity, should teach a lesson to every man, woman and child, just the reverse. Both by its laws and its examples, it should carefully maintain and enforce the sacredness of human life; teaching that retaliation and vengeance belong alone to a savage state; that to kill men because they have killed is but perpetrating the same evil; that it is better to suffer wrong than do wrong, and that clemency, forbearance, gentleness, are more divine, ennobling and blessed than retaliation and vengeance.

In every instance where a state or nation has exhibited *such* an example it has operated upon the people like leaven on meal, assimilating their hearts gradually but surely to its own divine nature. The officers of prisons in Belgium testified, that from "their experience the abolishment of Capital Punishment tended greatly to soften the disposition of the mass of the people." The same report comes from Russia and Tuscany. Such a thing in Maine as a murder is very uncommon; and the consequence is, when one occurs the whole community is shocked in its every nerve; while in California, where executions are almost of daily occurrence, the fact that a man has been murdered is received as coolly as the news of his marriage.

What a true philosophy calls for as a preventive to murder and protection against it is, not the gibbet—not the blood of the offender, but CORRECT MORAL SENTI-

MENT AMONG THE MASSES, AND ESPECIALLY A DEEP
REVERENCE FOR THE SACREDNESS OF HUMAN LIFE.
Let the State see to it that it sets the proper *example*,
and let all parents instil into the minds of their children,
from their very infancy, this reverence for human life,
and they are effectually armed against deeds of blood to
the last moments of their existence, as the consideration
of a single fact will be likely to convince them. The
Quakers, or Friends, are very particular in the education
of their children on this point. Their religion utterly
forbids the practice of war, duelling, hanging, or the destruction of human life for any consideration. In their
very *infancy* their children are impressed with this important truth; while always, in more advanced age, they
are strictly forbidden to attend an execution, or mingle
in the company of those who are familiar with crime.
Now is it not probable that if all children were educated
in the same principles we should have no need of gibbets
or State prisons. How seldom is a Quaker arraigned
for crime; and what is remarkable, *there is no account on
record of a murder committed by one of this sect.* Here is
the influence of early training and a correct moral sentiment. On the other hand, the fact is notorious that
those who have been guilty of the most villainous
crimes were familiar with criminals and scenes of blood
when young. An English writer records it as a fact, that
some of the most desperate assassins ever incarcerated in
the prison of the Old Bailey, in London, or hung beneath its walls, were the *children of parents who resided
in the alleys and courts in that vicinity and who were constantly about the prison and witnesses of every execution that
occurred.* Thousands transported to Botany Bay, took
their first lessons in crime at that place, and beneath the
very shadow of the gallows.

Thus have we demonstrated that the philosophy of Christianity is the best possible, as the basis of all human governments. Let us have faith in it and practically adopt it. "*Overcome evil with good.*" Would to God that men, especially *Christian* men, could give up the *devil*, as an incentive to purity, and confide more in the moral power of *God*—or goodness!

19

CHAPTER XV

TENTH REASON FOR ABOLISHMENT.

THE ENDS OF PUNISHMENT NOT ANSWERED.

Three objects of Punishment—Reformation—Example—Reparation—What Punishment is—What Revenge is—The Christian Law—Strangling Men will not Reform them—It is not an Example of Good—It cannot restore the life of the murdered Victim.

The gallows does not subserve any of the great objects of punishment.

This is our concluding reason for its abolishment. It is the last, but by no means the least in importance.

There can be but *three* proper objects of punishment, which are these, viz: First, the reformation of the offender; Second, an example for the benefit of others; and Third, restitution or compensation.

The first is the most important and legitimate object of punishment, which always implies *correction.* " Punishment is the infliction of pain in consequence of a neglect or violation of duty, *with a view to correct the evil.*" Hence, *endless* pain, or pain that results simply in the death of the body, is not punishment, for the reason that there can be no opportunity for correction. The apostle declares that " No chastening for the present seemeth to be joyous, but grievous; nevertheless *afterward* it yieldeth the peaceable fruits of righteousness unto them which are exercised thereby."* But if we "chasten" a man by strangling, or burning, or shooting him, what opportunity

* Heb. xii. 11.

(218)

has he for amendment. Christianity recognizes all men as *brethren* of one great family, and it demands that in devising punishments its votaries should be careful to adopt those only which will reclaim the vicious. The command is: "If thy brother be overtaken in a fault *restore* such an one;" not that we strangle the life out of him. Thus is it enjoined upon us to exert ourselves to rectify and soften the disposition of our brother; to correct whatever there is wrong in him, and raise up in his soul a power that shall be sufficient to counteract the power of future temptation. And can this be done by *killing* him? How unchristian is this whole system! If our brother is overtaken in a fault we say, "hang him! string him up! He has broken the law of God and man and deserves to be killed!" If he asks time for repentance we say, "give him no time!" "He is a murderer, and should die!" So we kill him, whether he is prepared for the great change or not. Now this is not *punishment*. Rather is it *revenge*, which is "the infliction of pain in consequence of the commission of injury, *with a view to gratify a malignant passion.*" Should *Christians* ever be controlled by malignant passion?

The second object of punishment mentioned above, is *example for the good of others.* We might pause here to argue the *right* of society to kill one man for the good of others, but though the principle involves an absurdity, and, therefore, is not, and cannot be legitimate, this is not the place for its discussion. Our object here is to show that the gallows does not subserve any of the great objects of punishment. As we have seen, killing a man does not *reform* him; and we come now to say, that though we may kill him as an example, for the good of others, to deter them from crime and thus purify society, the practical operation of the act is found, by universal experience, to produce a condition the *very opposite of that which we desire;* viz., instead of its being an example for *good*, it is an example for *evil*, as we have abundantly proven by an appeal to *facts*, during the progress of this work.*

The third object of punishment is, Restitution or Compensation. It is no more than right, if a thief steals my purse, or a robber enter my house and carry off my property, that he be made to restore it. I am aware that this principle is not recognized in our penal codes. A man may steal a thousand dollars, be convicted and serve out his time in the penitentiary, return to the world and become wealthy; but the law does not demand that he restore the stolen property. This is wrong. *Individual* as well as *general* interests should be recognized and taken care of by "the powers that be." Reparation should be made. Both the law of Moses and the Christian rule demand it. "If a man shall steal an ox or a sheep, and kill it, or sell it, he shall restore five oxen for an ox, and four sheep for a sheep."†

Now, if the principle of restitution were incorporated into our penal codes, and offenders should be made to recompense a fair equivalent, either in money or by their labor in prison, those whom they had wronged by theft or robbery, it would not only approve itself to their minds as an act of reason, but it would enforce a lesson of *justice*, which must prove beneficial, while at the same time it would serve, in part, as punishment for the offense.

But what we desire to say in this connection is, that even if our penal codes were based on the principle involved here, *the killing of one man could never restore the*

---

* See the xii. chapter of this work, in which this point is fully discussed.
† Exodus, xxii. 1.

life of his murdered victim. It could not give back to the weeping widow and sorrowing children, the slain husband and father. He is gone, and the sacrifice of ten thousand lives could not restore him to the arms of those beloved, or return him in health to society. No reparation can be made for this dreadful deed save it be by the positive repentance of the heart of the murderer, manifested in a constant desire to employ a whole life of labor for the welfare and happiness of those who specially suffered by the death of the slain victim. Thus do we see that all the legitimate aims of punishment are denied by the gallows. Strangling men on the gibbet till they are dead will neither reform them, prevent others from the committal of crime, nor bring back to life the murdered victim.

Now, with all these plain reasons against the Death Penalty, shall we still continue it upon our statute books? "I speak as unto wise men, judge ye what I say."

CHAPTER XVI.

OBJECTIONS CONSIDERED.

The Murderer not fit to Live—Give him time to Repent, then hang him—Not entitled to Live—Sufferings of the Innocent—Interesting Incident—Lecount and his Mother—Col. Hayne and his Son—James Dawson and his intended Bride—Conclusion.

We close what we have to offer in this work on the Death Penalty, by a consideration of a few objections which are sometimes brought in favor of the gallows.

"THE MURDERER IS NOT FIT TO LIVE!"

But is he fit to die? May be you are a professed Christian. Be cautious; you tread on dangerous ground here! Suppose the sentiment so generally taught in Christian books and Christian pulpits be true; viz: that the sinner who dies with his soul unregenerated by the power of the Holy Spirit, will be consigned to a hell of *infinite and endless anguish,* can you have it in your heart to hasten his exit from this state of probation? He is a murderer; and "ye know that no murderer HATH *eternal* life abiding in him!"* I appeal to you, fellow Christian, in the name of mercy, and of Him from whom *you* expect mercy, I ask, *will* you *hasten* the doom of the wretched victim? You have him safely secured by bolts and bars. He can no longer injure any living creature. Will you deny him the poor boon of life a little longer? It may be he is innocent. Will you take him from his stone cell, from his wife and children, from father and mother, and thrust

---

1 John iii. 15.

him *speedily* out of life, where he might have repented, down into a never dying hell, where repentance can *never*, NEVER come?

"BUT I WOULD GIVE HIM TIME TO REPENT."

Yes, you would give him time to repent:—you woulu *prepare* his soul for the purity and bliss of heaven ; make of him a saint fit for glory, and then with your Christian hands strangle the life out of him on a gibbet. Yes, if he were *innocent* you would do this, if you *conceived* him to be guilty. You would do it for your "brother in Christ." Many a Christian has been thus strangled by the hands of Christians:—In our own country, the act is perpetrated every year or month—whilst the "minister of God" stands by, with Bible in hand, and pronounces the doomed culprit a "hopeful subject of immortal felicity."

Now, to us there appears but little really Christian or necessary in all this. "*As I live saith the Lord, I have no pleasure in the death of the sinner* THAT REPENTETH, *but rather that he should turn and live.*" If *God* has no pleasure in the death of a REPENTANT *sinner*, why should man? Why should society? *Christian* society? especially when the offender is now a pure, good Christian with a heart full of love to God and love to man, and, therefore, *just fit to live.* How singular that we should conceive it either necessary or in harmony with the demands of Christianity to kill one who, after weeks or months of prayerful exertion, God has converted into a saint. He is no longer a murderer, but a brother Christian. Why should we kill him? "If thy brother trespass against thee seven times in a day, and seven times in a day turn again to thee saying, *I repent; thou shalt forgive him.*"* The friend of the gallows will give

*Luke xvii: 4.

the murderer *time* to repent, he says, but after he repents, what then? Will he "forgive" him? Not he. But he will administer to him the eucharist in his stone cell, then lead him, with a halter about the neck, to the gallows, make a hypocritical prayer over him, pull down the cap, give the hangman the wink, and as the drop falls and the body of his *brother* sways to and fro convulsed in death, he rolls his eyes up to heaven and asks *God* to have mercy on his *soul*, when he himself will have no mercy, not even on his *body*, for in an hour it will be cut down and sent to the dissecting room.

It may be said here that this same argument may be employed against the law that would *imprison* the repentant criminal. We answer, that the two cases are not parallel. Strangling or beheading or shooting a fellow creature is a work of blood and vengeance, and the worst and most unchristian use you can put him to: while by a proper imprisonment, he is taken on a sort of probation, and may be instructed, disciplined and blest, through the very means of confinement. Indeed, as we shall show in the second part of this work, this should be the leading object of punishment by imprisonment.

"BUT THE MURDERER IS NOT ENTITLED TO LIVE."

Would you say that, my Christian friend, if he were *your* father, or husband, or brother? Oh, my God, how heartless and inconsiderate we are! "When we see a man led to the gallows," says a thoughtful Christian writer of England, we should say, "there goes my father —there goes my son." If this were the spirit which pervaded society, could we say, "the murderer has no claims to life? Why should we be so indifferent to the wretchedness that is the necessary consequence of hanging, simply because those who suffer are strangers to us?

Every man who is executed holds endearing relationship with some one. "Is that *your* child?" asked a gentleman in the streets of Boston, of a woman who, at the peril of her own life, had saved a little child from death by a runaway team of furious horses;—" No sir," she replied,— "it is not *my* child, but it is *somebody's* child!" Every man who is executed is somebody's child; and no matter how low fallen he is in sin; no matter how degraded and wretched he has become, the heart of the parent still clings to him. Society may say that he has no claims to life; it may condemn him and strangle him, but the parent, the wife, the child, cannot give him up. I have seen enough of the wretchedness brought upon the innocent in consequence of the execution of the guilty. The day before the unfortunate Lecount was hung in Cincinnati, three years ago, I visited his cell to sympathize with, cheer, and strengthen him. He had just received the following message from his poor old mother, residing in Dayton, member of the Methodist Church, and now seventy-five years of age. "Oh, my son, my son, would to God I could die for thee, my son! my son!" Every member of the family was in agony for days and weeks. They could not sleep for thinking of the dreadful fate of the doomed man. How many thousands of innocent persons have dreadfully suffered from the same cause. It is recorded of Col. Hayne, of South Carolina, who was taken by the English during the American Revolution, that he was thrown into prison, loaded with chains, and afterward condemned to death. His son, who was permitted to remain with him, was overwhelmed with consternation and grief. His father endeavored to console him. "To-morrow," said he, "I set out for immortality; you will accompany me to the place of my execution : and when I am dead, take my body, and bury it by the side of your mother " The youth here fell on his father's neck, crying, " Oh, my father, my father, I will die with you! I will die with you!" The next morning Colonel Hayne was conducted to the place of execution. His son accompanied him. Soon as they came in sight of the gallows, the father strengthened himself, and said, " Now, my son, show yourself a man! That tree is the boundary of my life, and of all my life's sorrows. Beyond that, 'the wicked cease from troubling and the weary are at rest.' Don't lay too much at heart our separation; it will be short. 'Twas but lately your dear mother died. To-day I die. And you, my son, though but young, must shortly follow us." " Yes, my father," replied the broken-hearted youth, "I shall shortly follow you, for, indeed, I feel that I cannot live long." And his melancholy anticipation was fulfilled in a manner more dreadful than is implied in the mere extension of life. On seeing his father in the hands of the executioner, and then struggling in the halter, he stood like one transfixed and motionless with horror. Till then, proceeds the narration, he had wept incessantly; but soon as he saw that sight, the fountain of his tears was staunched, and he never wept more. He died insane; and in his last moments often called on his father, in terms that brought tears from the hardest hearts.

Hundreds of such incidents are on record. Some years ago, a young man by the name of James Dawson, with eighteen others, was executed in England for treason. At the time, he was strongly attached to a young lady to whom he expected to be wedded on the very day of his death.

"Not all the persuasions of her kindred could prevent her from going to the place of execution. She was determined to see the last hour- of a person so dear to her ;

and accordingly followed the sledges in a hackney coach, accompanied by a gentleman nearly related to her, and one female friend. She got near enough to see the fire kindled which was to consume that heart which she knew was so much devoted to her, and all the other dreadful preparations for his fate, without being guilty of any of those extravagances her friends had apprehended. But when all was over, and she found that he was no more, she drew her head back in the coach, and crying out, ' My dear, I follow thee—I follow thee!— sweet Jesus, receive both our souls together !'—fell on the neck of her companion, and expired in the very moment she was speaking."

Here we gather a glimpse of the wretchedness brought upon the innocent through the instrumentality of the Death Penalty. Would we then trample every vestige of mercy under our feet and strangle the life out of our fellow creatures, without regard to others whose hearts are full of affections, simply because we have conceived the idea that they are not entitled to life? It was once said that the burglar, the thief, and the robber were not entitled to life, but, thanks to God, that day of darkness has passed and a brighter and more hopeful has dawned.

In conclusion, then, I would say, my fellow Christian —or fellow mortal—for we are *all* mortal whatever our views—let us study and labor for the advancement of humanity. If the gallows is not a Christian institution, —if it is not neccessary—if it endangers the lives of the innocent—if it will not secure either individual or public safety—if executions are deleterious—if their influence is only to harden the heart and multiply crime—in a word, if we have proven what we have attempted in this work, why should the gallows exist a single day

longer in any State in our Union of States ? Down with
it, then! It belongs not to the present, but to a darker
age. If we are Christians let us trample under our feet
the very spirit which sustains and perpetuates it, and in
future look only to the cross of Christ for light to direct·
us. We need have no fears to go where he leads; for
he is the "Way, the Truth, and the Life." If we base *our*
laws upon *His* law of mercy and justice we shall be certain of securing the best good of ourselves and our fellow men.

> " The quality of mercy is not strained ;
> It droppeth as the gentle rain from heaven
> Upon the place beneath ; it is twice blessed ;
> *It blesseth him that giveth* and *him that takes ;*
> 'Tis mightiest in the mightiest ; it becomes
> The throned monarch better than his crown ;
> His sceptre shows the force of temporal power,
> The attribute to awe and majesty,
> Wherein doth sit the dread and fear of kings.
> But mercy is above the sceptred sway ;
> It is enthroned in the heart of kings ;
> It is an attribute of God himself ;—
> And earthly power doth show likest God's
> When *mercy* seasons justice."

THE PRISON.

The Prison of the Eighteenth Century.—Page 234.

THE PRISON.

CHAPTER I.

CRIME--THE CRIMINAL AND THE PRISON.

Crime in New-York City, Philadelphia, and the United States—Crime in Great Britain and France—Crime in Christendom—Five Hundred Thousand Criminals in the Christian World—What shall be done with them—Mad-Houses in the Past—Prisons in the Past—Treatment of Prisoners Regarded as Incurable—Dreadful Cruelty.

IN New-York city, during the year 1855, nearly 34,000 arrests were made; in Philadelphia, 38,657; in Cincinnati, 12,560; in Boston, 13,200; and in other cities nearly the same, in ratio to the population. A large portion of those arrested were discharged; while a large portion were guilty only of small offenses. In 1850, according to the United States Census, the penitentiaries of this country contained 5,646 convicts, while prisons of every description contained 40,000 criminals. In England and Wales, during the year 1853, there were 27,057 commitments to the various prisons for crime. In addition to this, it is estimated that London contains 30,000 vagrant men and women; that is, men and women who have no steady employment—who are corrupt in their morals, poor, filthy, intemperate, and many of them wretchedly loathsome. Paris, 20,000. New-York has nearly 4,000, Philadelphia 3,500, and Cincinnati 1,500 of this class. Following in their footsteps, there are 60,000 vagrant children in London and Paris, and nearly half this number in the three large American cities above named. These children obtain no instruction from our schools, though our school-houses are always open for their reception. They are poor, ragged, corrupt, vicious, and fast approaching the moral and physical condition of old offenders. These vagrant men, women and children, live chiefly by petty thieving. They never steal large amounts, but are guilty of pilfering any small thing upon which they can lay their hands and turn to immediate use. The parents of such children not unfrequently instruct them in the art of thieving, so that from this class come thousands of our most adroit pick-pockets and burglars.

In the foregoing we have mentioned only a few great cities of the Christian world. These classes exist, how-ever, in every city, town and country in Europe and America, and nearly to the extent, in ratio to the popu-lation, which we have mentioned. So that from these partial statistical facts it will be perceived that in a pop-ulation of 250,000,000, which is said to be the present population of Christendom, there must be, at least, 500,-000 human beings, young and old, guilty of various degrees of crime. What an army! And what are the demands of Christianity with reference to these classes? I write for *all*, but especially for *Christians*. Our States are professedly Christian States—our government a Christian government. I put the question to every Christian who reads this book, " *What shall be done with these classes of our fellow-creatures?*" And the question is one of exceeding importance and fraught with in-terest, not only to the criminal classes themselves, but to *all*, for individual security and happiness are in-separably connected with the purity of public morals;

and besides this, no man can tell how soon the question may interest him personally. His own son—or daughter—may soon be numbered with transgressors. We ask again, what shall be done with these classes?

We know what *was* done with them a brief time ago—and what *is* done with them in our day; and both the past and the present are full of prophecy for the future. In the past, men, *Christian* men, looked on criminals as voluntary enemies of mankind; and treated them, not as weak, or dull, or unfortunate *human* beings, but as beasts. Even lunatics were treated in the same spirit. "Mad-houses were simply stone pens, or jails, eucompassed by high and gloomy walls—without a tree or shrub, or blade of grass; without shade in the heat of summer, or protection from the cold of winter; with the hard, stony soil worn into hollows from the restless feet that trod it; and the only luxury there, a bench fastened to the wall with massive iron rings above it, so that even in the open air, force, instead of care, might rule the wretched inmates." Into these places, and iron cages, were the unfortunate creatures thrust, and there kept in nakedness and filth. If restless, they were chained with iron and beaten with whips. If they gnashed their teeth and tore their hair, and raved, they were beaten all the more, as if madmen were not our *brethren*, but *devils*. And what was the result? Were these wretches *cured* of their madness? Was their condition bettered? Not at all. *Such* results were never contemplated. But what a change a few years has wrought! "Now," as one has expressed it, "lunacy is a disease, to be prescribed for as fever or rheumatism. When we find an incurable case we do not kill the man, nor chain him, nor count him a devil. Yet lunacy is not curable by force, by jails, dungeons, and cages; only by the medicine of wise and

20

good men. What if Christ had met one demoniac with a whip, and another with chains!"

So with the criminal. All men regarded him, but a few years ago, as *incurable*, and worse than worthless—deserving only to be thrown into some wretched prison, or tortured, then killed, and buried in a dunghill. Criminals were scourged and mutilated and branded with red-hot iron—but never instructed, improved and blessed as the religion of Christ and a common humanity demand. The whole apparatus for punishing the offender, from the guillotine and the faggot down, was founded in the spirit of *revenge* and *force*, and never in *love* and *attraction*. Jesus never drives any body into his kingdom with whips and torture. His language is not *go*, but *come*. "Come unto me all ye that labor or are heavy laden." How then could the system of punishment practiced by our fathers have been Christian ?

Behold the prisons of Europe, but a single century ago! What was the design for which they were erected? Was it to safely keep the offender ; to treat him kindly; to convince him of his error, instruct, reform and bless him, and send him back to the world when his term of service expired, a better husband, or father, or son, and a more worthy citizen ? By no means.

This is an idea, what we have learned of it, of modern origin. Prisons, even of a comparatively recent era, as we have seen during the progress of these pages,* were simply dungeons of incarceration, into which men and women were thrown only to be abused and hidden from society. The most inhuman monsters were often appointed as keepers, and comfort or even kindness was seldom experienced by those whose misfortune or offense had placed them within the power of these men.

---

* See pages 36—7, extract from Macaulay.

All history attests to the fact that "torture in every variety; chains, stripes, solitary confinement in darkness, dampness and idleness; promiscuous crowding of offenders of every degree of guilt in the same loathsome, pestilential, narrow vaults; insufficient and unwholesome food; filth, illness of the body and sickness of the soul, are among the cruelties which have been inflicted, in every age, on the doomed criminal—whether guilty or innocent, as a punishment for his offense."* Where were the sympathies, where the wisdom of the Christian world during these ages? Where was the spirit, where the example of the blessed Jesus?

It was not till the last century that society manifested sufficient interest in the class of men of whom I am speaking, to inquire into their condition, or even ask if it could not be bettered; and it was then aroused from its lethargy mainly by the efforts of a single man. There were, indeed, previous noble examples of attention to those who were sick and in prison. The names of Carlo Borromeo, Claudius Bernard and St. Vincent De Paul are all bright with deeds of humanity. But their good acts were confined mostly to particular localities. Not so with those of the immortal HOWARD, a man whose name will live in the hearts of the humane, so long as sin and suffering afflict our earth. He conceived that the whole system of criminal punishment was based on a wrong principle—that the cruelty men endured in prison was not only unchristian but wrong in itself, and he went about the work of reform. From the year 1773 to 1790 —the year in which he died—he spent his whole time in visiting and inspecting prisons, first in England, Ireland and Scotland, and afterwards throughout Europe, and in endeavoring to ameliorate the condition of pris-

* Encyclopædia Americana, Vol. X. p. 342.

oners guilty of every degree of crime. In this sublime employment he chose to apply the fortune with which he was favored ; and when he disclosed to the world the sufferings and atrocities which everywhere prevailed in prisons, all Christendom was filled with horror and indignation. Thoughtful and Christian men were astonished at their own indifference ; and even those who exercised control over prisons showed by the guilty consciousness with which they shrank from the revelations of the cruelties committed under their authority, that they felt themselves accountable for the most dreadful outrages and wrongs, notwithstanding they were supported by custom.

CHAPTER II.

DEMANDS OF CHRISTIANITY.

What shall we do with the Criminal?—He belongs to the Body Politic—Christ the Head of every Man—Sentiments of Christians still destitute of Sympathy—No Patience for the Criminal—Patience of Christ—Patience of God—Story of Abraham and the Sinner—Imperfection of Humanity—God the Common Father—We are all Members of the same Family—Christ came to Bless all, especially the Sinful and Unfortunate—We are taught to do FOR them, as well as WITH them.

By the preceding chapter we get a glimpse of what *was* done with wicked men a little while ago. But the question returns what shall *we* do with them? They are still among us—the hardened criminal—the drunken vagrant—the young in crime—the degraded female—and thousands of vagrant boys and girls, as we have seen, inhabiting filthy cellars and garrets in our large cities—candidates for the jail and penitentiary. These are all in our midst and are so many members—corrupt members, but none the less members—of the " body politic." What shall we do with them?

There are yet those in society who say, " they are *worthless ;* cut them off and cast them away; the sooner we are rid of them the better " But is this Christian ? Is it best ? Would you sever the finger with a felon, or the foot containing a sore, so long as the surgeon gives promise of cure ? Would not amputation weaken the body and through sympathy injure its circulations ? The Sandwich Island savages once had a custom of killing their old men and women, because through age and weakness, they were a tax on the efforts and strength of the younger. But that was a *heathen* custom. We are

Christians. We are "all members one of another."
Christ is the HEAD of EVERY man; he died for ALL,
even for the most *corrupt* members of the great body of
humanity! Why, then, should any man—any Christian,
especially — say, cut off these base members forever
from all intercourse with humanity, truth, goodness and
happiness—hang them on a gibbet—plunge them into
dungeons—show them no pity—no mercy? Ah, Christian reader, do *you* not expect *mercy* at the hand of God?
You have "no patience," you say, "with wickedness."
No patience with those, even, who would strive, as Christ
did, to better the condition of these perishing ones.
"Why show sympathy for a thief?" you ask. "Why
talk, and preach, and speculate about, and strive to bless
those whom God has cursed?   Why build 'magnificent
prisons' for the *comfort* of such men? and expend millions to better their condition?   This is all mock sympathy, and I can have no patience with it."

But would this be your feeling, this your declaration,
if *your* father, or son, or brother were a convict?   And
has it never occurred to you how easy it is for human
nature to yield to temptation? and how possible it is for
even *you* to become a criminal?   Many professed ministers of Christ, who once scouted all kindness and sympathy for the wretched offender, are now inmates of our
penitentiaries.   "Who art thou, O man, that boasteth?
Let him that thinketh he standeth, take heed lest he fall."

Are you a Christian, and yet refuse to show mercy to
those out of the way?   Have you studied the history and
teachings of your Master?   Was he ever out of patience
with the wretched criminal?   Has he not instructed you
to visit those who were in prison? and behold his sympathy for the miserable thieves as he hung upon the

cross. Even in the midst of malediction he only blessed. *You* have no patience; and yet behold the patience of *Jesus*, and of *God* the Great Sovereign of the universe, "It is not the will of your Father which is in Heaven that one of these little ones should perish." When all had become wicked—all had gone out of the way—when "there was none good, no not one," God was not impatient, but he sent his only begotten and well beloved Son to die for the world as an example for man, and to commend his love to his great family.

"O, for grace our hearts to soften,
Teach us, Lord, like thee to love;
We forget, alas, too often,
What a friend we have above.

Hear the story of Abraham and the sinner, and learn a lesson of patience and humiliation:

"And it came to pass that Abraham sat in the door of his tent, about the going down of the sun. And behold, a man bent with age, came from the way of the wilderness, leaning on a staff. And Abraham arose and met him, and said unto him, turn in, I pray thee, and wash thy feet, and tarry all night; and thou shalt arise early in the morning and go on thy way. And the man said, nay, for I will abide under this tree. But Abraham pressed him greatly. So he arose and turned and they went into the tent. And Abraham baked unleavened bread and he did eat. And when Abraham saw that he blessed not God, he said unto him, Wherefore dost thou not worship the Most High God? And the man answered and said, I do not worship thy God but mine. And Abraham's zeal was enkindled against the man, and he arose and fell upon him and drove him forth with blows into the wilderness.

And God called unto Abraham, saying, Abraham where is the stranger? And Abraham answered, Lord he would not worship thee, neither would he call upon thy name; therefore have I driven him out from before my face into the wilderness.

And God said, have I borne with him these hundred and ninety and eight years, and nourished him and clothed him, notwithstanding his rebellion against me, and couldst not thou, *thyself a sinner*, bear with him *even one night ?"*

I know that we profess to be Christians, but how little, after all, do we cherish and practice what is Christ-like. How little do our criminal jurisprudence and our feelings toward the guilty partake of the nature of the Christian religion—a religion which recognizes God as a common Father, and all men as brethren—belonging to the same great family, possessing the same physical and moral nature; subjects of the same temptations, and destined, ultimately, to the same immortality. All are sinful. Perfection is not known to mortality; but some are more sinful than others—not innately, but from a difference in *organization, circumstances* and *education.* This is the history of man from the beginning. The weak and the strong, the righteous and the wicked, the rich and the poor mingle together, and the Lord is the maker of them all. Christianity contains the FATHER'S instructions for the government of his FAMILY. He would have them all happy, all blessed; and to this end he makes it the duty of the strong to assist the weak; the righteous to bear with and reclaim the wicked; and the rich to sympathize with and aid the poor. We gaze upon the loathsome, ragged vagrant—diseased externally and internally—or upon a herd of offenders against the laws of God and man, huddled in jail, or at work in the penitentiary, with guilt and self-abasement enstamped upon their features, and we say, "they are doomed objects of the law's vengeance, good enough for them—no matter how cruelly they are treated—they are not entitled to the sympathy or aid of good men!" But what a violation is this of the spirit and teachings, the history and death of the blessed Jesus! How did he labor for the little ones and the weak of earth's children. How kind was he to the unthankful and the evil. Follow him from city to city, over the mountains and along the valleys of Judea; see him in the hovels of the poor—the abodes of wretchedness—in the cells of the prisoner—and every where and always is he laboring for the doomed millions of God's family. It is for these that he specially toils. "I am not come to call the *righteous* but *sinners* to repentance."* "They that be *whole* need not a physician but they that be *sick*.†" "The spirit of the Lord is upon me, because he hath anointed me to preach the Gospel to the *poor;* he hath sent me to heal the *broken-hearted*, to preach deliverance to the *captives*, recovering of sight to the *blind*, ... and to set at liberty them that are *bruised*."‡

The classes that we have mentioned are wicked and dangerous—they lack moral principle—and are sometimes even desperate. Society has a right to secure them—to punish them. But it has no right to go beyond the dictates of mercy and justice and punish with vengeance. It has no right to debase one of its members any more than is absolutely necessary to the attainment of its design. It has no right to endanger the health or the intellect, or injure the remaining principles of any, even the most abandoned and desperate; but it should mete

---

* Matthew 9: 13.   † Matthew 9: 12.   ‡ Luke 4: 18.

21

out punishment *with an eye single to the good of the offender and public security.* This is the demand of the Christian religion. It will allow nothing short. The criminal is unfortunate. If there is a weakly born, or wayward, unfortunate child in the family, will the good parent, or brother or sister, cast him out and curse him? Would it not rather be a dictate of kindness and wisdom for all the family to unite their energies to instruct, improve, correct and bless him? And this is precisely what Christianity asks of you and me and *all* concerning our weakly organized, sinful and unfortunate brethren and sisters of the human race. And thus does it demand of us to do something *for* them, a truth which the great mass of Christians have yet to learn. They have conceived that if they have *done away* with them; they were performing their whole duty. " The Son of Man came not to *destroy* men's lives but to *save* them."

---
*Luke 9: 56.

CHAPTER III.

ABANDONED VAGRANT CHILDREN.

Crime in Embryo—Abandoned Vagrant Children—22,000 in N. York City—Dogma of Total Depravity False and Pernicious—Necessity of a Proper Culture—Good Seed and Soil in every Soul—How can we expect those educated in Depravity to bring forth Fruits of Virtue and Holiness—Interesting Incident at Long Island Farms—What the State is doing to Crush these Little Ones -Doing Nothing for them—Children seven years old in Jail—What it should do in their behalf—Ohio Penitentiary—New-York—Massachusetts—Vermont—Benevolent Societies—They are not Sufficient.

Having shown the demands of Christianity and a common humanity with reference to the classes of sinful beings we have enumerated, let us now proceed to state more definitely their condition, and what society *is* doing and *should* do in their behalf. And we begin where it is proper we should, viz: with ABANDONED VAGRANT CHILDREN, OR CRIME IN EMBRYO.

Think what a child is—*your* child—what it may be with a careful tender culture—what it is likely to be if abandoned to the temptations and wickedness of the world, and answer your own conscience if it is not the duty of the strong, the rich, the guardians of Christian society, to see to it that no child of this great family be left to perish for the lack of a home, kindness and profitable instruction? And yet, how sad is the thought that every great city contains thousands, some of them tens of thousands, who are thus abandoned. *Abandoned!* How little of Christ is in that word! Did *He* ever abandon any of the great family, young or old, no matter how sinful or wretched? And yet, all over the world, there are thousands of men and women, and even little children, abandoned by one another and by all men, to the

(243)

lust of hellish passions; to crime and to a career of sin, degradation and death.

During the year 1854, there were more than 10,000 arrests and 6,000 commitments of boys, and 12,000 arrests and 7,000 commitments of girls in the city of New-York alone, between the ages of *five* and *fifteen*. Great God! what a thought! *Twenty-two thousand* children of this description in *Christian* New-York! Think of the vice—the young depravity—the taint and moral desolation—the blasphemy, obscenity, drunkenness, wantonness—the rags and filth connected with these thousands, and the history of a life of crime, suffering and death which may follow, and if you have tears—weep!

Do you say—as many Christians have said, our fathers and mothers especially—that "these vagrants are born to crime—are full of evil—totally depraved—no one can benefit them—send them to the prison or the gibbet, they have no claim on our humanity!" But would you say this were your child or your son's child included? And he may be; who knows? Can you say it, and possess the spirit of Christ? Was *He* ever thus heartless? These children are depraved, sinful, wicked, but *in their nature* no more so than others. We visit the dark and narrow alleys of our great cities, where dwell hogs and filth—we enter the wretched cellars and garrets, and if we remain for any length of time, we may discover an exhibition of human nature most depraved and sorrowful to contemplate; but just what any man of sober judgment would expect *under the circumstances.*

The soil and the seed of virtue—of pure and generous emotions and principles—as well as their opposite, are in the nature of every child. What they need is *care* and *culture.* The moral development of the child depends almost wholly on this.

'Tis *Education* forms the common mind,
Just as the *twig* is bent the *tree's* inclined.

The abandoned outcast children we have described, whose mouths are full of blasphemy and bitterness, whose hearts are steeped in iniquity, and whose features are written all over with cunning, trickery and embryo villainy, perhaps have never listened to the words of persuasive kindness, or beheld a virtuous example. In the language of the Psalmist, " They were shapen in iniquity and brought forth in sin." The curse of POVERTY —an awful curse—is upon them. Their parents may have died or forsaken them in infancy, or, what is worse, may linger in drunkenness and crime. They extend not to their children the care and affection common to parents. They give them no good counsel. They put up no prayers in their behalf. They never send them to school or to the house of God; but, instead, *positively instruct them in the ways of depravity and the arts of crime.* There are thousands of children of this description in Cincinnati at this moment, from *five* to *fifteen* years of age, who have never seen the inside of a school-room, or heard a lesson in virtue, but whose entire existence has been in the service of depravity, in which they were educated by their parents and associates. Oh, how unfavorable has been their position, and the circumstances by which they are surrounded, for the culture of the good soil and seed of the soul. Instead, all the depraved passions and principles of their being have been developed. And what else could a reasonable man expect? These children are expert liars, thieves and pick-pockets, and by-and-by will be expert burglars, counterfeiters, robbers and murderers, but it would be a marvel if they, —or one in a dozen—became a good Christian or. citizen, or honest man, or virtuous woman.

Let one plant seed in the bottom of a cold, dark cellar, and he will raise no fruit. The man who should attempt it would be pronounced mad. The sunshine and showers and the hand of culture are necessary to insure the desired result. So with the moral elements and affectionate desires of the young soul. They need the warm sunshine of a careful and tender love, and the soft showers of goodness, and kindness and affectionate instruction. These will coax the better principles and desires forward into a healthful growth, no matter how cruelly the young soul has been neglected.

At a place called "Long Island Farms," not far from the city of New-York, there are 1200 once abandoned children, who were picked up in the vilest portions of that great metropolis, and are now supported and educated at the public expense. Not one of them is totally depraved. Their very natures contradict this foolish and pernicious old dogma. A change is at once observable in their looks and behavior as soon as they are fairly established in their new home, and feel, and see, and hear what they never before have felt, or seen, or heard, viz: the warm glow of human kindness, the beautiful picture of God's green earth, and the voice of real compassion.

"It is interesting," says one, "to see how suddenly their better natures are wrought upon by the touching, the beautiful, or by whatever is truly Christian. The glad face of nature—the shining stars by night—the sweet carol of the birds—the blooming flowers—the melody of music—the language of Jesus—the voice of love and instruction—all this finds a ready response in the young heart that is even supposed to be callous with evil, and will touch and subdue the soul and soften the affections, when many other sterner things would fail to accomplish the desired effect. All of which shows that the souls of abandoned vagrant children, as well as honest men's children, were formed for the pure and beautiful; as it also shows what is needed for the development, the culture, the full moral and spiritual growth of these perishing ones.

What is the *State* doing for this class? What *should* it do for them?

The State does nothing *for* these weak, abandoned creatures. It does much *against* them. I have seen a little, abandoned, ragged child, destitute of covering for head or feet, and but *seven years of age*, brought into court by a corpulent, savage officer, tried, condemned and thrown into jail, to be the companion of felons. What was his crime? Stealing silver spoons from a rich man's table, in obedience to the instructions of his mother. What was his history? Birth in a garret, amid wretchedness and want—the child of lust and crime—cradled in depravity, with the lullaby of drunken revelry—and schooled in deception and knavery. Already was he old in depravity. What else could you expect? And the State, instead of taking him at an earlier age, even, and becoming his guardian, sending him to good schools, instructing his heart and intellect in everything virtuous and useful, and thus helping him out of his degradation, by the above act it but plunged him in the more deeply. It made of him a felon—placed him in a college of felons, from whence he graduated but to spend the life of a degraded criminal—perchance to die in the penitentiary or on a gibbet. And this by a *Christian* State! Oh, for shame! for shame! And this is what every State in our Christian Union is doing in the middle of the Nineteenth Century, and in this age of Literature, Education, Morals, Common Sense, Christianity, and a

" world-wide humanity," for this class of perishing little ones. Massachusetts, New-York, Ohio, as *States*, all are employed in this same *wise* and *blessed* work. Last year New-York laid its strong arm on several little children, but five and six years of age. In the beginning of 1855 we visited the Ohio State Penitentiary, and were informed by the Warden that the prison contained 598 inmates. *Sixty-five* of the males were under 20 years of age. We had thought that the penitentiary was designed for old offenders; those of whose reform there was little or no hope, and against whose depredations it becomes necessary for society to secure itself by bars and bolts. But here we found this large number, too young to be desperate, and too young, also, to be given over to the buffetings of Satan. What hope can they have after years spent in the State Prison? What degradation! Who will trust or respect them? And how readily and unconcernedly the State thus casts away, and forever, the whole earthly existence of these unfortunate youth, without one effort for their salvation or improvement. But what we desire specially to record is, that we found, in the penitentiary, one lad *under thirteen* years of age, several under *fifteen*, and the day previous to our visit, *a little girl was brought there from Dayton, a prisoner, but thirteen years old.* We could not ascertain the name of the heathen judge who sentenced this child thus to a life of infamy. But this we know, that the State of Ohio, with its 4,000 Christian ministers and 50,000 Church members, sustains upon its statute book the law by which the abominable deed was perpetrated.

A Vermont paper * is placed on our table as we write, which contains the following:

"There have been confined in our jail, during the last

---

* Rutland *Herald.*

four or five months, two boys aged about thirteen years. Last week there was put into jail, a boy *seven years of age*, charged with the crime of stealing butternuts! In that jail are more than twenty persons confined for crime of all grades. There are confined there, also, three miserable prostitutes!

"Into such company, *in all the counties of this State, do the laws of Vermont throw children* who may, in their ignorance, have broken the letter of the law. Among criminals and hardened wretches, with nothing around them but barred doors, great hideous locks, grated windows, and everything which can remind them that they are rascals and villains! No moral instruction, no good influences are provided for them. No voice of kindness reaches their ears. Idleness, bars, bolts and the rough voices of desperate and cursing men are around them. The State does not expend one dollar to reform the children who are sent to the jail. They go in suspected rogues, and go out with the feeling and determination of rascals. Each old companion greets each juvenile offender who comes from the jail, with—'you've been to jail!' His eyes are pained with the full light. His limbs enervated with idleness. His body is full of pains from breathing foul air. His heart is faint with the taunts and gibes that greet him."

And this is what Vermont is doing *for* depraved children. We turn from an exhibition of these facts to inquire what *should* be done for them?

Some cities, and towns, and counties, and many individuals, are doing something in the right direction for these perishing ones. Hamilton county, Ohio, has its House of Refuge or Reform School, for vagrant children. ·It is an excellent Christian institution, and a monument of wisdom and benevolence. It takes the child guilty of

crime, and while it punishes him with confinement—not
limited, however, by the stone walls, bars and bolts of
the building, but by the grounds of the establishment—
it places him under the best and most judicious teachers
and keepers—furnishes him with a good home—with
good food and clothing, supports an excellent school, at
which he is put six hours in the day, and to Sabbath
School on Sunday, besides its chapel for preaching;—it
teaches him a good trade—instructs him in the importance of virtue and integrity—in short, the whole ma-
chinery of the institution is designed to aid, instruct and
bless those who become its inmates, so that they may
return to society improved and with hopefulness for the
future.   But what is that one institution for our county
and State?   It can accommodate only about three hundred pupils at a time, while Cincinnati alone will furnish more than three thousand.

A few such institutions only, can be found in our
Union; but in them we perceive the indications of the
remedy for the condition of these classes.   Benevolent
Societies are springing up here and there, with the same
object in view.   There is the "Ladies' Mission at the
Five Points," New-York, which has snatched large numbers of children from vice and ruin, and found them
good homes in the West; and the " Children's Aid
Society," in the same city, which has accomplished much
in the same direction.   "Its object is sufficiently indi-
cated by its name.   It seeks first to remove the poor
child from the coil of evil influences which have been
thrown around him, and which have been daily strengthened by the sharpest pressure of animal necessities.   It
comprehends the two-fold benefit of *education* and *labor*
in its system of "Industrial Schools."   Of these,*
at the present time, in New-York, there are eight, in

which a multitude of children are educated, taught to work, supplied with a warm dinner daily, and with such clothing as they can learn to make. In connection with these, there is one shoe-shop, in which thirty or forty boys earn a livelihood. Another object of this society is to find employment for its beneficiaries out of the city, and during the past year places in the country have been found for one hundred and twenty-five, where their employers treat them as their own children.

· These societies, we repeat, are based upon the proper principle, and are laboring in the true direction. "They aim to break up the old associations of the degraded child, to throw around him the atmosphere of a true home, and to blend intellectual, moral and religious training with that true charity which teaches one how to assert his true manliness, and support himself by the honest labors of his own hands." *

But a work like this—so important to the degraded classes themselves, and the purity of society generally, possessing moral and practical advantages so immense, should not be left to the caprice and uncertainty of voluntary benevolent societies alone.† The State is interested in the matter, and should move, and move effectually in it. There are 6000 children in Cincinnati who attend no school. This should not be permitted, unless they are engaged in some honorable employment. No vagrant or truant children should be allowed in our

---

* Humanity in the City, by Rev. E. H. Chapin.

† "The population of the Philadelphia House of Refuge at the beginning of the year," says the Annual Report of that institution, "was 364, and at its close 392. . The largest number under care at one time during the year was 457. Average daily number 385—about one-third being in the colored department. It is well for us that three or four hundred of our neglected vicious children are under reforming influences; but what hope is there for the FORTY-NINE FIFTIETHS that the report presents to us as the lowest estimate of the number who are 'growing up in idleness, vagrancy and crime?'"

streets or drinking cellars and saloons, around the levee or other public places, or even at home, without a proper excuse. Every family should be visited in each ward, by officers appointed and paid by the State—their condition noted, and the children obliged either to attend school or employ their time in some useful avocation. If the parents are poor, unable to spare their children from home, or to properly clothe them or furnish them with books, then let the State assist them—cautiously—judiciously—kindly, but determinedly, protecting their interests, and doing for them what they are not capable of doing for themselves.

Thus should the State become the GUARDIAN of all those ignorant, sinful and weak ones who have not sufficient ability or discretion, or the disposition, to manage their own affairs. In all great cities large numbers of men and women exist by receiving stolen property. Many of them keep second-hand stores, and encourage boys and girls of this description in stealing tools from workshops, produce from market wagons, goods from stores, clothing, spoons, knives and forks, and whatever they can lay their hands on, from dwellings and door-yards. Here is the school in which they receive their first lessons in crime. How important that all such schools should be utterly demolished, and children thus engaged should be made to spend their time in institutions of knowledge and under the tuition of teachers who would not only educate their minds in the important rudiments of learning, but their hearts in the principles of virtue and integrity. And all this can be accomplished only through the efforts and determinate action of the State, systematized and enforced by a judicious law covering the whole ground of need.

"But," says the objector, ".this would cost something."

So do our houses of correction, police courts, and jails, our criminal courts and penitentiaries, cost something. And is it not more humane and wise to *prevent* crime than to *punish* it? Most men of intelligence have come to know that crime finds its chief ally in ignorance, and that moral and mental abasement generally accompany each other. Formerly men were not of this opinion. A royal governor in Virginia once thanked God there were no public schools in that province. Facts show the connection between crime and ignorance. One half of the criminals in this country for the last forty years, could neither read nor write. In the several cities of the State of New York, from 1840 to 1848, there were 29,949 persons convicted of crime, as returned by the sheriffs of the several counties. Of the persons so convicted, 1182 are returned as having received a "common education;" 444 as "tolerably well educated," and 128 only, or one in about two hundred, as "well educated." Of the remaining 26,225, about *half* could barely read or write; *the residue were wholly destitute of literary instruction.* Of 1122 persons convicted in the same State in 1847, 1084 were utterly destitute of education. Of 134 persons convicted in 1848, twenty-three only had a "common education;" thirteen a "tolerably good education," and ten only were returned as "well educated," while eighty-eight could neither read nor write.

We have mentioned a single State. An examination into the statistics of other States shows nearly the same result. In the South, so far as we have the means of investigation, the comparative number of criminals utterly destitute of education, is still greater. And yet, notwithstanding these facts, with the existence of which every intelligent citizen should be familiar, every community contains men who look with distrust upon the increasing liberality of our public expenditures in the cause of general education; as if money expended by the State to educate the masses were a public loss. But if the masses grow up in ignorance we shall have a nation of criminals. Nineteen out of every twenty of the vagrant children, and men and women of our large cities, can neither read nor write. Nearly all the inmates of our state prisons are utterly destitute of education, while out of the 165 persons who were hanged in the United States, during 1854, *but seven* could read or write. The United States statistics for 1850 show, that the State of Maine has a larger number of children at school in proportion to the population than any country on the globe, and this State is freer from crime than any country on the globe. And besides all this, it is positively less expensive to educate paupers and vagrant children than to take care of them as criminals. The report of the Attorney-General of Ohio, for 1854, shows that the cost of trial and conviction of the criminals of this State, during that year, was a trifle over $73 each. " While the school tax levied under our present system, amounts to but $1,50 for each youth between five and twenty-one; and as three-fourths of these youth, or 600,000 attend school during some part of the year, the sum expended for the tuition of each is only $2,00. So that the cost of convicting these criminals would have instructed them in common schools for forty years; or it would have paid for their tuition and that of the next three generations of their successors (making 800 in all), for a period of nearly ten years each."*

How great an advantage, then, to community and the State, would be a law which should so thoroughly sys-

---

* The above is from an excellent article on this subject in the Ohio Journal of Education.

tematize a course of proceedure by officially appointed agents for each ward in our cities, and each town and plantation, as would secure the universal attendance of children at school, at least during a portion of the year.* It would not only keep them from much mischief and crime when young, but be the means of saving them from a life of ignorance and wretchedness, and make of them respectable and useful members of society. At the same time it would save expense to the State, lessen its number of criminals and paupers, increase the public security, and add to the purity and happiness of all. It is righteousness that exalteth a nation.

> " Ill fares the land to hastening ills a prey
> Where wealth increases, but where *men decay*."

Let not the State, then, think so much of saving *money* as of saving *men*, by looking after the mental and moral wants of her thousands of children and youth who were so unfortunately born as not to have the ability or disposition to look out for themselves. They are the weak and perishing ones. " *It is not the will of your Father in Heaven that one of these little ones should perish.*" They need not perish, if the State would look after their interest with half the zeal she exercises to get or retain political power. Political parties hold great conventions, make great speeches and sometimes get very drunk on the people's money, and all to secure to political demagogues the spoils of office. Would it not be very hopeful if, for once, they should meet to devise ways and means for aiding the weak ones of the "body politic" in their efforts to live honest lives, and thus escape the Peniten- .

---

* Of course we are speaking with reference to the Free States, where free schools are universally sustained at the public expense.

tiary and the gibbet; or in some similar way show their regard for the interest of society. A State Farm School for the class of whom we speak—ample, and conducted on truly philosophical and Christian principles—would be of more real value to a State, than many drunken, boisterous conventions. Ohio takes criminal parents and locks them in jail, while the children wander about the streets, sleep under carts, in door yards and hay-lofts, and furnish themselves the means of sustenance by theft. Would it not be well for her, at least to insti-tute a law by which these little ones shall be taken care of, and not left to perish utterly, under such circum-stances? Would not the act be *Christian*, though not *popular* with demagogues? " I speak as unto wise men, judge ye what I say."

CHAPTER IV.

THE CRIMINAL—HIS TREATMENT.

The Small Offender—Treatment not Reformatory—The Rookery—The House of Correction—The Jail—Unfortunate Females—Their Treatment—Should be Aided and Encouraged—The State never aids them—How it works in New-York, Philadelphia, Cincinnati—Experience of Isaac Hopper, the Philanthropist—Interesting Incident—Prisons for Small Offenders should resemble a House of Reform—The Duty of the State—Individual Effort not Sufficient.

WE leave crime in embryo, and pass to the consideration of the demands of humanity and Christianity, with reference to the real offender.

We will first notice the duty of the State toward those guilty of small offenses. These constitute a large majority of those who violate the law. Out of the 36,000 arrested in Philadelphia in the year 1855, but few were sentenced to the Penitentiary. So of other cities and towns. Thousands are annually brought before the police court of Cincinnati, while the number we furnish for the Columbus State prison is, comparatively, exceedingly limited. The youthful offender, guilty of larceny, the old vagrant, the drunken debauchee—the wretched prostitute—these go to swell the list upon the police record of every city, and constitute more than *six-sevenths* of all their arrests.

And what is the State doing *for* these classes? Literally nothing. Nothing to benefit or bless them, but all to injure and curse them. Let us look at the facts.

A man is a common vagrant. He is brought before the judge of the police court, and sentenced to what is designed to be the House of Correction, for five, ten, twenty or fifty days, on "bread and water." Female vagrants are brought in, in the same manner, and done for in the same way. Prostitutes, both old and young, who are a thousand times less guilty of any criminal offense, than the wretches who were instrumental in their ruin, are either sent to the house of correction or the common jail. Every morning exhibits a number of these classes in the police court of every great city. Monday morning, usually, presents the largest list. Fifty or eighty are sometimes brought before the mayor of Cincinnati in a single day. The common jail, or the rookery, or the house of correction receives them. But does the jail, or the rookery, or the house of correction, with its "bread and water" fare, *correct* them? Do they leave their place of punishment in the least improved morally, physically or intellectually? Are they put to some healthful and proper employment? Are they met with the voice of kindness and affectionate persuasion, in their prison? Are Christian men and women appointed by the State to oversee them, and employ every means which a benevolent wisdom has sought out to win them to the paths of virtue? Never. Instead, they are visited with harsh words, and ofttimes with positive cruelty and hatred. The State punishes as if its sole motive were vengeance. And it too often appoints men as overseers of these places of confinement who are utterly ignorant of any higher object in the discharge of their duties. Utterly regardless of the position of their victims as human beings, and entirely destitute of sympathy for them, they either treat them with heartless indifference, or heap upon them curses, and torture them with blows. So that when they return to the world, it is not with chastened affections and a resolve on amendment, but rather with a more bitter and vindictive spirit and a stronger determination to follow in the paths of crime and pollution. So that a few days only inter-vene, ere they are again brought before the mayor for another trial, and sentenced to ten, or twenty, or fifty, or a hundred days at the house of correction; and each time they are forewarned by the court, that if again found in violation of the law, it will be under the neces-sity of enforcing a more stringent punishment. The number of days are, therefore, increased, and the treat-ment rendered more and more severe. But they are never improved by such treatment. Over and over again are they subjected to the same ordeal; so that it is no unfrequent thing for old offenders to have been thus sentenced thirty, fifty, or even a hundred times. A man in Troy, New-York, was imprisoned one hundred and sixty-eight times for drunkenness, and a woman in Phil-adelphia over two hundred times. Is it said, that they are so depraved by nature that no power on earth can improve them? This is simply an error. The very man whom we just mentioned as having been imprisoned one hundred and sixty-eight times for drunkenness, and whom every body said no power on earth could improve, was effectually reclaimed by the kindness, assistance and affectionate persuasion of the Washingtonians twelve years ago, and to this day is an industrious and sober man, and good citizen, husband and father.

By the employment of the same means, (which are simply those that God has ordained through Christ, or in other words *Christian*,) the State could have reclaimed him fifteen years earlier, and thus saved him and his, from a life of infamy, and itself a heavy expense.

But perhaps the worst feature in our present system is the injury done to the young and comparatively innocent, by placing them in the company of the most **depraved and polluted**. All are made to herd in common together. In all populous cities there are large numbers of both sexes out of employment. By a careful inquiry, it has been ascertained that there are on an average 1500 females, of this description, in New-York, 1300 in Philadelphia, and 500 in Cincinnati. Many of them are *orphans*, and are homeless and friendless, and in consequence of the emergency that want brings, they are frequently subjected to fraud, imposition, deception, and, at length, to ignominy, pollution and death. We have been informed by an old physician of Cincinnati, that he has known scores of beautiful young orphan females to be led down, step by step, to ruin, purely from the simple fact of their position as orphans, destitute and friendless, with no kind father or mother to counsel and protect. The base deceiver, taking advantage of the destitution and isolated position of his victim, by honeyed flattery, the most earnest protestations of love, and the offer of rich presents, and a pretty little home all their own, in some retired place in the city, allures her to destruction. She yields to his embrace, and awakens, at length, only to find herself deserted, and in her own eyes and the eyes of the world—especially the *Christian* world—utterly and hopelessly ruined; and the consequence is, in many cases, alas, how many! she plunges deeper and deeper down into the vortex of infamy.

Now, for all such, careful Christian provision should be made, by the State, to save them. But there is no such provision. They are thrown into the *alms house*, the *house of correction*, or the *jail*, in company with old, drunken, profane hags, and, no matter how young, made to listen to the most disgusting and awful blasphemy and obscenity. By the Report of the Prison Society in

New-York, we learn that there is constantly an average of one hundred females, old and young, in the prison in that city called the Tombs, all of whom are without any employment whatever while there, and are left to spend their time in such conversation and acts as their depraved lives might suggest. " Here, we found in the upper rooms," says the committee, "a number of young girls, from ten to twenty years of age, associating together. It was a sad sight to see the little vagrant of ten or twelve years, committed for her destitution, and the want of a proper home and care-takers, cast into companionship with those whose conduct and habits had taken from them a name in respectable society, and whose corrupting influence must be powerful over those neglected and unfortunate children. In the yard of the prison were about thirty women, seated on benches, many (perhaps the greater number) showing by their wretched, bloated faces, a positive proof of the cause of their incarceration. Others were in the cells, or walking in the entries, but with every opportunity to circulate the poison that festered in their own minds, and created a malaria wherever they moved or breathed."

This committee also visited the prison for the same classes on Blackwell's Island, in the vicinity of New-York, and speak as follows of what they saw and heard: " To this prison women are sent, who are sentenced to periods of confinement, of from one to six months. A large majority of these cases are from disorderly houses : women, (many of them young,) to whom the glass, profane oath, and licentious practices, are the habits of daily life. To some of these, the constant changes are from the abode of drunkenness and debauchery to the almshouse and the prison. Cases have been known, where women have been thus imprisoned *forty* times, and in their midst were *several young girls, whose countenances, manners and histories, told that the blight of the destroyer had but lately passed over them.* From the Matron we learned, that there were two hundred and sixty women there; one hundred in the hospital; and one hundred and sixty in a frame shantee, shut up together during the day, often without employment, and corrupting, by this dreadful association, the good that still might remain in some." Could any place or position be devised that would more certainly quench the remaining sparks of goodness in the young, prostrate all hope of reform, and lead to certain ruin, than this? And here we discover the wisdom and the Christianity of the State.

"It was a sadly distressing scene to witness, and to know," says the committee, "that so little effort was made to cultivate industrious habits, or reform the morals of that degraded company; to the most of whom, perhaps to all, Providence had given the capacity to be useful, respectable, religious women. From occasional visits to these prisons, benevolent, earnest minds have seen the necessity, not only of efforts to remedy these evils, but that a *preventive power* could, and would effect great benefits to the unfortunate daughters of poverty, ignorance, and crime."

This is true; and what we contend for, is that there should be a reform in this entire department of police operations. The unfortunate beings above described should never be ranked with common criminals, and shut out from the world by the stone walls, bars and bolts of the gloomy prison. They never can be improved or saved by any such means. On the contrary, it proves, in many instances, the direct and positive agency of ruin, by sundering the last link which binds them to society and gives them a feeling of right to make an effort for virtue.

What they need is encouragement, counsel, protection and some place they can call HOME, where such protection and encouragement can be felt and realized by them, and where they can feel some security against want. Whenever and wherever such means have been employed in their behalf, the result has been most salutary. A Quaker gentleman of great humanity, who was long connected with the criminal courts of Philadelphia and New-York,* relates that many years ago, when he was inspector of the prison in the former city, a middle-aged woman by the name of Norris was frequently recommitted. On one occasion, she begged of him to intercede for her that she might get out.

"I am afraid thou wouldst soon come back again," said he.

"Very likely. I expect to be brought soon," she replied.

"Then where will be the use of letting thee out?"

"I should like to go out," said she. "It would seem so good to feel free, if for only a little while, to look up to the bright heavens, and enjoy the open free air."

"But if thou enjoys liberty so much, why dost thou allow thyself to be brought back again?"

"How can I help it? When I go out from prison no one will employ me. I feel that everybody shuns me. No respectable people will permit me to go into their houses. I must go to such friends as I have. If they steal or do wrong, I am taken with them; whether guilty or not, is of no consequence. Nobody will believe me innocent. They will all say, 'She is an old offender; send her back to prison; *that* is the best place for *her*.'"

It touched his feelings to hear her speak thus; and he

---

* Isaac T. Hopper, who died in New-York city two years ago, much lamented by every friend of Humanity in the north.

said: "But if I should obtain steady employment for thee and a good *home*, where thou wouldst be treated kindly, and be paid for thy services, wouldst thou really try to behave well?"

Her countenance brightened, as she eagerly exclaimed, "Oh, yes indeed, *indeed* I would! But is there any place on earth that will receive me, and be to me a HOME, and can you help me to it? If so, God bless you!"

"I think there is, and I will try what I can do. But thee must not expect too much, as thee may be disappointed."

"I used my influence," said he, "to procure her dismissal, and succeeded in obtaining a good place for her as head nurse in the hospital for the poor, and the consequence was that *she remained there more than seventeen years, discharging the duties of her situation so faithfully that she gained the entire respect and confidence of all who knew her.*"

"I have aided and encouraged," said he, "more than fifty younger females, who had become fallen and degraded, by means similar to those I have mentioned, and it is a great satisfaction to me to be able to state to the world, that *only two* disappointed my expectations."

Aid and encouragement, we repeat, are what they need to benefit and bless them. And this is what the true Christian will strive to afford. Behold Christ. When the woman who had been taken in the very act of violating the Jewish law—a law which demanded her life for the offense—was brought into the presence of Jesus, and her sin proven upon her, and all men condemned her, what was the language and the dealings of that pure and exalted being toward her? Did he, by cruel words, and more cruel acts, crush out of her heart whatever feelings of self-respect or principle of virtue might have lingered there? Not at all. He aided and encouraged her. " Neither do I condemn thee; go thy way and sin no more."

Now the State, as we have shown, acts upon no such principle in its dealings with these classes. Though it professes to be Christian, the element of Christianity, love, kindness, is utterly wanting in its entire system of operations. In New-York there is a " Home for Friendless Females ;" and in Boston a " Penitent Females' Refuge ;" but they were not established by the State, or county, or city, but by a few Christian men and women organized into Benevolent Associations. They obtained the means of erecting their buildings by begging of individuals the stingy sums that are usually given for such purposes, and by Church contributions. The consequence is, they have been struggling with pecuniary difficulties from the beginning, and are not yet relieved. Expenses are constantly accruing, and how is it possible that such institutions can be sustained by charity alone? Benevolent men will give for a single year or two, but by constant drafts upon their resources, they become discouraged. Moreover, all institutions of this description erected in our large cities, are entirely too limited in their accommodations, to answer the wants of the communities in which they are located. That in Boston has an average only of twenty inmates. Those in New-York and Philadelphia but thirty or forty. In all other cities the average is about the same in ratio to the population. This, in itself, is well as far as it goes; but it is not enough. Thousands are sentenced to the jail, the house of correction and the rookery, every month, who need the good instruction, the encouragement and fostering aid, which these institutions might afford if sufficiently ample for their accommodation, and were

23

owned or managed by the State or county. They should be located out of the city, in some rural district, with gardens and ample grounds, school-room for the younger, and chapel for all; and while they should be so constructed as to prevent any from escaping, they should resemble a House of Reform and Industry, more than a jail or huge prison.*

The philosophy that would *degrade* while it punishes, is wholly wrong and unchristian. The classes of whom we speak, when guilty, should be sent, or, if you please, sentenced to such an institution as we have described, not through revenge, but for improvement. It should be a place, not of idleness like our common jail, but of the most perfectly systematized industry. The inmates should not be put to the most degraded forms of female drudgery, but to employments suited to their sex, and so far as is consistent, congenial with their taste. Such a place might be made the manufactory of a thousand useful articles of trade; such as straw hats and bonnets, wearing apparel for men and boys, mattresses and bedding, millinery and dresses for ladies, collars, artificial flowers, light shoes, hose, and many other things. And care should be taken that all who enter destitute of a knowledge of some kind of work, whereby they can obtian the support of life, should be given good trades, so that when their term of time expires, they may not be returned to the world destitute of the means of sustenance.

---

* We perceive that New-York is moving in the right direction so far as concerns its inmates. The Committee on *State Charitable Institutions* of the New-York Legislature, reported a bill, lately, incorporating the "Home for Inebriates" in the village of Geneva. This corporation is allowed to hold 250 acres of land, or property to the amount of $250,000, in shares of $20 each. The Home to be managed by nine trustees—the first set to be appointed by the Governor and Senate, and the successors of six of them to be appointed by the stockholders, and the successors of the other three by the Governor and Senate. The bill also appropriates $10,000 to the use of the corporation when $5,000 have been subscribed.

We confidently believe that such an institution, with kind and judicious Christian men and women to oversee and control its movements, would be an immense saving to every large city, not only on the score of economy, but of true charity, and that five-eighths of those who might be thus aided, while they were punished, would be saved from idleness, want and utter ruin; and "instead of living to prey upon and curse society, enduring in their own souls the unavailing anguish of remorse, they might live to honor and bless the sphere in which they move." This would be a humane, Christian and desirable work. Why should not the State engage in it?

CHAPTER V.

THE JAIL AND THE PENITENTIARY.

Need of Reform in the Common Jail—Congregated System injurious—Jail in Cincinnati—The Influence of the Old Criminal on the Young—Present System makes Criminals—Facts related—Importance of Labor—Expense of maintaining the Prisoner in Idleness—Reformation of the Offender the most important Consideration—The Penitentiary—The Old System—Progress already made—More to be done—Work of Howard the Philanthropist—Eastern Penitentiary of Peunsylvania—Separate System—Its Advantages—Ignorance the Cause of Crime—Reform needed in the Educational Department—Also in the Disciplinary—Power of Kindness—Prisoners should be Encouraged when in Prison and when they return to the World—Interesting Facts.

THERE is great need of reform in the management of the common jail, in this country. The present system of herding together culprits of all ages and of every degree of crime, and permitting them to remain in idleness, indulging in gambling and profanity, reading obscene books, recounting their deeds of daring and profligacy, and instructing each other in all the arts of crime, is the most injurious and damning possible.

Take, for instance, the jail in Cincinnati, for the county of Hamilton, which consists mainly of a room say fifty feet in length by forty in breadth, with stone floor and walls, and with cells for the safe keeping of the prisoners by night. Each morning the doors of the cells are opened, and *all the prisoners*, without regard to age, complexion, education, or degree of guilt, have the free range of the large room. From fifty to one hundred and fifty are its constant occupants. There, may be seen at any time the old offender steeped in crime, and learned in all the mysteries of theft and burglary, side by side with the lad of fifteen whom an unfortunate and

(268)

trifling deviation from the right, has brought into this position. He may be there only for a few weeks; he may be detained merely as a witness, but behold how the tempter, as he sits before him dealing his cards, recounting his exploits in crime, his association with dissolute females, and describing his easy, jovial, pleasant life, is luring him to temptation, and sowing the seeds of crime. For days, weeks, it may be months, is he taught in this school of crime. Nothing better presents itself to occupy his attention. Not a day nor an hour's work is performed by the whole motley crew during their entire term of imprisonment. Constantly do they lounge in idleness, with no checks upon their tongues or passions. Under such circumstances, what could reasonably be expected, but that old villains should lead the young offender in the evil way? If it were one of the main objects of the government to sow broad-cast the seeds of crime, it could scarcely devise means better fitted to its end, than is exhibited in the system of imprisonment which most of our county jails present. Hundreds of well-attested cases might be cited to show the truth of this declaration, some of which have come under our own observation; but we have space for but one, which we extract from a voluminous letter just published, from the Corresponding Secretary of the " Prison Association of New-York," to one of the Vice-Presidents, on " The Cause of Crime." Among other facts, he presents the following :—

" We once visited the jail of Columbia county, (N. Y.) and found among the inmates a boy of fifteen years old, who had been put there for a breach of some corporation ordinance—we believe it was firing crackers in the streets; he was undoubtedly a bad, mischievous child, **but he never dreamed of committing a crime. A few** months afterwards, on visiting the same jail, we found him there again; and on inquiring we learned that an old burglar, who was in the jail at the time of his first confinement, had taken a fancy to the lad and inflamed his mind with images of the free and easy life that men of his profession led—their exemption from labor, the magnitude of their gains, and the pleasure they had in spending them. When he had fully succeeded in rousing the boy's ambition to enter a career of lawlessness and crime, he taught him all the details of lock-picking and pocket-picking, taught him how to elude the watchfulness of housekeepers and storekeepers, how to dispose of troublesome dogs, and how to conceal and dispose of stolen property; thus in a few short weeks, a wild boy, *through the agency of a common jail*, was ripened into a bold and consummate rogue, whose life was fully dedicated to the work of preying on the property and perhaps the lives of his fellow-men. On leaving the prison the burglar furnished him with a letter to a confederate, and together they soon planned a burglary; the boy entered the store—the other remaining outside to watch —but before he had secured his booty the proprietor entered the store through a private passage and secured him, while his confederate escaped; and he was now in jail waiting for his trial, which was certain to end in conviction !"

This is but an isolated case. Hundreds very similar are constantly occurring. Nearly 10,000 different persons in the State of Ohio, and 30,000 in the State of New-York, as many more in Pennsylvania, and all other States in ratio to their population, pass through the corrupting ordeal of the county jail, annually; and when we consider how large a portion of these are really or legally innocent, or are detained only to testify to the criminal acts of others, and must necessarily be contaminated more or less by the influences which surround them, we behold the positive *inhumanity* of the system ; a consideration which is sufficient to condemn it, aside from all considerations of public policy. " Why, sir," exclaimed a convict to us in the Cincinnati jail not long since, when questioning him on this subject, " Why, sir, bring a man to this room as pure as an angel, and let him mingle in this company six months, and he *will go out a devil*, AND CAN'T HELP HIMSELF !" It is singular that the public have not everywhere discovered, that the inevitable tendency of this system is to multiply criminals instead of lessening them.

In addition to all this, *it is an exceedingly expensive method of punishing crime.* Every criminal, no matter how long he has to remain in confinement, must be supported *in idleness* at the cost of the State. James Summons, charged with the committal of a most revolting murder, has lived a gentleman, for more than six years in the Cincinnati jail, at the expense of our citizens, and during the whole time has not so much as lifted a finger toward his support. The annual expense to our State for the support of our county jails, cannot be less than $300,000 ; in New-York, $600,000, and in Pennsylvania about the same amount. Now this need not be.

" But how can it be remedied?" inquires the reader. I answer, Reform the construction of your jails; especially, those of large cities. Make them equally safe, but more ample, with workshops, and rooms fitted for different descriptions of employment. The shoemaker, carpenter, blacksmith, locksmith, turner, tailor, engraver, printer might be put to work. Indeed, no man, or woman, if in health, need remain in idleness. Some simple employment could be furnished them, by which they could at least be made to earn their board, after deducting the interest on the cost of the establishment, and the salary of the keepers. In the Cincinnati jail we have on an average at least one hundred in constant confinement. Allowing 313 working days in a year, the average loss of time in idleness is 31,300 days, which at 80 cents per day would amount to an aggregate of $25,040. The time squandered in the Tombs in New-York city, is worth $50,000 annually. The same loss is sustained in the jails of all our large towns and cities, in ratio to the population; while at the same time honest citizens are taxed to maintain these delinquents in their idleness. Why should this state of things remain?

Do you say, that many of them are not yet convicted of crime, but are detained in jail for trial, or as witnesses against other criminals, and that the State has no right to force them to labor, or if it has, such compulsion would be unjust and inhuman? I answer, first, The State has the same right to compel them to labor, that it has to deprive them of liberty; and second, It is positively inhuman, and most injurious to their morals, as we have shown, to permit them to remain in idleness. If guilty of crime, it is but just that they should be made to pay the expense of their maintenance; and if on examination, their innocence is established, or if they are detained as witnesses, justice would demand that the county should refund a fair equivalent for their services. In this way they would be made to earn something for themselves, during their confinement. Thus, viewing the subject as we may, the advantages are altogether in favor of the change which we have described. We are satisfied, that so far as economy is concerned, the weight of the argument is on the side of a change; while all must allow that the moral advantages secured by the

change would be invaluable to the delinquents themselves. The great thing to be accomplished in the punishment of offenders, is their reformation. The question
of *economy*, notwithstanding what we have said, therefore,
is not one of moment. The true system of prison discipline to adopt, is that which possesses the greatest
reformatory power. No system should be countenanced
that makes bad men worse, and instructs the youthful
offender in all the subtile arts of villainy; which, as we
have seen, is the inevitable result of our present system.

THE PENITENTIARY.

WE have said, during the progress of these pages,
that sixty years ago prisons were simply dungeons of
incarceration and filth, into which men and women were
thrown only to be abused and hidden from society. The
great mass of men regarded the convict as incurable and
worse than worthless, deserving only to be tortured, then
killed and buried in a dunghill.

Such were the prevailing opinions, and the condition
of prisons in England and France, when the attention of
the benevolent Howard was turned to a consideration of
this important subject. He argued that the criminal,
notwithstanding his offense, is still a child of God and a
member of the human family. He had violated the law
and become a convict, but this was no just reason why
he should be the proscribed object of public vengeance,
and utterly destroyed. On the contrary, it was the duty
of society, while it punished, to endeavor to reclaim and
restore the offender. But this was impossible in prisons
constructed simply with reference to a dungeon confinement, where existed but little or no light, no ventilation
or cleanliness; no instruction or labor, no sympathy or
kind words, nor prayerful admonitions; and it was at his

suggestion that prisons were constructed on enlarged and more humane plans, with separate cells, chapels and healthful circulation of air.

Acting on the hints of this friend of humanity, the work of improvement has progressed from that day to the present, in all Christian countries, till now, many prisons are aiming to be what humanity and Christianity demand, viz: SCHOOLS OF REFORM, at the head of which are some of the kindest and most Christian men the world has ever known.

Probably the most humanely constructed and best regulated prison in the world is the Eastern Penitentiary of Pennsylvania. It is arranged on the separate plan, a principle of discipline which originated in Pennsylvania and was first applied and tested in that prison. No prisoner is allowed to mingle with others. Each man has a cell by himself, which is about 17 feet square and 12 feet high—large enough to admit a weaver's loom, hydrant, bed, snug and convenient water closet, and whatever else is necessary to the health and comfort of the prisoner. To each cell there is attached a yard of the same dimensions, where he is allowed to exercise one hour each day, and in which he cultivates peaches, flowers, grape vines and shrubbery.

Some benevolent men have condemned the " separate cell" system as inhuman, unnatural and awful. But they have condemned without investigation. They suppose the prisoner exists in perpetual solitude—is destitute of light, and that he has no employment but that of brooding over his own fate. But instead of this, it allows him plenty of light, and permits any and every degree of association with him, except that of other convicts. His friends can call to see him, and converse with him at any hour as long as they desire. Each day his task is assigned him—his overseer and chaplain visit him for instruction and encouragement, and he is furnished good books, and permitted to employ a certain amount of time for their perusal, and for educational purposes. As his old associations with the corrupt are broken up, and he is not permitted to mingle with them for his term of improvement, there can be no question but the probabilities of the reformation of a prisoner in a separate prison, under such a government, are a hundred fold greater than in a congregate prison. Indeed, this system has been faithfully tested, and with signal and acknowledged success.

This is the principle we would recommend for all States to adopt in the construction of their Penitentiaries, as speedily as the nature of their circumstances will allow. It is the principle on which our county prisons for large towns and cities, should be erected. As says the "Pennsylvania Journal of Prison Discipline," in its advocacy of this system:—

" When a man is arrested for crime, the legal presumption that he is innocent, should protect him from all degrading and polluting associates. Hence, he should be secluded from all others charged with or convicted of crime, as one entitled to the sympathy and companionship of the honest and good.

" If he is acquitted, it shall be no fault of the government if he does not return to society without any stain which was not on him when he was arrested.

" If he is convicted, the same care is demanded by right and justice, as well as by sound public policy, that he shall enjoy every opportunity to reinstate himself in the confidence of his fellow-citizens, and that nothing shall be done to him or suffered by him, that can possibly contribute to his further deterioration, . and that all means are used to encourage him in efforts to retrieve his character. Among these the first and chief is, *a complete change of company*—absolute separation from convict society, and all needful association with the honest and upright. This we regard as the *sine qua non* of every rational, humane or reformatory system of prison discipline."

But notwithstanding the progression of which we have spoken, in the improvement of prisons and treatment of prisoners, there remains much yet to be accomplished in that direction. Neither the benevolence of Christianity, nor the ingenuity of humanity, has arrived at the *ne plus ultra* of effort.

In what we have further to say on this subject, we desire to specify four departments in which there is still need of more marked attention; viz: the *Educational*— the *Disciplinary—Encouragement of the offender*, and *care over him when discharged.*

1. *The Educational Department.* We are aware that some men sneer at the idea of instructing a "State prison bird." They don't want to live to see the day when the penitentiary for convicts and felons shall be changed into a college. They will never consent that the public money shall be appropriated for any such purpose! But such persons, though they may profess to be overstocked with the Christian religion and a true philosophy, have but precious little of either. We have no desire to see our penitentiaries literally turned into colleges; but yet while they are places of confinement, labor and punishment, both Christianity and a true policy demand that they should be places of instruction.

As we have shown,* one great cause of crime is IGNORANCE. Seven-eighths of all the criminals in Christen-

---

* See statistical facts mentioned in third chapter.

.dom, have but little or no education. Many of them
from infancy, were so circumstanced that it was beyond
their power to obtain even the rudiments of learning.
Their parents themselves were criminals, or crushed
with poverty, or existing in profligacy and drunkenness.
They had no care over their children, who grew up in
idleness and vagrancy ; were instructed in crime by their
parents and early companions, and the State prison or
penitentiary is their end. There is no difficulty in showing, from the statistics of crime in the United States for
the last twenty years, that a large majority of State-
prison criminals could neither read nor write. And in
the report of the British and Foreign School Society, a
few years ago, we are informed that "out of nearly 700
prisoners put on trial in four counties, upwards of *two
hundred and sixty* were as ignorant as the savages of the
desert—they could not read a single letter. Of the
whole 700, only 150 could write, or even read with ease;
and nearly the whole number were totally ignorant with
regard to the nature and obligations of true religion."
In the reports of the Society, for 1832-3, it is affirmed,
"In September, 1831, out of fifty prisoners put on trial,
at Bedford, only *four* could read. At Wisbeach, in the
Isle of Ely, out of nineteen prisoners put on-trial, only
six were able to read and write, and the capital offenses
were committed by persons in a state of the most debas-
ing ignorance." When a jailor was describing his
prisoners to Leigh Hunt, he termed them, "*poor, ignorant
creatures.*" Now this phrase describes the condition of
nearly all the inmates of our penitentiaries in the United
States. There is now and then an educated man among
them, it is true, but generally they are a set of "*poor,
ignorant creatures.*" If they had been properly educated
when young, some of them would have been honorable

and high-minded men, a blessing to themselves and an honor to their race.

And evidently what they need is instruction, to prevent a repetition of crime. Why should they not have it, even in their prisons? The true object of punishment is the *correction* of the offender. But how can we correct him if his mind is enshrouded in ignorance; if he is low and groveling in all his conceptions, and, therefore, has no appreciation of moral truth, and what is really for his happiness? Our common schools are established and supported by taxation, on the basis of universal intelligence as the safeguard against moral depravity. Our States have assumed, that it is wiser to pay for the instruction of poor children, than to maintain them in crime; and Great Britain is following in our footsteps. She has learned that it does not cost the United States so much by *four hundred per cent* to educate our children, as it does her own nation to support her paupers and her criminals; and hence recommendations have come from the proper sources in that country to insure the establishment of free schools somewhat similar to our own in the free States.

If, then, it is in harmony with a wise policy to educate children, to keep them out of crime, why is it not equally wise to educate them in prison, to prevent a repetition of crime? And surely this is what Christianity demands. If we are Christians we must not—we *cannot* punish crime out of revenge. Instead of this the obligations of our benevolence teach us that while we punish the offender to prevent a repetition of crime, we must do him all the good in our power. Christianity is not merely prohibitory—directing us to avoid "working ill" to another—but amendatory, requiring us to do him good. And we may rest assured, that the legislator whose laws are contrived only for the detection and punishment of offenders, fulfils but half his duty. If he would conform to the *Christian* plan, he must also labor and provide for their *reformation*.

Much has been accomplished already in many prisons, in the educational department. But not enough. All our penitentiaries should be so regulated and managed, that every man, woman and child, with common mental capacity, should be necessitated to learn to read and write, if the term of his or her sentence would admit of it. They should also be carefully instructed in the principles of morals and religion—not the religion of a sect, or creed, but the Christian religion, which consists in love to God as a Father, and to man as a brother. To this end, the most judicious and Christian teachers should be selected, who would faithfully discharge their duties. A few hundred dollars additional salary is a matter of slight consideration.* The right men should, by all means, be employed; for as far as the experiment has been tried, the result of furnishing such men and spending an hour or two each day in instructing the convict, has been most salutary.

In New-York, teachers are employed in all the prisons. In a recent report they say : " In discharging our duties as teachers, we think we have been able to discern the wisdom which prompted to the establishment of means for the instruction of convicts confined in our prisons.

---

* Last winter our Ohio Legislature made a move in the right direction for the advancement of the Columbus penitentiary convicts. A bill for the thorough reorganization of that institution passed through the House Committee of the Whole, which contained some excellent provisions. Among other things, it was provided that the chaplain be a tutor, at a salary of $800 per annum, and to have an assistant at $300 if necessary. We were glad to see this, as it was an advancement upon the old system. Still it was not advancement enough. To spend all their time in their duties, if the right kind of men, they should at least have $400 added to the above sums ; while it should have been positively settled that an assistant is "necessary."

The eagerness to learn, which has been manifest on the part of the criminals who needed instruction—the attention and application which they have evinced, and the improvement which they have made, are exceedingly gratifying."

A young man writing to his brother, from the Eastern Penitentiary of Pennsylvania, where the criminals are not only instructed in good trades, but in reading, writing, arithmetic, religion, &c., says:—

" I can now make a good shoe, and the improvement of my mind, I leave you to judge by comparing my letter to sister of some time since, with this. My mind is the main point at which I am aiming. I am determined to master the arithmetic, and other books. This imprisonment will be the most useful of all my life spent so far, and I assure you I shall try to improve by it whenever the opportunity offers itself. When I am liberated, instead of wasting my evenings with engine companies, I will attend some useful lecture at the Franklin Institute, or in reading books from which I can derive some useful information. My eyes are now open, and I see the disgrace of being ignorant. I shall always look upon this imprisonment as the greatest benefit I ever had, and when that happy time arrives that I can be able to call myself worthy of my relatives, then I will look back on these walls, and thank God that I ever inhabited them."

2.   In the *Disciplinary Department,* reform is also still needed.

Prisons are too generally controlled by brute force. Blows, chains, the lash, kicking, the screw, the shower-bath, and other barbarous and cruel treatment has been employed as a means to control and subdue the offender, instead of persuasion and kind, Christian, moral means.

The benevolent Howard beheld this wherever he went; and he saw no good resulting from it, but, on the contrary, it but increased the desperation of the offender hardened in crime, and utterly froze all his better feelings to their very fountain. He, therefore, resolved to be governed only by kindness and tenderness in his visits to the wretched criminal " Overcome evil with good," he believed to be the true principle; and "experience soon convinced him that there was no man so debased, or his feelings so callous, but that he could be reached and softened by Christian kindness. Blows, kicks, starvation and neglect, only turned the heart to iron ; but no sooner was the angel voice of this Christ-like man heard, and his kindness felt, than the long-sealed feelings were opened, the dried up sources of tears were filled, the waters of sorrow flowed, and the heart of sin became radiated with deep and undying love for his benevolent visitor."*

Such are the effects of the law of Love, in all prisons where it has been made the governing element. Says an intelligent gentleman,† in describing what he saw and heard during a visit to the Pennsylvania Institution a few years ago: " I was greatly pleased to witness the effects of kindness, in the gratitude and reverence manifested toward the warden. We were shown to, and into perhaps a score of the cells in one of the wards—not by selection, but by succession—and we did not see a single instance which would create suspicion of the existence of any other law than kindness (associated, of course, with firmness.) The address of the warden, a mild and kind Quaker, was indeed fatherly;—as, for example, he would say, when he let down the iron wicket:

---

* Montgomery's Law of Kindness.
† Rev. A. C. Thomas, Philadelphia.

24

" 'Well, Ned, how does thee get along to-day, my boy? Does the work go to suit thee?' To another, who was lying down and was striving to rise quickly, when he heard the wicket open—'There, there, lie still, Sammy, I am afraid thee don't feel well to-day. I am bringing some friends to see thee, Sammy.' And thus from cell to cell we went to see and converse with the prisoners—some of them committed for terrible crimes—and the good warden was ever the same kind friend, as the evident gratitude and respect of the convicts denoted.

" The punishments, aside from separate confinement and the necessity of work, are only two in number; in minor offenses a withholding of food for one or more days, and in aggravated cases a removal to what is termed the dark cell. Of the latter description, during a year, out of more than 400 prisoners, only 15 were thus treated."

" When he took charge of the prison, he was informed of a very hard subject—a stout, violent and very profane mariner. He was told that nothing short of great sternness and severity could tame this rebellious spirit—and so it seemed likely to prove, for offenses in violation of rules of order, were reported daily of 'Ben.' After a week had elapsed, the warden went to the grating of his room, and simply said: " Now, Ben, thee must go to the dark cell."

The keepers ironed and removed him as directed. He was perfectly furious, and broke out into the most violent imprecations, which continued, with scarce an interruption, for hours.

In this state, affairs remained until the next day, and taking the advantage of a quiet spell, the warden opened the wicket. Ben saluted him with a terrible storm of abuse ;—but the warden merely looked at him in silence. "For full ten minutes, I should think," said the worthy man in relating the incident, "Ben continued his bitter tirade of abuse—and I continued to look at him in silence. The truth is, I was querying with my-self whether I had not taken wrong means to subdue this violent man, and was striving to discover some way of mending the error. But by-and-bye he was worried out with his own vehemence, and he heaved a deep sigh and was quiet.

"Thee has noted such states in children, I suppose. I knew it was a tender time with him, and so I said kindly,

"'Ben, has thee a mother?'

"The strong man was subdued in an instant, and sobbed like a child.

"I saw he was melted, and ordered the keepers to take off his irons and return him to his cell. Visiting him immediately after, I had a long private opportunity with him—and to good effect, for he was afterward an orderly and well-behaved man. And when his time expired he left us with tears. I do not say that he was altogether a changed man; *but I do think that kindness and tenderness did for Ben what nothing else on earth could have accomplished.*"

Many facts of a similar nature, going to show what power there is in the principle of love, to overcome the most ignorant and depraved, might be adduced, had we space. All the prison keepers, both of this country and Europe, who have been at all successful in "taming the savage breast," have owed their success to it. They could accomplish nothing with vengeance. Some men think that *philosophy* is better than *Christianity*. They are not aware that Christianity is the truest philosophy. "God made us and not we ourselves." He knows, therefore, what is in us and what will answer our moral and spiritual wants. And when Christ said, "Bless them that curse you," and Paul exclaimed, "Overcome evil with good," a principle of moral philosophy was enforced, which has been found by actual demonstration, *to be the only power that will soften the heart of the criminal and fill him with better desires and holier resolves.*

Perhaps no man ever lived who was more successful in reclaiming and subduing the savage spirit, than Captain Pillsbury, of the Weathersfield Prison, in Connecticut. Previous to his connection with the prison, the convicts were visited with the most shameful cruelty. The rooms were filthy, whipping was frequent and severe, while many of the convicts were kept continually in irons. This state of things was not only detrimental to industry, for the institution run the State in debt every year, but its effect upon the temper of the convicts was very injurious, producing in them "a deep-rooted and settled malignity." And there were so many recommitments to this and other prisons, of convicts who had been sentenced to it in the first instance, as to demonstrate that such treatment did not produce reformation. But when Captain Pillsbury took charge of the new prison in Weathersfield, and the convicts were removed to it from Newgate, he instituted a very different course of treatment. He was kind in every respect, yet inflexibly firm in the discharge of his duty. He substituted the law of kindness for severity. Says the Report, " He mingles authority and affection in his government and instructions, so that the principles of obedience and affection flow almost spontaneously towards him from the hearts of the convicts." The consequences of such a course, were immediate and obvious. The convicts were liberated from their irons; their respect and obedience to the agent were gained, and the institution began to pay for itself by its own labors. There was no institution of the kind in the whole country so successful. The most desperate criminals, who could be tamed nowhere else, were sent to Captain Pillsbury, to be charmed into staying their term of time out. Even the most ferocious were subdued—and all by kindness, confidence and love. The most desperately bitter could not stir feelings of unkindness within him. If sick, he would watch over them with the greatest assiduity by night and by day. This was the man, "who, on being told that a desperate prisoner had sworn to murder him, speedily sent for him to shave him, allowing no one to be present. He eyed the man, pointed to the razor, and desired him to proceed. The prisoner's hand trembled, but he went through it very well. When he had done, the Captain said, 'I have been told you meant to murder me, but I thought I might trust you.' 'God bless you, sir! you may,' replied the regenerated man. Such is the power of faith in man."

Thus should the spirit of Christianity govern among the most sinful. No other principle will reclaim them. How important, then, that each State should look carefully after the true interests of its criminals in this respect. We are happy to know that Ohio is moving in the right direction.* Let other States follow her example, or, what is better, lead the way. Great care should be employed in selecting proper keepers and teachers. Politics should not govern. Profane, wicked, unfeeling demagogues, who may work well for a party, will not do

---

* Section 16 of the bill before mentioned, does away with whipping, and forbids the striking of a prisoner with a stick, or kicking of him, except where necessary in self-defense. All the officers to demean themselves in as kind, humane and forbearing a manner as is consistent with the enforcement of strict discipline—*forbids the use of the shower-bath as punishment,* except with the consent of a physician. Punishment is to be confinement in a dark cell, on bread and water diet.

here. Their influence is decidedly deleterious. Regard should be had to moral purity. The man who occupies this position must possess that love which "suffereth long and is kind." Honor or emolument must not be the leading motive with him in seeking the place. He must feel that his work is a kind of mission, under God, of good to his race—and one which he must not, and dare not leave just to get more salary, more leisure, less worry or less confinement. "Such a man," says an English philanthropist, "conducts his work in the spirit, and by the instruments of the missionary. Not only teaching, but praying; not only admonishing and advising, but giving the daily example of patience, kindness, industry, endurance, and devotion in his personal life. Before such men the stubborn tempers bend, the hard hearts soften, the idols of vice and crime are cast down. They need not be men of extraordinary talent, but they must be men of *earnestness, love, and a sound mind.*"

3. *Criminals should be more encouraged* than they are, while suffering for their offenses. If kind, obedient, faithful, and guilty of no infraction of the rules of the prison, they should have the credit and the advantage of such behavior. Their term of service should be shortened; they should be furnished with a certificate of good behavior by the warden, on leaving the institution, and acquire again the rights of citizenship.* In addition to this, the prisoner should have his work allotted him, and all he earned over the actual expenses of his imprisonment should be given for the support of his family,†

---

* All this is provided for in the new bill for the Ohio Penitentiary, to which we have before alluded. This is truly Christian, and will have a salutary effect.

† Says Prof. Stowe, in his Report on Education in Prussia, of the provision made for the children of criminals :—" When I was in Berlin I went into the public prison, and visited every part of the establishment. At last I was introduced to a very large hall, which was full of children,

who were deprived of his assistance by his imprisonment; or, if he had no family, it should be paid to himself on leaving the prison, that he might have the means of support till he could find employment.

The State prison convict has little enough, at best, to encourage him, as he toils in his dismal confinement. To know that he is laboring for his wife and children, whom his wickedness has made to suffer, would fill his heart with gratitude; and to feel that when his term of imprisonment expired, he would be restored to citizen-ship and would possess something which his own hands had earned, to support him while he sought in the cold and unforgiving world for an honest livelihood, would cheer him in his gloom, and encourage him to strive for that reputation which he had sacrificed by the perpetra-tion of crime. The influence of such encouragement could not but prove beneficial to all who might be exer-cised by it.

4. *Reform is needed in the treatment which the public generally bestows on discharged convicts.* No matter how pure his desires and sincere his resolves to amend his life, on his return to the world, he is met with so much coldness and distrust on every hand, and he finds it so difficult everywhere he is known, to obtain employment in consequence of this state of feeling, that he not unfre-quently becomes enraged against society; and for the double purpose of obtaining the means of living, and to avenge himself on those who seem determined on his

---

with their books and teachers, and having all the appearance of a common Prussian school-room. 'What,' said I, 'is it possible that all these chil-dren are imprisoned here for crime ?' 'Oh no,' said my conductor, smiling at my simplicity; 'but if a parent is imprisoned for crime, and, on that account, his children are left destitute of the means of education, and liable to grow up in ignorance and crime, the government has them taken here, and maintained and educated for useful employment.' The thought brought tears to my eyes."

ruin, he plunges again into crime, utterly regardless of the consequences.

A young man in writing from his cell in the Eastern Penitentiary in Pennsylvania, to his sister, speaks in the following confident language: "I am resolved in my soul never again to be guilty of crime. Much have I reflected on my course since I have been an inmate of this cell, and the kindness of my dear mother and sister, and I feel sure that I can regain my good name. You say uncle is well disposed toward me. I am glad to hear it. I am young yet, and I thank God that my eyes are open. What is there to hinder me from not only regaining *his* regard, but the regard of *all* that know me? Nothing. I shall try to do so with all my power, and those hearts that have been almost broken by my heedlessness, will heave for joy when they see what a difference this will make in me."

This may have been sincere. At least, it is the duty of the Christian to look upon such a case with favor, and confide in the subject until he is proven again to be deceptive. Some say that all "State prison birds" are deeply dyed villains—can never be anything else; and, therefore, should never be harbored by any decent family. But what a mistake—and how unchristian, nay, inhuman the declaration. Thousands have been reclaimed. I know a man in my native State, who was guilty of robbery to a large amount. He served out his term in the State prison, and for more than thirty years has been an honest, upright Christian—good father, husband and citizen—in possession of a fine farm, and is as much respected as any man in the neighborhood.

Says a gentleman* of Boston, who, for the last twelve

---

* Rev. Charles Spear, Universalist clergyman. He publishes a valuable monthly in Boston, called the PRISONER'S FRIEND, which is patron-

years, has made it his chief labor to find good homes for discharged convicts: " I could give hundreds of cases where the criminal has been restored to society and the confidence of his fellow-men. This whole movement is one of the most sublime charity. Heaven must smile on the efforts of any one, who in the smallest degree shows kindness, and contributes toward the saving of the erring and the fallen."

Suppose, now, that the young man who penned the excellent resolves mentioned above, on returning to society, should be met only with coldness, distrust, sneers and curses; would not such treatment be unchristian, nay, positively cruel? And could its effects be other than injurious upon his soul? See how deplorable the condition of such a man, as described by himself:

" Though his heart be as pure as the dew of heaven yet unfallen, yet the gaze of suspicion is immovably fixed upon him. The very circle which contains all his sympathics and his affections is destitute of sociality, of pleasure, and consolation. Does he ask forgiveness in charity for the past?—not a feeling bosom aspirates a pardoning response. Does he give an assurance of propriety in the future?—even that is sneered at with immovable disbelief. The inhuman deride him, and snicker at his misfortunes; the unfeeling calumniate him, and are not sparing in their invectives. He has no hour of peace. Has he a wife?—she is inconstant, or despises him. Has he children?—they scorn to call him father. Had he a home?—it is now a lonely ruin. God help the

---

ized by humane gentlemen, who always favor discharged convicts, until they have reason to doubt their sincerity. Through these friends of Humanity, by advertising in his paper, Mr. Spear finds homes and employment for the blacksmiths, shoemakers, cabinet makers, &c., &c., of Charlestown Prison, against their term of imprisonment expires, which is an invaluable favor to these unfortunate men.

'poor man when affliction thus comes upon him!' His
consolation is scanty, his grief more than plentiful.'

This picture may be overdrawn, but there is much,
very much that is true in it. And is it just or humane?
Reader, remember, " It is your Father's good pleasure
that not one of these little ones should perish."

Such are our views of the Prison and the duty of the
State and of every individual, toward the prisoner. The
reader may condemn them; but we are certain that the
more he reflects upon them in connection with the
Christian religion, and a true philosophy, the better will
he be convinced that they have claims upon his affections
and his influence, which he must not disregard. Oh,
that the great world would awaken to a sense of what is
really divine, and for the good of the human race! Why
distrust the power of love? Why be afraid to exercise
that charity which is kind, and without which " though
we give our bodies to be burned," " we are nothing ?"
But this shall not always be. The human family is fast
moving in the direction of Him who went about doing
good, and who was "kind to the unthankful and the
evil." ALL MEN shall soon be embraced by the Christian's arms of affection.

> " God loves from whole to parts; but human soul
> Must rise from individual to the whole.
> Self-love but serves the virtuous mind to wake,
> As the small pebble stirs the peaceful lake ;
> The centre mov'd, a circle straight succeeds,
> Another still, and still another spreads ;
> Friend, parent, neighbor, first it will embrace;
> His country next—and next all human race :
> Wide and more wide, th' overflowings of the mind
> Take every creature in, of every kind :
> Earth smiles around, with boundless bounty blest,
> And heaven beholds its image in his breast."

THE POOR HOUSE.

A Christian Mother and Children, perishing with cold and starvation, in the great City, and in the very midst of the extravagance of wealth. Page 297.

THE POOR-HOUSE.

CHAPTER I.

PERISHING ONES.

Poverty in Christian Lands—England, France, Ireland, Scotland—United States—London—New York—Pauperism—Beggary—Needle Women—Interesting Incident—Death by Starvation in Philadelphia and Cincinnati—Romance of a Shirt—Suffering in Philadelphia—Working Classes in Great Britain—United States—Many of them Slaves—Family Stowage in New-York—Inhumanity of Christians.

THE author of these pages cannot send them forth without offering a plea—brief though it is—in behalf of the doomed victims of poverty, that everywhere exist, especially in civilized, *Christian* lands.

" The POOR ye have always." What millions are scattered abroad in Christendom ! As we look out upon the great world, how do we behold them coming up from the dens and kennels—the cellars and garrets—the alleys and lanes of great cities; and from the jails and poorhouses, the highways and by-ways of our earth !

We contemplate Europe—England, France, Ireland, Scotland, Spain, Germany, Russia—and wherever we turn our attention, what an army of perishing creatures, in rags and wretchedness, rise up before us ! In England, every sixteenth man is a pauper. In France, nearly 5,000,000 are beggars and paupers. In Ireland, from the Government report of July 3, 1847, there were 3,030,712 who subsisted on public alms. In Scotland, " thirteen per cent of the population are paupers

(299)

and live on the charities of their fellow-men." In Great
Britain (England, Ireland and Scotland), an immense
number of ragged, starving creatures, lie down every
night on their bundle of straw, or the damp earth, not
knowing where they may repose the succeeding night,
nor how to procure a loaf of bread to prevent utter starvation. In London alone, there are 30,000 professional
beggars. The census for 1854, taken in that city in the
night, shows over 20,000 destitute of a roof to cover
them. Fourteen thousand were "sleeping on doorsteps,
in hay-lofts and alleys, and under boxes, casks and carts,
and in barges, boats and other vessels." In Paris there
are 40,000 of the same description of perishing ones, and
in all the cities of Europe nearly as many, in ratio to
the population.

How vast the number in Europe, then, that are thus
cursed with POVERTY. What mind can conceive, or
tongue tell, or pen describe, the amount of mental and
physical suffering connected with it

When we turn to a contemplation of our own country,
the scene is less gloomy and sorrowful, but bad enough.
The report for the State of New-York in 1855, shows the
county paupers in that state to be 84,934; town paupers,
18,412; the number temporarily relieved, 159,092;—total
number relieved and supported, 204,161, at an aggregate
expense of $1,279,959.51. Taking New-York for a
basis, and our country contains not less than 500,000
paupers. Beggars, of course, are not included in this
estimate. In all our large cities this class is numerous.
Said the " New-York Journal of Commerce," two years
ago: " Those of our city who have good homes, and
habitually lay their heads upon comfortable pillows, can
scarcely believe that every night hundreds of men and
women are wandering houseless about the streets of this

great metropolis, without a place to shelter them. The Chief of Police reports that during six months preceding last November, 21,620 persons were furnished with lodgings in the various station houses in our city. This would give us more than 43,000 for the year. But probably not half of the number destitute of homes were found and assisted by the police : so that really there were more than 100,000 souls in this city during the year, destitute of a place of repose for the night. What an amazing amount of misery is concentrated in this single fact."

But the *paupers* and the *beggars* do not constitute the sum total of the POOR. Would to God they did. The great mass of the poor are those who are struggling by toil, privation, and even in destitution, to get bread and clothing for themselves and children, and a place to shelter them from the cold and the storm, *without begging, or calling upon the public authorities for aid.* Oh, my God! How many thousands exist everywhere in Christendom, of this description! I see them now, in the city—the village—the country. I see them living— suffering in garrets and cellars—and pent-up rooms— with no ventilation ; damp, filthy, destructive to health and happiness. I see the widow and the orphan—and the honest poor man, with a large family—weak and sickly himself from long and constant toil to furnish bread and clothing for his dear ones. I behold them all in poverty; at times positively suffering for the want of bread and fuel; and yet toiling on and on, from week to week, year in and year out, perhaps without a murmur, and yet with no hope of relief.

Cincinnati contains more than 6000 females, who earn a scanty subsistence with the needle by working from fourteen to seventeen hours per day. The youthful, already broken down with intense toil, and the aged, with wrinkled brow and tottering steps and husky voice, are among the number. Some of them once lived in affluence. But their riches have taken wings and flown, and the husband and the children have passed to "the land of rest." We met one of this description a few days since in a grocery, where she was purchasing her half-pound of sugar and a very little flour and tea. She was "in mourning." For long years had she worn the same faded bonnet and little black shawl—for long years had passed since the last dear son had been claimed by the destroying scourge as it passed through the land. A lonely widow is she now, "with no kin in the country." She had rented a room in the fourth story of a building situated ten squares, or a mile and a half from the shop of her employer, who keeps a clothing establishment For this man she manufactures vests at 20 cents each.

"Eight a week, by working *very* late of nights," said she, "is the best I can do. That gives me $1.60, out of which I have to pay one dollar a week for my rent and fuel; which leaves me only 60 cents for bread and clothes. Oh, sir, sometimes I feel that I cannot hold out much longer.* I am now *seventy-one* years of age, and have to get up and down the stairs *four stories*, which is very wearisome. sir!"

She had upon her arm her eight vests, which her toil had finished, and she continued:

"Do you not think my employer very hard, sir? I

---

* How much sympathy should be shown this class of virtuous and industrious persons—aged and infirm widows. The late Mr. Graham, of Brooklyn, New-York, has established on a scale of princely munificence, a spacious Public Hospital, now nearly completed, on Raymond street; and an asylum, four or five blocks off, for Poor Aged Women! Beautiful deed! What monuments must such works as these be, so far beyond columns of brass, or statues of marble, or *even legacies to the Board of Foreign Missions.*

have been all the way to his store on this hot day, to take these vests, and he refused to receive them and pay me for them, *because I was one day before my time.* I must go again to-morrow, which will require half the day, besides climbing the stairs. Indeed, sir, it is very hard. I fear I shall not hold out much longer. God knows what will become of me when that time arrives. I cannot beg—and how *can* I go to the poor-house! But I must not repine. God is my shepherd and I shall not want."

Ah, me! a man feels to weep when he listens to such tales, and *knows them to be true*, though it is not *his* mother who thus toils and suffers. An aged woman of this description literally starved to death in the city of Philadelphia, in the winter of 1842, for the want of the means of procuring bread. These words were found upon her table: "*I cannot steal, and to beg I am ashamed.*" During the same week the following appeared in one of the daily papers* of Cincinnati :—

A Case of Starvation.—Night before last about 9 o'clock, as J. H. Singer, a shoe dealer on Fifth street, was passing along Water street, near Vine, his attention was attracted to a little girl not over eight years of age, who just then issued from an old desolate-looking frame house, crying piteously. The forlorn appearance of the child, together with the real anguish which seemed to weigh upon her so heavily, induced Mr. S. to approach and enquire the cause of her tears. She started with evident fear at the sound of his voice, but in a moment perceiving he was a stranger, besought him to give her four cents to buy a loaf of bread. "O, pray do, sir," said the poor child, "mother is sick and so hungry," and

---

* Cincinnati Daily Times.

again her tears fell. Where is your mother? enquired Mr. S., who felt the full force of this appeal.

"Here, here, come, I will show you," cried the child. Mr. S. did as desired, and after traversing a filthy passage and descending a broken stairway, looked upon one of the most harrowing scenes of human misery, such as would have softened with pity the hardest heart. The apartment was part of a dark, damp cellar, without a spark of fire, and bare of the most trifling article conducive to comfort—not a chair, table, or indeed anything save an old trunk and mattress lying in the middle of the floor, could be seen to denote the abode of any living being.

On the mattress, however, lay the form of a woman about 25 years of age, reduced almost to a skeleton. At first sight Mr. S. thought her dead, but on observing her more closely he discovered she was still alive, though unable to move hand or foot. Directing the girl to remain where she was for a few minutes, he went out and purchased a small bottle of cordial and some little articles of food, with which he immediately returned to the wretched habitation. Mixing a portion of the cordial with water, he applied it to the unfortunate woman's lips, but for some moments without effect. At length, however, she opened her eyes, and with evidently a painful effort, faintly articulated the word " bread." Mr. S. gave it to her at first in very small pieces dipped in the cordial. Soon, under this kind treatment, she began to regain a little strength, and finally, in about three hours after the little girl's affecting supplication for her parent, she was able to converse and move her limbs.

She proved to be a widow, whom poverty and ill-health had reduced to this sad extremity. " It was *so* hard to ask for assistance," she said. And when the truth was known, it was ascertained that she had stinted herself to feed her children, till death was about to relieve her of her sufferings!

And all this in the very midst of abundance, wealth, luxury, and a hundred Christian Churches, whose spires pierce the clouds.

These are isolated cases, we know. But few literally starve for the want of bread; but, oh, God! how many *suffer!* How many perish inch by inch, as the heart's blood oozes out drop by drop! How many are doomed to toil all their days, and at last cry out to the cold, un-feeling world, "Give me bread—Oh, give me bread, or I die!" In every great city of our beloved country and of the world, thousands of this description can be found: notwithstanding the profusion of wealth and professions of humanity and Christian charity which everywhere abound. Behold a scene, as painted by another:*

"Look yonder! Is it not a magnificent festival that flashes along the wide hall, with its pillars, its draperies, its columns! Ah! it is a gay scene! Elegantly dressed men and beautiful women swaying gently along the bounding floor, while the music of a full band bursts upon your ears. This world is not so bad, after all. Who talks of misery and rags in Philadelphia, while these rich wines flow, these satins glisten, and these jewels flash from panting bosoms?

"But hold; let me tell you a romance connected with this ball-room: yes, a romance of a shirt: and, mark ye, those who may laugh at the title of this romance may pray God to forgive them for it, ere I have done.

'Let me tell you, then, the Romance of a Shirt. Yes, that elegant shirt, clothing the bosom of yonder gay, good-humored man—his pleasant face grows pleasanter

---

* From the writings of George Lippard, Philadelphia.

with genial champagne—in the ball-room: let me tell you the Romance of this Shirt. You smile: it is indeed a laughable thing—to look upon that Shirt and remember that every stitch has been drenched with a widow's tears—every thread along its carefully wrought surface has been baptized with the sighs of a breaking heart: that candle, held in the skeleton hand of Poverty, has lighted the White Slave and shone on her hot eye-balls, as she listened to the moans of a child for bread, and worked on, at the Shirt, sixteen weary hours; and all for—just enough to ' *keep body and soul together.*'

"Come with me now through this spacious street, flashing with a thousand lights; the Theatre glaring here, and the Rum Palace there: let us at once dive into the recesses of yonder darkened court.

" Into this old house, with rags and straw stuffed in the window panes—up the dark stairs, that creak be-neath our tread—into this lonely room.

" Ah! there is not much of romance in this scene.

" A lonely woman, clad in faded attire, sitting there by a flaring light, working away, with hot eyeballs and fe-verish hands, at the very Shirt which you have seen in yonder ball-room!

" Thus she has toiled for twelve long hours: and now, while her orphan children are lying there, moaning in their hungry sleep, there sits the mother, without bread or fire, toiling on with hot eyeballs and trembling fin-gers—toiling on all day and all the night for this tre-mendous sum—a single ELEVEN-PENNY BIT! Twelve and a half cents for one long winter's day of hunger, toil, and cold—laughable, is it not?

" And that flaring light glares in her face—shows the shrunken outlines—the eyes unnaturally large and dark —the under lip quivering, and quivering, as the poor

Widow tries to choke down the deep agony mounting to her throat.

"This faded woman once dwelt amid scenes of comfort—luxury. She never dreamed that the lot of the poor Child of Toil would be hers; never for a moment thought that the splendid mansion would dwindle into a dark, cold room; the dazzling chandelier into this flickering candle; the light of a husband's smile into this gloom of hopeless toil; the warm, happy forms of childhood into those starved and ragged things in yonder corner!—The husband died suddenly; his estate was insolvent: and now the story is clear. What claim has the widow on the tenderness of society? Poor—she must toil, and toil for the task-master, who chooses to reap his profit—that is the word—from the loss of her health, the nakedness of her children.

"An isolated case? Cherish the idea, if it saves you the expense of a blush. But still the fact festers on the forehead of your barbarous city civilization. *There are at least Ten Thousand poor and virtuous women in Philadelphia, who, suddenly impoverished by the death of a husband, a father, or a brother, are forced to toil at various occupations for just such a pittance as* 'WILL KEEP BODY AND SOUL TOGETHER!'

"Beautiful lady, darling of Chestnut street, now floating in the dance in yonder ball-room, can you tell me how much agony was woven up with the threads of that splendid robe which envelops your voluptuous form?

"Wear it; and while your bosom pants beneath it, forget if you can your Slave Sister, who toiled sixteen hours a day on this very dress, and now, while you bound in the dance, clutches the pittance in her consumptive hand, and goes to her crust—to her sick mother—to her desolate home.

" Laugh, my gay beauty: it will show the ivory white-ness of your teeth: but remember—a whisper in your ear—to-night your father is stricken with an apoplectic fit—his wealth wrecked in hopeless insolvency—and to-morrow you must become the White Slave, make shirts for twelve and a half cents, vests for a quarter of a dollar, dresses like the one you now wear for just enough to buy your bread, or——

" Shall I picture the alternative ? There is a great deal of luxury to be had in this large city for the mere sacrifice of a woman's virtue."

High wrought as is this description, those who know best affirm that it is not far from the truth. All over the world, the same classes are to be found. In New-York, Boston, New-Orleans, London, Paris, "their name is legion." With the other sex the same condition pre-vails. The census of London for 1855 shows that there are in that city " 20,000 journeyman tailors, of whom 14,000 earn a miserable existence by working 14 hours a day, *at twenty cents*, including Sunday. There are also in the same city, 30,000 sewing women, who, on an average, make only 5½d, or 9 cents a day, by working 14 hours—not quite three-fourths of a cent per hour." Throughout Great Britain, France and, indeed, nearly all Europe, the same condition prevails among the labor-ing classes. They are simply *slaves*. In the collieries and workshops of England, men toil for a mere pittance, half clad, living upon the most wretched fare; while in the factories their condition is no better, but more dreadful. Six pence or a shilling a day is the extent of a man's earnings. The consequence is, that if he has a wife and children, all must go into the factory, in order to obtain the means of subsistence. " Thousands of lit-

tle children not over six years of age, from the very poverty of their parents, who have been employed from
infancy in the same trade, are obliged to enter these
places of toil, and there delve from twelve to sixteen
hours per day, or die with starvation. Indeed, these
factories are the homes of vast numbers of the suffering
poor in England. Half starved, and half clad, they toil
through the day, and rest their weary bodies at night
upon their chairs or stools, or lie down wherever they
chance to be, upon the hard, bare floor."

> " Work—work—work !
> From weary chime to chime ;
> Work—work—work !
> As prisoners work, for crime !
> And what its wages ? *A bed of straw,*
> *A crust of bread and rags.*"

This is the condition of more than 50,000,000 of our
fellow creatures in Christian Europe. No wonder they
look to America, the Land of Promise, for " rest and a
competence."

But even here, as we have seen, Poverty stalks abroad
all over the land. " The destruction of the poor is—
their poverty." They are ignorant, not from choice but
from necessity. They are the " hewers of wood and
drawers of water." Men of mind and energy use them
as tools, and out of their sweat and sinews coin gold—
the American GOD. Their toil furnishes the luxuries of
the rich man's table, and builds charming mansions for
rich men's families—while they and theirs subsist on the
coarsest food, and are huddled together in miserable

dens,* comfortless and squalid, which they rent at extravagant prices from their rich employers. Such is the
condition of the world—and our own blessed country is
not exempt.

---

* A recent official investigation into the occupation of what are
known as "tenement houses" in New-York, has resulted in showing
(not for the first time) a most prolific cause of crime and degradation.
In many cases five-story houses were found to contain from twenty to
thirty families—mostly of a low order and filthy habits. In one of the
wards one hundred and twenty-one tenement houses were found to contain two thousand two hundred and thirty-seven families, or eighteen and
a half families to each house, and in many of the houses a portion of the
ground floor is used for a shop. In one house one hundred and twelve
families were found!

CHAPTER II.

JESUS AND THE POOR.

IN the preceding chapter we have presented a bird's-eye view of the condition of the perishing classes in Christendom, where Churches dedicated to Him who "came to preach the Gospel to the poor," are in every hamlet and upon every hillside;—where ministers of this same Gospel are as numberless as the stars of heaven—where Bibles and prayer books can be had for nothing, and a cart load of tracts thrown in—and where $10,000,-000 can be spared annually to send the Gospel to the heathen, while in Christian lands there are 50,000,000 of God's children, who cannot read his word, and are pleading with hearts of anguish, not for wealth, nor even comfort, but for bread to prevent starvation, and for rags to cover their nakedness.

Cannot this condition of things be bettered?

Certainly. There is no difficulty in the way, if we would only be Christians.

But how?

By paying our working classes better;—by making laws for the improvement of the homes of the poor, and doing more for their education;—by taking away from work its curse of shame, and by looking more after the

26   (305)

affairs of the millions of "little ones and weak" who have no eyes to look for themselves.

All this can be done; and we repeat, it would be done, and done very speedily, if all those who profess to be the followers of Christ, but possessed his spirit and practiced his doctrines.

To know what Christianity *was*, and what it required when Jesus lived and labored on earth, and what it *should be* in the nineteenth century, we should look to Him—his life, spirit, teachings and acts.

And what was the life and spirit of Christ? All have read the lives of the great and renowned—a Cæsar, an Alexander, a Napoleon—but what was the life and spirit of Jesus.

Did he seek wealth or fame? Was he led by worldly ambition, and did he study to secure the favor of the great and influential? Did he repose in the luxury of rich men's palaces, or pass his days in idleness and sensuality? Oh, no! Never! He dwelt rather in the hovels of the poor, and the dens of misery. The weak, the ignorant, the widow and the fatherless, the mourning and suffering, shared his attention as he went about doing good, ever intent upon the great object of his mission, to comfort and bless the poor, the unfortunate, the ignorant and the suffering.

Behold Him in his HUMILITY—his LOVE—his WISDOM. He wears no silk, or purple, or glittering diadem. A coarse robe falls from his shoulders, and his feet are shod with worn and tattered and dusty sandals. He is all humility; and it is the humility of love and wisdom.

See him as he wends his way along the highways, and through the valleys of Galilee, on his errand of mercy to the poor and the afflicted. Behold him at the pool of Bethsaida, amidst the sick and lame and dying; at the grave of Lazarus, weeping with the afflicted; in the poor widow's hut, sharing her scanty crust with orphans, and breathing words of encouragement into their ears. Everywhere and always he is the same kind, compassionate and benevolent Being, toiling and suffering to improve and bless the little ones and the weak of the human race. Oh, yes! He was consecrated by the Father for this very purpose. Hear him exclaiming to the proud Pharisees in the midst of the splendor and beauty of a sumptuous synagogue—" The spirit of the Lord is upon me, for he hath anointed me to preach the Gospel to the poor. He hath sent me to heal the broken-hearted, to preach deliverance to the captive, recovering of sight to the blind, to set at liberty them that are bruised, and to preach the acceptable year of the Lord." Here we behold the design of Christianity. Jesus was consecrated, not to distract men with cold formulas, or frighten them with awful declarations of God's wrath, or torment them with the mysteries of subtile creeds, or save their souls from some dreadful doom in the world of spirits; but to raise up and encourage the oppressed, to strengthen the weak, to bless the poor, heal the broken-hearted, and give all a hope of a happy immortality; in a word, *to show sympathy for, and render assistance to the very classes that needed assistance and could obtain it from no other source.*

And how constantly and faithfully was he devoted to the heavenly mission entrusted to his care. I see the blind beggar, covered with rags—the maniac, foaming with madness—the sick, sinful, and the victims of outrage and wrong, all pressing around him with hope and joy; and as he lays his hands upon them and exerts his heaven-derived power in their behalf, what a thrill of joy runs from heart to heart, and how are the souls of the once doomed and despairing overflowing with gratitude and peace!

This was the Christianity of Christ—the blessed Son of God—the Savior of the world. *It should be the Christianity of our day.* But, alas! how little do we see of Jesus in the Christian world—or Church, after a lapse of eighteen centuries! Where is the spirit—where the example of Christ? Fellow Christian, I put this question to you. The poor, the unfortunate, are still with us; but is Jesus with us? Do we cultivate a desire to visit the abodes of squallor and wretchedness? Do we say, " Come, our Master has taught us by his own spirit and example to go out into the by-ways and alleys of our city, and seek for the kennels where starvation, leprosy, and rags are mingled, and where the bitterness of despair is experienced? Let us go and do them good." Nay, nay! But we are ashamed of the very classes whom Christ delighted to bless, and has instructed us to assist. Behold the rich, the most fashionable and the most influential portion of the Christian Church, looking down with contempt on the poor and suffering. Some are positively mad with vexation, when called from the luxury of a divan in a sumptuous parlor, to listen at the kitchen door to the tale of some poor widow whose orphan children are starving for bread. They "wonder what these straggling wretches were made for," and why they are permitted to "disturb respectable folks in their houses." If the Lord Jesus himself were on earth, clad in his coarse raiment, with feet torn by the road-side flint, and hair matted with the dews and rains of heaven, and the dust from rich men's chariots, he would be driven from the dwellings and the Churches of these fashionable Christians—and perhaps shut up in the poor-house or jail, with felons.

The doctrine of Christ is in perfect harmony with his spirit and acts. He taught that God is the common Father of the human race. "Have we not all one Father, hath not one God created us?" This interesting question, asked by one of the ancient servants of God, was answered in the affirmative by Jesus. All, therefore, are children of the same Father—members of the same household—BRETHREN. Here is the great central principle of the Christian religion. It should cement the whole family of man in one holy bond of sympathy and interest. We are brethren and sisters; all subjects of the same infirmities, governed by the same laws, liable to the same afflictions, and destined to the same immortality. Should there not be union, sympathy and mutual aid among the members of this household? Will the brother who has an abundance, stand unmoved at the poverty and suffering of some weakly-born or ignorant member of his Father's household? That would be unnatural—inhuman. The strong must provide for and protect the weak. God works by means; and here is the means he has instituted to secure the preservation of those who, through sickness or weakness or misfortune, cannot take care of themselves. Everywhere in the inspired word has he plainly enforced this duty. " The rich and the poor dwell together, and the Lord is the Maker of them all." We are " one body of many members," of whom Christ is the head. " Whoso hath this world's goods, and seeth his brother have need, and shutteth up his bowels of compassion, how dwelleth the love of God in him? My little children, let us not love in word and in tongue, *but in deed and in truth!*"*
Again: " What doth it profit, my brethren, though a man say he hath faith, and have not works? Can faith

---

*1 John, 3: 17.

save him? If a brother or sister be naked and destitute
of daily food, and one of you say unto them, Depart in
peace, be ye warmed and filled, notwithstanding ye give
them not those things which are needful to the body,
what doth it profit?"*

From all this, it is clear that Christianity demands
the physical comfort, as well as spiritual good, of those
for whom it was designed. It would "provide things
needful for the *body*," as well as look after the wants of
the *soul*. How can men and women, whose bodies are
actually perishing with cold and hunger, give proper
heed to the aspirations of religion? And yet, our doctors of divinity, our clergymen, and the Church everywhere, are praying day and night, and laboring with the
utmost diligence for the salvation of immortal souls
from hell and from purgatory, while they will not move
a finger to relieve poor, suffering, mortal bodies! Millions of dollars are raised, annually, in England and
America, to save the souls of the benighted heathen in
foreign lands, while in our own cities and around our
own homes, the bodies of thousands of poor women and
orphan children are perishing, inch by inch, for bread.
The minister of God, when called to the bed-side of
some poor dying wretch, whose very sickness is the consequence of his poverty, and the suffering of his starving
wife and children, prays with the most holy unction, an
hour and a half, for the salvation of the soul of the gasping sufferer; but he says nothing—he thinks nothing,
about the physical wants of this man and his family.

Behold the millions annually extorted by Catholic
priests from the poor of her Church, for the purpose of
erecting gorgeous temples, and other costly edifices,
where the souls of the Church are to be cared for; but

---

* James, 2 : 14—17.

how seldom do they look after the physical wants of her millions of perishing votaries. A poor Irish woman, in deep distress, once called on the author of these pages, for assistance. He investigated her case, gave according to his scanty means, and suggested that her priest would do something in her behalf. "Ah, sir," exclaimed the suffering creature, "*the priest takes all, but gives nothing.*" In many instances this is literally true. He takes the last dollar from the ignorant and superstitious, for looking after the wants of their *souls*, and then turns them over to the *world*, to look after their starving, ragged *bodies*. And this is the Christianity of the nineteenth century. Great God what a farce! How long to its end?

CHAPTER III.

CHARACTER OF OUR CHRISTIANITY.

Personal and National Pride and Fashion hold Rule in the Church—Charity thrust out—Landed Estates of Great Britain in Possession of the Aristocracy—Twenty-Six Millions destitute of a foot of Territory—The Church the Aristocracy—Cost of maintaining it comes upon the Poor—Enormous Expense of maintaining the Royal Family—Facts stated—Christ and the British Queen—France and her Millions expended for Ornament—Spain and her Christianity—Strange Charity of a Queen—What America is doing.

WE repeat, the condition of the POOR would be looked after, their wants supplied, the workers better paid—their homes improved, their minds and hearts benefitted, if Christians were what they profess to be—THE FOLLOWERS OF CHRIST. There is no insurmountable barrier in the way. God's earth is sufficiently spacious for all. It can be made to produce enough for the subsistence of five hundred times its present population. The *means* to accomplish the work of improving the poor are abundant. All we lack is *disposition*. But, alas! how great is this lack! While we profess to love Christ and humanity, and desire to worship only these, we trample them in the very dust of the earth in our eagerness to approach the altars of Power, Ambition, Gold and Fashion! These are the gods we worship!

Look at the facts.

The question which concerns the happiness of the 50,000,000 beggars, paupers and toiling sufferers in Christendom, is one of exceeding importance. But do sovereigns or kingly assemblies ever consider it for the purpose of devising ways and means for their relief?

(312)

Never. It is not their policy. Great Britain contains 27,000,000 of inhabitants; 26,400,000 of whom *own not one inch of landed property.* All the territory of that realm is in the possession of less than 60,000 families; so that more than *twenty-six millions* of the people of that nation, the most *enlightened, Christian* and *wealthy* on the face of the earth, are the vassals and slaves of an aristocracy. And the blackest feature of the whole abominable system is exhibited in the fact that the Church of England constitutes that aristocracy.

The established religion is Episcopacy. The king is the supreme head, and the Church is governed by two archbishops and twenty-five bishops, who have seats in the House of Lords, and are styled *spiritual lords.* The archbishops have the title of *Grace and most reverend father in God by divine permission,* and are "*enthroned.*" Bishops are addressed with the title, *Lord and right reverend father in God by divine permission,* and are simply *installed.* These men really have no sympathy for the poor and suffering classes of God's children. They live in the most princely style, enjoying an annual income each, of from $50,000 to $1,000,000; so that instead of assisting the poor, the Church aristocracy of England grinds them to dust. The greatest curse that the poor of that realm ever felt, was the law established through the influence of the Church itself, which required one-tenth of their annual income for the support of the clergy.

The entire government of England is equally crushing, and the poor have no possible means of redress. When Victoria, "the Defender of the Faith," ascended the throne, she had the pleasure, as youthful as she was, of giving her official sanction to an act of Parliament, settling nearly $2,000,000 a year upon herself for life;

27

at the same time, the allowance to her mother was increased to $40,000 a year.   The Queen now draws from
the civil list of Ireland and Scotland, poor and wretched
as they are, the sum of $1,415,000, in addition to the
amount voted her by Parliament, making an annual income of $3,340,000.   Besides all this, the income fixed
by Parliament for the maintenance of Albert, the husband of the Queen, is $150,000 annually; and the Queen
has heaped upon him lucrative appointments to such an
extent, that the aggregate of their entire income is now
$4,988,650 every year, simply for *personal and domestic
expenditure.*   So that the cost of the government of England, for the maintenance of the Queen, her royal husband and royal children, is at least FIVE MILLIONS OF
DOLLARS A YEAR!   Look at that now, and consider that
while $800,000 are appropriated annually to replenish
the table and wine cellar of the Royal Family, there are
in the city of London, and almost within sight of the
Royal Palace, 30,000 professional beggars, and more than
50,000 widows, orphan children, and toiling poor, who
are slowly wasting into their rude graves for the want of
a sufficiency of wholesome food.   Look at that, and consider that while the Queen has three magnificent palaces
appropriated to her use, within the borders of her realm
there are millions existing in wretched shantees, cellars
and garrets, in filth and vermin, with disease which festers and rankles within them, many of whom are ready
at any moment, to "curse God and die."   Look at that,
and remember that the Queen of England is a professed
Christian, and at the head of the Church of England,
which *professedly* is the Church of *Christ,* the friend of
the poor.   Look upon the splendor of her throne, the
gold and purple and costly jewels which glitter and flash
upon her person, and then think of Christ, her great

spiritual King, with his tattered robe all covered with the dust of rich men's chariots, and his unsandalled feet, torn and bruised by the road-side flint, as he hastened from place to place "to preach the Gospel to the poor, and bind up the bleeding heart." How dissimilar, when contrasted, do they appear. The one in poverty and rags, but comforting and protecting the "little ones and the weak" of God's earth—and the other, clothed with wealth, glittering with fashion and splendor, but with her heel treading upon the necks, and pressing the life's blood from the hearts of these same perishing ones. And the Church and Parliament and aristocracy of Great Britain sanction, sustain and perpetuate this condition of things: which shows that the Church worships *power*, *fashion*, *national pride*, rather than *Christ.**

So with any nation in Christendom. France, for instance, Christian though she professes, with her 180,242 regular and secular clergy and nuns, and $700,000,000 of Church property, while she enslaves her poor and grinds them to powder, makes gods of her rich and influential. Nothing can exceed the extravagance of her court. More than $500,000,000 are expended annually for ornament and show, by the people of Paris, and yet France has nearly 5,000,000 of paupers and beggars within her borders. At the birth of the royal Prince, a short time since, presents to the amount of nearly 2,000,000 francs were forwarded to the Empress for the royal infant; while the starving and perishing of the

---

* The Queen of England is unquestionably a benevolent woman, naturally. The facts presented above show the love of power and the force of education. The sin of Great Britain in lavishing so much upon the crown, while it starves its poor, is enormous. A few months since the Queen called on Parliament for an appropriation of $32,000 a year, to maintain the stables of the young Prince; which is $7,000 more than is appropriated annually by the United States to maintain the White House at Washington.

nation were forgotten.* Prof. Paul Dubois, the attending physician, received 30,000 francs for his services, and the public demonstrations of joy at the event cost $500,000.

Spain, so far as her means will permit, shows that her Christianity is in keeping with that of France and England, though more superstitious. She never legislates *for* the poor, but always *against* them. A short time since the Queen of that country, forgetting the wants of her suffering subjects, gave a new cloak, ornamented with garnets to the value of 200,000 reals, to a statue of the Virgin Sonons. In this strange act is exhibited the character not only of her charity, but her Christianity. Famishing and perishing human beings, by thousands, are at her very feet begging for aid, and she passes by them all to bestow her gifts on a cold, lifeless statue.

In our own country, the inconsistency of our Christianity is apparent, though not of the same character. Our form of government is more republican. The White House in Washington is not so gorgeous as the Queen's Palace in London; and the Presidential Chair yields but $25,000 a year, instead of $5,000,000, for which we should be duly grateful to God and the wisdom of our ancestors. Yet such is the character of our government, the want of true Christian sentiment, and the spirit of patriotism among the leading politicians and law-makers of our nation, that while we economize in the President's salary, we permit millions of the public moneys to be squandered in electioneering purposes. How much effort is made, and time and means spent by legislative bodies, to aggrandize " the party," extend the borders of the Republic, and build up personal and selfish interests; but how little in aid of any cause of real humanity. We

---

* With honor be it remembered, that the Emperor had many of the presents, or an equivalent, appropriated to the wants of the poor.

have no money for benevolence; no time to pass laws for the improvement of the homes of our poor, or benefitting the social condition of the unfortunate—but time enough to annex new States, to quarrel with our neighbors, legislate ourselves into bloody wars with them, and millions at command to defray all expenses.

By thus glancing at the ruling motives of some of the leading nations in Christendom, in the administration of government, we behold the inconsistency of our Christianity. The truth is, there is no government on earth that is, in the slightest degree, entitled to the name Christian. The plea offered both by nations and individuals, for the neglect of the doomed millions of our earth, is *a want of means to assist them.* England, France and Russia have always presented this ostensibly as an apology for their apathy; and yet France herself acknowledged that the Russian war, while it raged during the last two years, cost in the aggregate the enormous sum of *one million of dollars per day,* or over *one thousand millions* during the war. If this money had been expended for the moral, intellectual, social and physical improvement of the 50,000,000 beggars and paupers of Europe, how vast the amount of happiness would it have secured. But instead, it paid for cutting men's throats, blowing them to atoms—plundering, pillaging, burning towns, and destroying public buildings: in a word, it paid for all the horrid evils of a bloody and terrible war, during which more than 300,000 Christians *were slain by their brother Christians.* And this is the Christianity of the nineteenth century. We have no means to educate the ignorant, feed the starving, clothe the naked, and improve the dwellings of our millions of perishing brethren and sisters of the human race; but means enough to press them into the national service, and grind them to powder! means enough to lay waste green fields, destroy dwellings, and drench whole towns in the blood of our brethren!

And this is not all; the Christianity of social life is even more inconsistent than that which pervades national governments. Consider, a moment, the *extravagance* of *fashion* in London, Paris, New-York, Philadelphia and Cincinnati. We have already glanced at this subject. "*No means to assist the poor;*" and yet what millions are annually expended by the rich and fashionable of the Church, for mere show. What sumptuous dwellings, rich furniture, splendid carriages and costly churches! Visit the church* of Bishop Bloomfield in London, on the Sabbath, and you will behold gold and jewels sufficient to purchase all the poor of London good houses, food, clothing and fuel for twenty years to come. One of the leading journals of Paris, in speaking of the growing disposition to extravagance in that city, says:

"The Parisian ladies seem to be afflicted this season with a perfect mania for magnificent toilettes; indeed, extravagance and sinful profuseness are carried to the extreme. An instance of this is furnished in the preparation of a 'layette,' (a new-born infant's trousseau,) intended for a private family. The robe for the baptismal ceremony is of white silk, covered with three flounces of deep point d'angleterre lace; the body and sleeves of the same material, and the whole ornamented with bows of broad white ribbon. The cloak is gorgeously embroidered with silk, with a deep lace flounce, and the hood is composed of silk lace and feathers. The whole of the child's toilette is in the same style of magnificence, and probably will not cost much short of *eighteen or twenty thousand dollars!*

---

* Where the Royal Household attend.

Even the fans in use this season are marked by elaborateness of workmanship, and cost as high as $2,000 each. Twenty or thirty dollars is considered the merest trifle for one of these highly decorated, carved, and enriched articles."

And yet, these fashionable Christian ladies havn't the *means* of assisting some starving wretch with a crust of bread; but if he should apply at their sumptuous establishments for aid, would drive him off with dogs or send him to the watch-house—indignantly exclaiming: "Why are these pests of society permitted to trouble honest people? Do they think we are made of gold?"

In New-York, Philadelphia and Cincinnati the same extravagance exists. The duties on imported silks, lace, artificial flowers and other articles of ornament, are *sufficient alone* to relieve and maintain all the poor of our land. In New-York it is no uncommon thing for a lady —*member of the Church*—to expend $10,000 a year in dress and ornament; while she has not a dollar for the poor, and *screws down her servants' wages to the lowest mill. That* is our Christianity.

In that city bridal presents have become fashionable. Sometimes gifts to the amount of $20,000 are bestowed, on the nuptials, in articles that can never be used, while the money with which they are purchased *is wrung from the blood and sweat of perishing ones, who are doomed to toil early and late, as we have seen, for a mere pittance* Here is the Christianity of the nineteenth century.

Says the *Philadelphia Ledger:* " A fashionable dry-goods dealer advertises a lace scarf worth fifteen hundred dollars. Another has a bridal dress, for which he asks twelve hundred dollars. Bonnets at two hundred dollars are not unfrequently sold. Cashmeres from three hundred dollars and upward are seen by dozens in a walk along Broadway. A hundred dollars is quite a common price for a silk gown. In a word, extravagance in dress has reached a height which would have frightened our prudent grandmothers and appalled their husbands. A fashionable lady spends annually on her milliner, mantua-maker and lace-dealer a sum that would have supported an entire household, even in her own rank in life, in the days of Mrs. Washington. Add to this the expenditure for opera tickets, for a summer trip to the springs, and for a score of little inevitable *et ceteras*, and the reader gets some idea of the comparatively wanton waste of money, carried on year after year, by thousands, if not tens of thousands, of American women."

Yes, and while millions of toiling poor are suffering all around them for the common necessaries of life. We repeat, *this* is our Christianity!

"In Cincinnati, we havn't the means to do a work of humanity." Last Christmas a great and general effort was made by the friends of the Cincinnati Orphan Asylum, (an excellent Christian institution,) to obtain aid for the further usefulness of the institution. All the Protestant clergymen in the city were appealed to, who in turn appealed to the hearts and pockets of their fashionable Christian hearers, on the Sabbath previous to Christmas, and called upon them in the name of all that was beautiful and divine, to assist in this good work to the utmost. Collections were taken in *every Church;* and the entire aggregate amounted to *just one-fifth of the annual expenditure of a single fashionable Christian lady of our city, for dress,** viz: $1,013.69. From all the merchants on Pearl street,† there was collected $374.00.

---

* We have been informed, from a source we have no reason to doubt that the expense of some ladies in this city for personal decoration, is not less than $6,000 a year.

† Wholesale Dealers.

From various other persons and associations, $180.00. Total, $1,567.69—for which the managers of the institution "returned their grateful acknowledgments;" more than intimating that notwithstanding the great need of the "institution for a much larger sum," this "far exceeded their most sanguine expectations:" and yet the sum total was not equal to what some one of our fashionable Christians throws away every year for extravagance, or expends in a single ornament for the person or the parlor.

A few years since, the fashionables from different parts of the country, stopping at Newport, R. I., during the warm season, had a "Grand National Fancy Ball." It was styled "a magnificent affair." The Ocean House hall was decorated for the occasion, at an expense of $1,200. The tickets of admission were $18 each, and there were six hundred persons present. The whole expense of "this glorious occasion," said the reporters, "could not have been less than $30,000. The *belle* of the party was the youthful, elegant and fascinating Madame Laverte, of Alabama. Her dress was a superb satin, ornamented with pearls and gold embroidery, and cost $6,000. Many other dresses were equally beautiful and costly. What a magnificent entertainment! How brilliant!—how enchanting!" To be sure. And we make no war upon the custom of social life that sanctions such displays. This is not the design of this book. But while we look upon an entertainment so magnificent, we would not forget the thousands in our country, clothed in rags and starving for bread; and above all, we would not have the participators in all the extravagance we have described, repeat that they, and Christian society generally, *have no means to assist the poor. It is false!* We have means enough; all we want is the disposition.

Tell me not that Cincinnati, where the hardiest enterprise prevails, and which has the means to build a thousand miles of railroad, dig down or tunnel mountains, fill valleys, build steam-ships and bridges and stores, and expend $5,000,000 annually in extravagance, has no means *to assist the poor*. What she needs is the *will*. So of other cities, States, and the nation. God has given us the most plentiful land on the globe. We have an abundance. Let us cultivate a disposition, and the perishing classes will rise up and call us blessed.

CHAPTER IV

AN APPEAL.

Oneness of the Human Family—Dependence of all Classes mutual—Appeal to Members of our National Councils—To Christian Ministers, Lawyers, Doctors, Teachers, Artists, Farmers, Mechanics, Traders, the Old and Young, Learned and Ignorant, to help in the good Work—Brighter Day dawning—Conclusion.

In conclusion, we affectionately appeal to our fellow-creatures of all classes and both sexes, especially to professed Christians, to assist in the furtherance of the principles advocated in this volume, so far as you believe them to be in harmony with true Christian philosophy, and for the happiness and well-being of the human family. "God hath created of one blood all the nations of men to dwell on all the face of the earth." The dependence and happiness of all classes are mutual. "As we have many members in one body and all members have not the same office, so we being many are one body in Christ Jesus, and *every one members one of another.*"* Here the human form is made to represent the human race. The head, the eyes, the hands, the feet, are all members of the same body, and though each has its distinct office, all are but one body, and every one members one of another. Some men operate by *skill;* others, by *capital;* and others still, by *labor:* but each of these classes is necessary to the others' happiness. Infinite Wisdom hath appointed this diversity for the general good, as the apostle declares: "Now hath God set the members every one of them in the body as it *hath*

---

* Rom. 12 : 4—5.

pleased him, * * and *tempered them together.* The eye cannot say unto the hand, I have no need of thee; nor again the *head* to the *feet,* I have no need of you. Nay, even those members of the body which seem to be more feeble, are necessary; and those which we think are less honorable, are worthy of more abundant honor."

Remember, then, my reader, that every other human being is a portion of the great BODY OF HUMANITY, of which you are a constituent member; and that it is impossible for you to wrong or oppress any brother or sister of the human race, however abject or culpable, without injuring yourself. "God hath tempered the whole body together, that the members should have the same care one of another. And whether one member suffer, all the members suffer with it; or one member be honored, all the members be honored with it."* Quaint old Fuller says: "Let him who expects one class of society to prosper in the highest degree while the other is in distress, try whether one side of his face can smile, while the other is pinched. The thing is impossible!".

Let members of our national councils and all our legislative bodies, then, in making laws for the punishment and suppression of crime, and for the government of the people generally, see to it, that while the criminal is punished as the nature of his deeds demands, that he is not utterly crushed, but, if possible. improved; and that the poor and ignorant—the toiling and suffering classes, are favored as their situation and a prudent wisdom may dictate. The happiest people on earth have been those who were governed by mild and humane sovereigns, who studied for the improvement and happiness of the weak ones of the body politic. Let the whole body be "tempered together," and all legislation be had with an eye

---

* 1 Cor. 12: 26—27.

single to the welfare and happiness of every member of the body, and prosperity and a general elevation must be the result.

To the ministers of the Gospel, we would appeal for their hearty co-operation in extending the principles advanced here, if in harmony with their convictions of the Christian religion. Let us not be Christians in *name* only, but "in deed and in truth." Let us study to apply the teachings of Christ to the wants of humanity, for this is the very object of the Christian religion. Take, then, the great subject with you into the pulpit, my brother, and you have Christ there with out-stretched arms, blessing the poor, the unfortunate and sinful of our earth.

To all the generous, loving and hopeful, we appeal, whether in the Church or out, who have charity for the imperfections of humanity, and confidence in the moral power of goodness; and we beseech you to give countenance and favor to the principles we enforce. Make them practical as opportunity may offer, that they may be the more truly known and *felt* among men. What you need is a heart to work. God give it to you, for if you have hearts, you *will* work, and the world will be Christianized, which is what it needs.

To men of all professions—the lawyer, the physician, the teacher, the farmer, the mechanic, the trader, the seaman, the artist—the young and the old—the learned and the ignorant—male and female, we appeal. Do not turn away from this subject as if of no importance, or condemn it without a faithful examination. The doomed classes of which we have spoken, are your brethren and sisters. To mitigate their sufferings and rectify the evils and errors of society, is so palpably your duty that you dare not deny it. Will you not, then, go about

your duty? What hinders you? It may be avarice, or
ambition, or pride, or fashion. But these have no right
to a place in your heart, to the injury of others, and
should be rooted up. A few years, at most, and we shall
all lie on a level, low in the dust of the earth;—or
rather, be translated into a brighter world of immortality.
Why not, then, work for Humanity while our day lasts?
Is there anything better for us to do? Is there not
something divine in lifting up the criminal and perishing classes? Was not Christ found in this very employment? Ah! the day approaches when the true spirit
and design of Christianity will be known and felt.
"Onward, upward irresistibly, shall move the spirit of
Reform, abasing the proud, exalting the lowly, until
Oppression and Tyranny, Sloth and Selfishness, Want
and Ignorance, Cruelty and Inhumanity shall be swept
from the face of the earth, and a Golden Age of Knowledge, of Virtue, of Plenty and Happiness shall dawn upon our sinning and suffering race." God help us to
engage with alacrity in whatever labor is necessary to
produce a consummation so hopeful.

> "A brighter morn awaits the human day,
> When every transfer of Earth's natural gifts
> Shall be a commerce of good words and works;
> When poverty and wealth, the thirst of fame,
> The fear of infamy, disease, and woe,
> War with its million horrors, and fierce hell
> Shall live but in the memory of time,
> Who, like a penitent libertine, shall start,
> Look back, and shudder at his younger years."

Lightning Source UK Ltd.
Milton Keynes UK
UKOW06f1832110915

258510UK00009B/167/P